Accounting
for Payroll

Accounting for Payroll

A COMPREHENSIVE GUIDE

Steven M. Bragg

John Wiley & Sons, Inc.

Library of Congress Cataloging-in-Publication Data
Bragg, Steven M.
  Accounting for payroll : a comprehensive guide / Steven M. Bragg.
    p. cm.
  Includes bibliographical references and index.
  ISBN 0-471-25108-9 (cloth)
    1. Wages—Accounting—Handbooks, manuals, etc.   I. Title.
HF5681.W3B7 2004
657'.742--dc22

2003027634

Printed in the United States of America

10 9 8 7 6 5 4 3 2 1

Subscriber
Update
Service

BECOME A SUBSCRIBER!
Did you purchase this product from a bookstore?

If you did, it's important for you to become a subscriber. John Wiley & Sons, Inc. may publish, on a periodic basis, supplements and new editions to reflect the latest changes in the subject matter that you *need to know* in order to stay competitive in this ever-changing industry. By contacting the Wiley office nearest you, you'll receive any current update at no additional charge. In addition, you'll receive future updates and revised or related volumes on a 30-day examination review.

If you purchased this product directly from John Wiley & Sons, Inc., we have already recorded your subscription for this update service.

To become a subscriber, please call **1-800-225-5945** or send your name, company name (if applicable), address, and the title of the product to:

mailing address: **Supplement Department**
John Wiley & Sons, Inc.
One Wiley Drive
Somerset, NJ 08875

e-mail: **subscriber@wiley.com**
fax: **1-732-302-2300**
online: **www.wiley.com**

For customers outside the United States, please contact the Wiley office nearest you:

Professional & Reference Division
John Wiley & Sons Canada, Ltd.
22 Worcester Road
Rexdale, Ontario M9W 1L1
CANADA
(416) 675-3580
Phone: 1-800-567-4797
Fax: 1-800-565-6802
canada@jwiley.com

John Wiley & Sons, Ltd.
Baffins Lane
      Chichester
West Sussex, PO19 1UD
ENGLAND
Phone: (44) 1243 779777
Fax: (44) 1243 770638
cs-books@wiley.co.uk

Jacaranda Wiley Ltd.
PRT Division
P.O. Box 174
North Ryde, NSW 2113
AUSTRALIA
Phone: (02) 805-1100
Fax: (02) 805-1597
headoffice@jacwiley.com.au

John Wiley & Sons (SEA) Pte. Ltd.
2 Clementi Loop #02-01
SINGAPORE 129809
Phone: 65 463 2400
Fax: 65 463 4605; 65 463 4604
wiley@singnet.com.sg

Dedication

*To Andrea, whose enhanced communication skills
will undoubtedly land her in either a human resources
or payroll department.*

Acknowledgment

Many thanks to John DeRemigis, who can process a book proposal faster than anyone on the planet.

Contents

Preface

When I wrote *Essentials of Payroll*, I realized that the limitations of Wiley's shorter "Essentials" softcover series did not provide enough room for the wide range of topics required to present a really thorough treatment of the payroll topic. Even though the *Essentials of Payroll* manuscript became the longest Essentials book ever issued, I still wanted to jam in more information. This book alleviates my need to "go long" by adding to the original Essentials book an additional eight chapters and two appendices. Extra topics now include payroll measurements and reports, record keeping, journal entries, payroll-related laws, outsourcing, and international payroll issues, plus coverage of how to create a payroll department from scratch, government payroll-related publications and tax forms, Internet payroll sources, and a dictionary of payroll terms.

This book is designed for accountants who are setting up a payroll system, improving the efficiency of an existing system, or who need answers to the inevitable variety of compensation, tax, deduction, benefits, international, and record keeping issues associated with payroll.

The book covers three main areas. The first is the overall set of policies and procedures, controls, best practices, and measurements that comprise a payroll system. The second part addresses the processing of specific transactions, encompassing compensation benefits, taxes, deductions, and other related issues. The third area is reference-oriented, with discussions of laws, government publications and forms, Internet sources, and a dictionary of payroll terms. The chapters are:

Chapter 1: Creating a Payroll System. This chapter covers outsourced and in-house payroll systems, emphasizing both manual and computerized systems. Flowcharts are given for each type of system and for the control points used with each one.

Chapter 2: Accumulating Time Worked. This chapter describes a variety of manual and automated methods for collecting time worked and notes the situations in which each solution is most viable.

Chapter 3: Payroll Procedures and Controls. This chapter contains detailed policies and procedures for the primary payroll functions, which can be easily adapted to suit one's individual circumstances.

Chapter 4: Payroll Best Practices. This chapter describes a number of payroll *best practices*, which are highly efficient methods for operating the payroll function. They are especially useful for any business that is striving to reduce its administrative costs in this area.

Chapter 5: Payroll Measurements and Internal Reports. This chapter addresses a number of measurements useful for determining the efficiency of the payroll function, as well as a number of payroll reports not normally found in the standard report package that accompanies most payroll systems.

Chapter 6: Compensation. This chapter covers such key topics as the status of contractors, wage exemption and payment guidelines, temporary workers, the minimum wage, compensation computations, tips, back pay, and a variety of business expense reimbursements.

Chapter 7: Payroll Deductions. This chapter covers the calculation and related regulations for a number of payroll deductions related to asset purchases, charitable contributions, child support, pay advances, tax levies, and other items.

Chapter 8: Payroll Taxes and Remittances. This chapter discusses the calculation of federal, Social Security, Medicare, and state income taxes, as well as taxation issues for resident aliens and citizens working abroad. It also covers the timing, reporting format, and related penalties for tax remittances.

Chapter 9: Benefits. This chapter covers a number of payroll issues related to employee benefits, such as cafeteria plans, insurance, pension plans, sick pay, stock options, and workers' compensation.

Chapter 10: Payments to Employees. This chapter addresses the specific procedures for paying employees, using either cash, check, or direct deposit payments, as well as state regulations related to the frequency and timing of both regular and termination payments to employees.

Chapter 11: Unemployment Insurance. This chapter addresses the structure of the federal unemployment tax system, as well as the calculation of unemployment taxes at the state level. It also covers the completion and proper depositing of related tax forms.

Chapter 12: Payroll Recordkeeping. This chapter describes the record keeping standards in such areas as unemployment taxes, new employees, garnishments, leaves of absence, and unclaimed wages.

Chapter 13: Payroll Journal Entries. This chapter covers every payroll-related journal entry a payroll staff is likely to need, including accruals for benefits, bonuses, vacations, and wages, as well as cafeteria plan transactions and manual payroll checks. The chapter also addresses how to ensure journal entry accuracy and ways to reduce the number of account codes used.

Chapter 14: Payroll-Related Laws. This chapter summarizes 21 key laws impacting the payroll department, sorted into the following categories: employment eligibility, garnishments, health insurance, pensions, taxes, and wages.

Chapter 15: Outsourcing Payroll. This chapter covers the advantages and disadvantages of outsourcing the payroll function, as well as conversion, transition, control, measurement, management, and service issues.

Chapter 16: International Payroll Issues. This chapter addresses a variety of payroll issues related to the employment of U.S. citizens in foreign countries.

Chapter 17: Setting Up the Payroll Department. This chapter gives a clear itemization of all steps required to both set up and fine tune the payroll department.

Chapter 18: Government Payroll Publications and Forms. This chapter notes the primary IRS publications and forms that a payroll department is most likely to use, as well as the lesser requirements imposed by several other government agencies.

Appendix A: Sources of Payroll Information. This appendix contains several dozen information sources on the Internet for payroll processing, general payroll information, payroll-related trade organizations, and the complete or summarized texts of numerous payroll-related laws.

Appendix B: Dictionary of Payroll Terms. This appendix contains definitions for almost 100 payroll terms.

For those new to the payroll function, this book is best read in sequential order from cover to cover. For those who are implementing a new payroll system, Chapters 1–4, 12, 13, and 17 will be the most useful, while for those who want to improve their current systems, Chapters 4, 5, and 15 are highly recommended. For those who are searching for answers to daily payroll-related questions about compensation or benefits, Chapters 6–9, 14, 16, and 18 are the most useful. In general, this book can also be used as a refresher class for those who have been involved in payroll issues for a long time, but who have not updated their skills recently.

May 2004
Centennial, Colorado

About the Author

Steven Bragg, CPA, CMA, CIA, CPIM, has been the chief financial officer or controller of four companies, as well as a consulting manager at Ernst & Young and auditor at Deloitte & Touche. He received a master's degree in finance from Bentley College, an MBA from Babson College, and a bachelor's degree in Economics from the University of Maine. He has been the two-time president of the 10,000-member Colorado Mountain Club and is an avid alpine skier, mountain biker, and rescue diver. Mr. Bragg resides in Centennial, Colorado. He has written the following books:

Accounting and Finance for Your Small Business (Wiley)
Accounting Best Practices (Wiley)
Accounting Reference Desktop (Wiley)
Advanced Accounting Systems
Business Ratios and Formulas (Wiley)
Controller's Guide to Planning and Controlling Operations (Wiley)
Controllership (Wiley)
Cost Accounting (Wiley)
Design and Maintenance of Accounting Manuals (Wiley)
Essentials of Payroll (Wiley)
Financial Analysis (Wiley)
Just-in-Time Accounting (Wiley)
Managing Explosive Corporate Growth (Wiley)
Outsourcing (Wiley)
Sales and Operations for Your Small Business (Wiley)
The Controller's Function (Wiley)
The New CFO Financial Leadership Manual (Wiley)

1

Creating a Payroll System

Introduction

This chapter[*] provides an overview of how the payroll process typically functions, using a payroll supplier, an in-house payroll process assisted by computer systems, or an in-house system that is entirely processed by hand. These descriptions also include flowcharts of each process and coverage of the exact controls that are most useful for each situation. Additionally, the chapter covers the types of documents used to set up a new employee in the payroll system, how to organize this information into a personnel folder, and how to process changes to employee information through the payroll system. As noted in the summary, the information in this chapter is supplemented with more detailed descriptions of specific payroll issues in later chapters.

Overview of the General Payroll Process

The next three sections describe how the payroll process flows for specific types of systems—outsourced payroll, in-house computerized payroll, and in-house manual payroll. In this section, we cover the general beginning-to-end processing of payroll, step-by-step, irrespective of the specific payroll system, in order to show the general process flow. Though some of these steps will not apply to each of the processes noted in later sections, it gives a good feel for how a payroll is completed. The steps:

1. *Set up new employees.* New employees must fill out payroll-specific information as part of the hiring process, such as the W-4 form and medical insurance forms that may require payroll deductions. Copies of this information should be set aside in the payroll department in anticipation of its inclusion in the next payroll.

2. *Collect timecard information.* Salaried employees require no change in wages paid for each payroll, but an employer must collect and interpret information about hours worked for nonexempt employees. This may involve

---

[*] This chapter is derived with permission from Chapter 1 of Bragg, *Essentials of Payroll* (Hoboken, NJ: John Wiley & Sons, 2003).

having employees scan a badge through a computerized time clock, punch a card in a stamp clock, or manually fill out a time sheet (see Chapter 2, "Accumulating Time Worked").

3. *Verify timecard information.* Whatever the type of data collection system used in the last step, the payroll staff must summarize this information and verify that employees have recorded the correct amount of time. This typically involves having supervisors review the information after it has been summarized, though more advanced computerized timekeeping systems can perform most of these tasks automatically.

4. *Summarize wages due.* This should be a straightforward process of multiplying the number of hours worked by an employee's standard wage rate. However, it can be complicated by overtime wages, shift differentials, bonuses, or the presence of a wage change partway through the reporting period (see Chapter 6, "Compensation").

5. *Enter employee changes.* Employees may ask to have changes made to their paychecks, typically in the form of alterations to the number of tax exemptions allowed, pension deductions, or medical deductions. Much of this information must be recorded for payroll processing purposes, since it may alter the amount of taxes or other types of deductions (see Chapter 7, "Payroll Deductions").

6. *Calculate applicable taxes.* The payroll staff must either use IRS-supplied tax tables to manually calculate tax withholdings or have a computerized system or a supplier determine this information. Taxes will vary not only by wage levels and tax allowances taken but also by the amount of wages that have already been earned for the year-to-date (see Chapter 8, "Payroll Taxes and Remittances").

7. *Calculate applicable wage deductions.* There are both voluntary and involuntary deductions. Voluntary deductions include payments into pension and medical plans, while involuntary ones include garnishments and union dues. These can be made in regular amounts for each paycheck, once a month, in arrears, or prospectively. The payroll staff must also track goal amounts for some deductions, such as loans or garnishments, in order to know when to stop making deductions when required totals have been reached (see Chapter 7, "Payroll Deductions").

8. *Account for separate manual payments.* There will inevitably be cases where the payroll staff has issued manual paychecks to employees between payrolls. This may be caused by an incorrect prior paycheck, an advance, or perhaps a termination. Whatever the case, the amount of each manual check should be included in the regular payroll, at least so that it can be included in the formal payroll register for reporting purposes, and sometimes to ensure that the proper amount of employer-specific taxes are also withheld to accompany the amounts deducted for the employee.

9. *Create a payroll register.* Summarize the wage and deduction information for each employee on a payroll register, which can then be used to compile a journal entry for inclusion in the general ledger, prepare tax reports, and for general research purposes. This document is always prepared automatically by payroll suppliers or by in-house computerized systems.

10. *Verify wage and tax amounts.* Conduct a final cross-check of all wage calculations and deductions. This can involve a comparison to the same amounts for prior periods, or a general check for both missing information and numbers that are clearly out of line with expectations.

11. *Print paychecks.* Print paychecks, either manually on individual checks or, much more commonly, through a computer printer, with the printouts using a standard format that itemizes all wage calculations and deductions on the remittance advice. If direct deposits are made, a remittance advice should still be printed and issued.

12. *Enter payroll information in general ledger.* Use the information in the payroll register to compile a journal entry that transfers the payroll expense, all deductions, and the reduction in cash to the general ledger (see Chapter 13, "Payroll Journal Entries").

13. *Send out direct deposit notifications.* If a company arranges with a local bank to issue payments directly to employee accounts, then a notification of the accounts to which payments are to be sent and the amounts to be paid must be assembled, stored on tape or other media, and sent to the bank (see Chapter 10, "Payments to Employees").

14. *Deposit withheld taxes.* The employer must deposit all related payroll tax deductions and employer-matched taxes at a local bank that is authorized to handle these transactions. The IRS imposes a rigid deposit schedule and format for making deposits that must be followed in order to avoid penalties (see Chapter 8, "Payroll Taxes and Remittances").

15. *Issue paychecks.* Paychecks should, at least occasionally, be handed out directly to employees, with proof of identification required; this is a useful control point in larger companies where the payroll staff may not know each employee by name, and where there is, therefore, some risk of paychecks being created for people who no longer work for the company (see Chapter 10, "Payments to Employees").

16. *Issue government payroll reports.* The government requires several payroll-related reports at regular intervals, which require information on the payroll register to complete. These reports are discussed in Chapters 8 and 11.

Overview of the Outsourced Payroll Process

Outsourcing the payroll processing function shifts a number of key payroll processing tasks to a supplier, resulting in a significant drop in the payroll department's workload, its required level of expertise in operating computer software, and in the risk that payroll taxes will not be remitted to the government in a timely manner. For these and other reasons, outsourcing payroll is an extremely popular option, especially for smaller businesses that do not have in-house payroll expertise on hand. This subject is covered in much more detail in Chapter 15, "Outsourcing Payroll."

The basic process flow for an outsourced payroll function is shown in Exhibit 1.1. The key items in the exhibit are the tasks that are *not* shown because they have been taken over by the payroll supplier. These tasks include processing the payroll transactions, printing payroll reports and paychecks, and making tax deposits and reports to the government on behalf of the company. By removing these activities, the payroll staff is reduced to compiling and verifying incoming data about hours worked, loading it into the supplier's payroll system, and verifying that the results are accurate.

The process tasks noted in Exhibit 1.1 can be streamlined by taking several additional steps. First, use a computerized timekeeping system that will prevent unauthorized overtime and automatically issue reports that highlight hours that were not logged in by employees, thereby eliminating two steps from the data collection part of the process. Second, some payroll suppliers sell computerized timekeeping systems that link directly into their systems, so there is no need to manually load this information into the supplier's system (or call it in to a data-entry person). Third, a company can pay the supplier to create customized summary-level reports that can be used as the foundation for journal entries, which eliminates additional work. Finally, some suppliers now issue payroll reports on compact disc, which nearly eliminates the filing chore. By taking advantage of these additional outsourcing features, the payroll process can become a very efficient system.

Controls over the outsourced payroll process are fewer than required for other systems because there is no need to control the check stock or signature plates, which are handled by the supplier. Consequently, the primary controls tend to be at the beginning and end of the process. As shown in Exhibit 1.2, there should be an approval process for overtime hours worked, as well as for negative deductions; a negative deduction is essentially a payment to an employee, and if used repeatedly, even incrementally small amounts could add up to a significant pay increase for an employee. For larger companies with many employees, one should also compare the addresses on the employee paychecks to see if a fake employee has been added to the system, with the check being mailed to a current employee's address to be cashed by that person. One can also issue a list of people receiving paychecks to the department supervisors to see if any fake names or the names of departed employees crop up. Finally, fake employees can also be spotted by handing out checks directly to employees and having them show some form of identification before they receive their checks. Though not all of these controls are necessary, one should select those that make the most sense for a company's specific circumstances.

Exhibit 1.1 Flowchart of the Outsourced Payroll Process

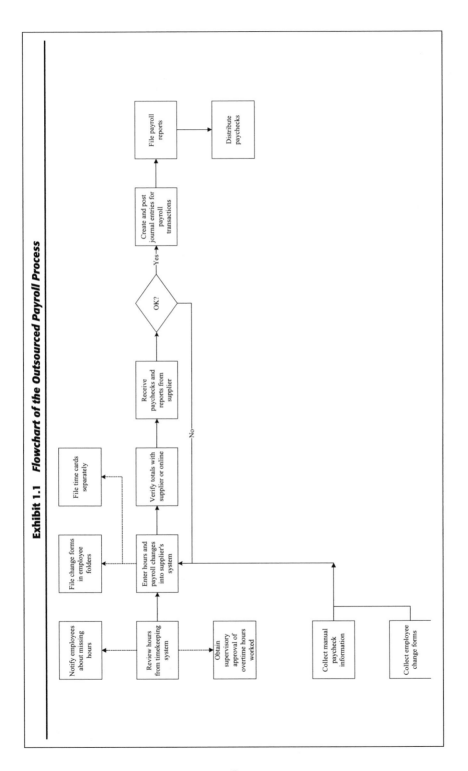

Exhibit 1.2   Controls for the Outsourced Payroll Process

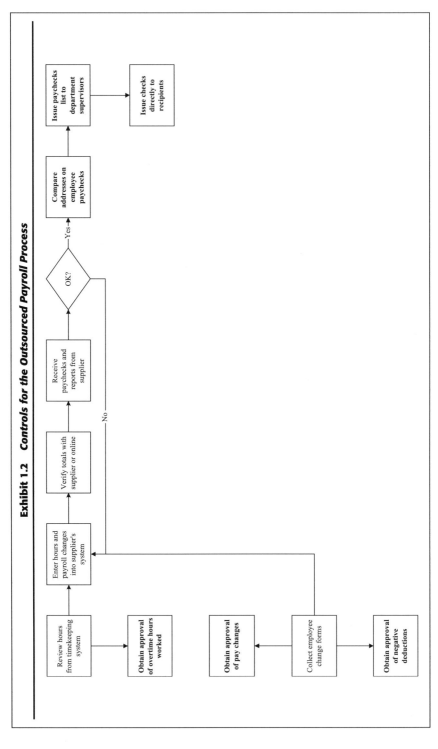

Overview of the In-House Computerized Payroll Process

A payroll system that is just as popular as outsourcing is the in-house computerized system. Payroll software is very inexpensive, as it is now bundled with accounting software that costs just a few hundred dollars. More comprehensive systems that can be used for large numbers of employees are much more expensive, but are a cost-effective solution for large entities.

The basic process flow for an in-house computerized payroll process is shown in Exhibit 1.3. A fully automated process involves the review and verification of hours worked and other changes as entered by the employees, followed by the processing and printing of payroll reports, filing of direct deposit information and payroll taxes, and the distribution of paychecks.

The flowchart assumes a complete automation of all key payroll functions. For example, a computerized timekeeping system is assumed. This system, as described in Chapter 2, requires employees to run a badge through a time clock that can reject the scan if the employee is clocking in at the wrong time or attempting to work during an unauthorized overtime period. By using such a system, the payroll process is considerably reduced at the front end, with the payroll staff only having to investigate missing badge scans. Also, the process flow assumes that employees can make their own deduction and address changes through an interface to the payroll software, so that the payroll staff only has to review these changes. Further, the process flow assumes that the timekeeping database used by the time clock computer feeds directly into the in-house payroll software, which eliminates the keypunching of payroll data. If any of these automation elements are not present, then the process flowchart appears as a mix between in-house computerization and a manual system, which is shown later in Exhibit 1.5.

There are several key differences between the automated in-house system shown in Exhibit 1.3 and the outsourced solution shown earlier in Exhibit 1.1. One difference is that an in-house system requires the payroll department to file several tax returns, which would otherwise have been filed by the payroll supplier. These include the quarterly federal tax return, the annual federal unemployment tax return, and annual W-2 forms to employees. There may also be a variety of state reports to file. Further, an in-house system that uses direct deposit requires the payroll staff to create a database of direct deposit information and send it to the company's bank, which uses it to process direct deposits to employees; this would have been handled by a payroll supplier. Third, the in-house payroll database must be backed up and stored, which is normally handled by the payroll supplier. Finally, an in-house system requires the payroll staff to summarize all tax deposits, fill out remittance forms, and file payments with the federal and state governments at regular intervals. Consequently, no matter how much control a company may feel it has by using an in-house computerized system, the payroll staff will have a number of additional tasks to perform.

Controls for the in-house computerized payroll process are noted in Exhibit 1.4. Based on the assumption that a computerized timekeeping system is being used, we further assume that there are no controls required for timekeeping activ-

Exhibit 1.3 Flowchart of the In-House Computerized Payroll Process

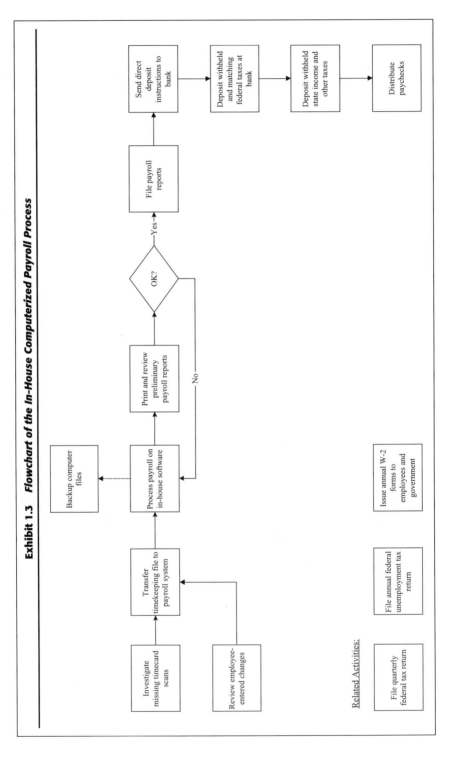

Exhibit 1.4   Controls for the In-House Computerized Payroll Process

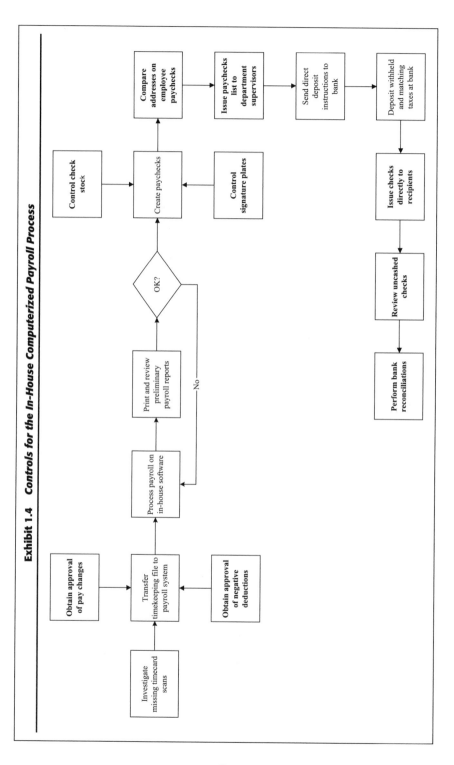

Exhibit 1.5 The In-House Manual Payroll Process

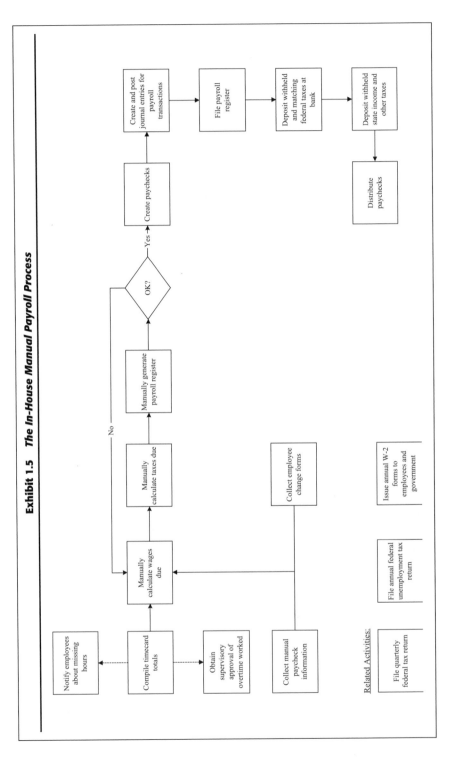

ities, since the computer can spot them. If your company does not have such a system, then please review either the outsourced or manual control systems in Exhibits 1.2 or 1.6 for the controls covering this area. Besides those controls shown earlier for the outsourced system, new controls are also needed for check stock and signature plates, both of which should be securely locked up at all times. Also, at the very end of the process flowchart are controls for reviewing uncashed checks and performing bank reconciliations. These controls are designed to spot payments made to employees who are no longer with the company and who, therefore, never received the checks (which were probably issued in error). These two controls can also be added to the earlier outsourced payroll system, though some suppliers will notify a company of any uncashed checks, depending on the outsourcing arrangement.

Overview of the In-House Manual Payroll Process

An increasingly rare payroll system is the completely manual approach that avoids all use of payroll suppliers or in-house computer systems. This system is most commonly found in very small organizations where the additional labor required to calculate wages and taxes is not too onerous for the small accounting staff.

The manual process requires extra labor in three key areas. First, employees are filling out timecards by hand or with a punch clock, so the payroll staff must use a calculator to add up the hours worked, verify the calculations (since this task is highly subject to errors), notify employees about missing time entries, and have supervisors approve any overtime hours worked. Second, the payroll staff must multiply hours worked by hourly pay rates to determine wages for the nonexempt employees and then use IRS-provided tax tables to determine the amount of taxes to withhold, plus the amount of matching taxes to be remitted by the company. This task is also subject to a high error rate and should be reviewed with care. Third, the payroll staff must create paychecks from the prior information and manually summarize the results into a payroll register. Since employees want to see all deductions broken out on their paychecks, the paycheck writing process is lengthy. In comparison to the outsourcing and in-house computer system solutions described previously, the manual payroll process is painfully slow and is at risk of so many errors that the payroll staff will find itself taking a disproportionate amount of its time to ensure that outputs from the process are correct. The manual payroll process is shown in the flowchart in Exhibit 1.5.

The flowchart does not mention the preparation of a direct deposit database that can be forwarded to a bank, since it is most unlikely that a company without means to calculate its payroll on a computer will be able to create the direct deposit database. Also, the three types of reports shown in the lower left corner of Exhibit 1.5 will require manual completion, which would not necessarily be the case if an in-house computerized system were used, since such systems can have the capability to produce these standard tax reports at the touch of a button.

The controls for an in-house manual payroll process are shown in Exhibit 1.6. Since there is an assumption of having no automated timekeeping system in place,

Exhibit 1.6   Controls for the In-House Manual Payroll Process

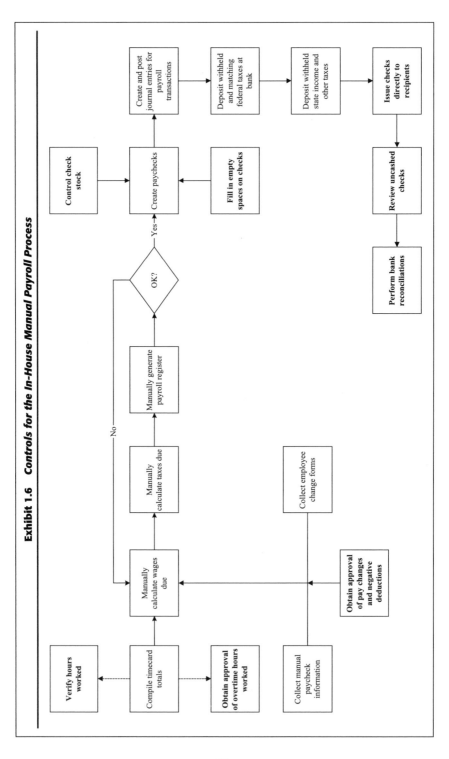

two key controls are verifying total hours worked and obtaining supervisory approval of overtime hours worked. Other controls later in the process are similar to those found in the computerized in-house system, since some watch over check stock and signature plates must be maintained. However, some of the reviews for fake employees at the end of the process, such as comparing addresses on checks, can probably be discarded, since this type of process is typically used for companies so small that the payroll staff knows exactly who works for the company.

Setting Up the New Employee

When a new employee is hired, the human resources staff will go over a variety of paperwork with the person and forward to the payroll department any items required by the payroll staff to calculate the person's wages, taxes, and other deductions. However, it is common in a smaller firm with no human resources staff for the payroll department to perform this function. If the latter situation is the case, the payroll staff should be aware of the variety of forms that are typically included in the new employee packet. Though some forms may be specific to an individual business, the following forms will be found in most cases:

- *Check-Off Sheet.* Each new employee packet should begin with a check-off list that itemizes all documents that should be contained within the packet. By using it to verify a complete package, there is minimal risk that employees will not be issued critical information. It is also useful to include the latest form release date on this sheet, so one can use it to verify the document dates contained within the packet.
- *Company Go-To List.* A new employee has no idea who to approach regarding basic daily issues, such as phone and network problems, pension plan enrollments, expense reports, and so on. This list should itemize which people to approach about each type of problem, as well as a backup person.
- *Company Phone List.* For a smaller company, this list should itemize not only the work number for each employee, but also the cell phone or other number at which they can be most easily reached. It is also increasingly customary to include e-mail addresses on this list. For larger companies with massive phone lists, the phone list for the department to which an employee belongs may be sufficient.
- *Company Seating Chart.* For a smaller company, it is quite useful to issue a seating chart that lists every person in the company. Once again, a larger company may be forced to issue a chart for smaller subsets of the company. This chart will require a reasonable amount of maintenance, given the number of moves typically experienced.
- *Insurance Enrollment Forms.* Enrollment forms for a variety of insurance types can be issued to a new employee at a later date if there is a waiting period before they go into effect. However, it is possible for some employees to

fall between the cracks and never be issued the forms. Consequently, a better approach is to issue them at the same time that an employee receives all other paperwork, so there is no chance of them being missed. Enrollment forms can cover medical, vision, dental, life, supplemental life, short-term disability, and long-term disability insurance. Some insurance carriers provide a wide range of coverages with a single application, but this is the exception—be prepared to issue a large number of documents.

■ *Veterans Check-Off Form.* Companies are required to submit the VETS-100 form to the federal government once a year, which specifies the proportion of military veterans in the corporate workforce. It is easiest to track this information by having new employees fill out a simple check-off form that itemizes whether or not they have been engaged in military service in the past.

■ *Employee Manual.* There should be a comprehensive employee manual in the new employee packet that includes a tear-out acknowledgement of receipt. The employee signs this receipt to indicate that he or she has received and read the employee manual; the receipt goes into the employee's personnel file. This is useful in case an issue regarding employee benefits or rights arises at a later date and an employee claims to have no knowledge of the issue, even when it is stated in the employee manual.

■ *Pay Period Schedule.* The pay period schedule may be obvious for salaried personnel, since it should always fall on the same date. However, employees who are paid on an hourly basis must know when a pay period ends, which can vary in relation to the pay date. This is an especially common problem when the timekeeping system is on a weekly basis and the payroll system is on some other system, such as biweekly.

■ *Form W-4.* All employees must fill out the IRS Form W-4, in which they claim a certain number of allowances and possibly additional tax withholdings. This information is needed in order to compute their income tax withholdings. Turn to Chapter 8, "Payroll Taxes and Remittances," for a more in-depth discussion of this form.

■ *Form I-9.* The Immigration and Naturalization Service requires all new employees to fill out the Form I-9, the Employment Eligibility Verification form. A sample copy of the form and its instruction sheet are shown in Exhibit 1.7. This form serves two purposes. First, it requires the employer to establish the identity of a new employee, which can be done with a driver's license, a variety of government identification cards, a voter's registration card, or a Native American tribal document. Second, it requires the employer to establish that a new employee is eligible to work, which can be done with a Social Security card, birth certificate, Native American tribal document, or an unexpired employment authorization document. These two requirements can be satisfied with a single document, such as a U.S. passport, certificate of U.S. citizenship or naturalization, unexpired temporary resident card, or several other documents that are specified in Exhibit 1.7.

Exhibit 1.7 *The Employment Eligibility Verification Form*

U.S. Department of Justice
Immigration and Naturalization Service

OMB No. 1115-0136
Employment Eligibility Verification

Please read instructions carefully before completing this form. The instructions must be available during completion of this form. ANTI-DISCRIMINATION NOTICE: It is illegal to discriminate against work eligible individuals. Employers CANNOT specify which document(s) they will accept from an employee. The refusal to hire an individual because of a future expiration date may also constitute illegal discrimination.

Section 1. Employee Information and Verification.   To be completed and signed by employee at the time employment begins.

Print Name: Last	First	Middle Initial	Maiden Name

Address (Street Name and Number)	Apt. #	Date of Birth (month/day/year)

City	State	Zip Code	Social Security #

I am aware that federal law provides for imprisonment and/or fines for false statements or use of false documents in connection with the completion of this form.

I attest, under penalty of per jury, that I am (check one of the following):
☐ A citizen or national of the United States
☐ A Lawful Permanent Resident (Alien # A _____
☐ An alien authorized to work until ___/___/___
(Alien # or Admission #) _____

Employee's Signature	Date (month/day/year)

Preparer and/or Translator Certification.   (To be completed and signed if Section 1 is prepared by a person other than the employee.) I attest, under penalty of perjury, that I have assisted in the completion of this form and that to the best of my knowledge the information is true and correct.

Preparer's/Translator's Signature	Print Name

Address (Street Name and Number, City, State, Zip Code)	Date (month/day/year)

Section 2. Employer Review and Verification.   To be completed and signed by employer. Examine one document from List A OR examine one document from List B and one from List C, as listed on the reverse of this form, and record the title, number and expiration date, if any, of the document(s)

List A	OR	List B	AND	List C
Document title: _____		_____		_____
Issuing authority: _____		_____		_____
Document #: _____		_____		_____
Expiration Date (if any): ___/___/___		___/___/___		___/___/___
Document #: _____				
Expiration Date (if any): ___/___/___				

CERTIFICATION - I attest, under penalty of perjury, that I have examined the document(s) presented by the above-named employee, that the above-listed document(s) appear to be genuine and to relate to the employee named, that the employee began employment on   (month/day/year)   ___/___/___ and that to the best of my knowledge the employee is eligible to work in the United States. (State employment agencies may omit the date the employee began employment.)

Signature of Employer or Authorized Representative	Print Name	Title

Business or Organization Name	Address (Street Name and Number, City, State, Zip Code)	Date (month/day/year)

Section 3. Updating and Reverification . To be completed and signed by employer.

A. New Name (if applicable)	B. Date of rehire (month/day/year) (if applicable)

C. If employee's previous grant of work authorization has expired, provide the information below for the document that establishes current employment eligibility.

Document Title: _____   Document #: _____   Expiration Date (if any): ___/___/___

I attest, under penalty of perjury, that to the best of my knowledge, this employee is eligible to work in the United States, and if the employee presented document(s), the document(s) I have examined appear to be genuine and to relate to the individual.

Signature of Employer or Authorized Representative	Date (month/day/year)

Form I-9 (Rev. 11-21-91)N Page 2

To fill out the I-9 form, have the employee fill out the "Employee Information and Verification" information in Section 1. This section must be signed by the employee and may require a preparer's or translator's signature as well if such a person assisted with the document. The employer fills out Section 2, which requires the examination of one or more original documents, as previously noted and as described in more detail on the second page of the exhibit. The reviewing person must then sign at the bottom of Section 2. Section 3 of the form is only used to update the information if an employee subsequently changes names, quit and was rehired within three years of the original form being completed, or has obtained a new work authorization.

Creating the Personnel File

When a new employee starts work, either the human resources or payroll staffs should create a personnel folder in which all employee-related documents are stored. This folder should be capable of holding several hundred pages of documents and also have multiple dividers, so that information can be logically divided and easily accessed. Information can be grouped in a variety of ways within the folder; here are some common subsets of information to consider:

- *Deduction Information.* One block of information will be the deductions related to all types of benefits, such as medical, life, and dental insurance. This means that the sign-up or waiver sheets for each type of insurance should be included in the folder.
- *Employee Correspondence.* Employees may communicate with the payroll or human resources departments from time to time, perhaps to make complaints, notify the company of time off for various reasons (such as jury duty), or ask for special treatment in some manner. If these communications are in writing, they should be included in the folder. If they are verbal, the person receiving the information may include them in a memo if the matter appears sufficiently important, and store them in the folder.
- *Employee Reviews.* All employee reviews should be kept in the folder. They are particularly important if employees later file suit against the company in the event of a termination, since the company must be able to prove that an employee was terminated for cause. Also, one should note if both the reviewer and the employee have signed a review, and if possible obtain these signatures if either one is missing, so that additional proof of employee receipt is made.
- *Garnishment Information.* If there are court orders for garnishing an employee's pay for any reason (e.g., tax levies, creditor levies, child support, or alimony), then a copy of each one should be included in the folder.
- *Tax-Related Information.* Tax deductions can only be made from an employee's wages if prior written authorization has been made by the employee. The employer should retain proof of these requests (nearly always in the form of a W-4 form) in the folder.

It is absolutely essential that the entire set of personnel files for all employees be kept under the strictest security at all times. These files contain potentially damaging information about employees, such as job reviews, medical information, or

Exhibit 1.8 *Company Name–Employee Change/New Form*

Employee Name: _____   Social Security #: _____

Reason: _____

Categories	Changes/New	Effective Date
Name		
Address		
Phone		
Gender		
Birth Date		
Hire Date		
Term Date		
Title		
Salary		
Status		
Married/Single		
Federal Exempt		
State Lived in		
State Worked in		
Medical Deduction		
Dental Deduction		
LTD		
STD		
Supp Life		
401K% or $		
Dependent Flex Deduction		
Dependent Flex Goal		
Medical Flex Deduction		
Medical Flex Goal		
Direct Deposit Routing #/Account #		

Comments: _____

_____

_____

_____

Completed by: Date:

court orders that could be embarrassing or job-threatening if the information were to become public knowledge. Employees rely on the employer to keep this information secret, and the employer should fulfill this expectation.

The Payroll Change System

There will be changes in employees' lives that require them to constantly ask for changes to the information used to create their paychecks. For example, an employee may have a baby, which requires an alteration in that person's medical insurance from two adults (which is at one price) to a family plan (which is at another price); this change will probably require a different payroll deduction for the employee's portion of the insurance expense, which must be reflected in his or her paycheck. As another example, an employee is diagnosed with a long-term medical problem that will require a great deal of medication, so this person enrolls in a cafeteria plan in order to deduct the medication cost from his or her pretax wages. These and other scenarios will occur constantly, so the payroll staff must have a procedure in place for handling them. One approach is to create a separate form for each type of payroll change, but this can result in a blizzard of paperwork. A better approach is a single summary-level change document such as the one shown in Exhibit 1.8.

This employee change form can be used as the source document for new employees, as well as for each incremental change requested by existing employees. In the latter case, one enters just the information relating to a specific request (such as a change in short-term disability, supplemental life insurance, or a 401k deduction), has the employee sign it to confirm the transaction, and submits it to the payroll staff for processing. The completed form is then filed in the employee's personnel folder.

Summary

The information in this chapter only covers the general process flow of several types of payroll systems, setting up new employees, and changing their information in the system over time. Other chapters contain a great deal of supplementary information. For example, Chapter 2, "Accumulating Time Worked," describes systems for collecting and summarizing employee hours in a variety of ways. Chapter 3, "Payroll Procedures and Controls," describes a number of payroll processing procedures in detail, and also describes a number of key control points that will reduce the risk of payroll errors or fraud. Chapter 13, "Payroll Journal Entries," describes the exact entries that should be transferred from the payroll system to the general ledger. Finally, Chapter 15, "Outsourcing Payroll," describes the advantages, disadvantages, management issues, and implementation problems associated with shifting the payroll processing function to an outside entity. All of these chapters should be read in order to obtain a better understanding of the payroll process.

2

Accumulating Time Worked

The Need for Time Tracking

This chapter* discusses the three types of costs incurred by any organization—direct materials, overhead, and direct labor. Historically, the largest of these three types of cost was either direct materials or labor necessitating the creation of elaborate tracking mechanisms for these two cost categories, while overhead costs were largely ignored. However, with the advent of technology, the cost of overhead has skyrocketed while direct labor costs have shrunk. As a result, much of the accounting literature has advocated the complete elimination of direct labor cost tracking on the grounds that the tracking mechanism is too expensive in relation to the amount of direct labor cost currently incurred.

In reality, a company's specific circumstances may still require the use of detailed direct labor tracking. This is certainly the case if the proportion of direct labor to total company costs remains high, such as 30 percent or more of total company costs. Given this large percentage, it is crucial that management know what variances are being incurred and how to reduce them. Another case is when a company is located in such a competitive industry that shifts in costs of as little as one percent will have a drastic impact on overall profitability. Finally, the decision to use a detailed labor tracking mechanism can be driven less by the total direct labor cost and more by the level of efficiency of the tracking system. For example, if a company's data-tracking costs bear the relationship to the proportions of total company costs that is noted in Exhibit 2.1, then there is a strong need to reduce the labor tracking system.

In the exhibit, the cost of direct labor is very low while the cost of collecting all associated data is much higher than the combined tracking costs for the other two cost types. The proportions shown here are quite common. If this is true for a given company, then the data tracking system for direct labor is probably not worth the cost of administration. However, if this data-tracking system can be made more efficient, perhaps with the data collection methods noted in the next

---

* This chapter is derived with permission from Chapter 5 of Bragg, *Cost Accounting* (Hoboken, NJ: John Wiley & Sons, 2001).

Exhibit 2.1 *Data Tracking Costs by Cost Type*		
Cost Type	Proportion of Total Costs	Proportion of Total Tracking Costs
Direct Materials	40%	15%
Direct Labor	10%	65%
Overhead	50%	20%
Totals	**100%**	**100%**

section, then it may still be worthwhile to use a reasonably detailed timekeeping system.

In short, it makes sense to employ a relatively detailed time-tracking system for direct labor if the proportion of total company costs is heavily skewed in favor of direct labor costs, if profit pressures are high, or if the cost of the timekeeping system is relatively low in proportion to the amount of direct labor cost incurred.

Data Collection Methods

In most cases, a company's total direct labor cost is not so high that it warrants the creation of an elaborate data collection system. Instead, the company can either focus on a simple system that collects only the most basic data or install a system that utilizes a greater degree of automated data collection, thereby keeping costs low while still obtaining a high degree of detailed information.

If a simple data collection system is needed, the easiest possible system to implement is one where employees are assumed to work 40 hours per week and the only need for logging hours is to record overtime, which is recorded on an exception basis and forwarded to the payroll staff who enter the additional overtime costs into the payroll system and generate payments to employees. This approach is most useful when a company has a relatively fixed base of direct labor employees who rarely work any additional hours and who also rarely work less than a fixed number of hours per week. A further justification for this approach is when a company has such a small amount of direct labor cost that any more elaborate timekeeping system would not be worth the effort to implement. This system yields no information whatsoever regarding how the cost of labor is being charged to various jobs. It has the singular benefit of being very inexpensive to maintain but at the cost of providing no costing information to management.

A slightly more complex system is to have direct labor employees fill out timecards that itemize their hours worked each week. These timecards are reviewed by the direct labor supervisors for accuracy and then forwarded to the payroll staff, who compile the information and key-punch it into the payroll system. This approach is most useful when there is a significant amount of variation in the number of hours worked per week resulting in continuing variations in employee pay from week to week. This approach requires considerably more administrative labor because of the large amount of data entry involved; additional labor is also needed to verify the entries made by employees and to investigate and correct any errors.

One step up from this entirely manual system is the addition of a time clock. In its simplest form, a $100 to $500 time clock can be mounted on a wall. Employees insert their timecards into it to punch their "in" or "out" times. This approach makes timecards easier to read and also controls the recording of times worked, so there is less chance of any deliberate alteration of times worked. This approach is highly recommended, since the additional cost is minimal and is easily justified by the increased level of data accuracy.

The next step up in system complexity involves the use of a computerized time clock. This is a device that is also mounted on a wall for employee access. However, it contains two additional features. One is the use of a bar-coded or magnetically coded employee card that is swiped through a channel on the side of the clock whenever an employee clocks in or out. This card contains the employee's identifying number, so that the system will record, with complete accuracy, the person's identification and all associated times worked. The second innovation is that the clock contains a computer that is linked back to a central payroll computer. This feedback mechanism allows the time clock to reject employee swipes if they are made at the wrong times (such as during the wrong break times), or if swipes are made for employees who are not supposed to be working during specified shifts (i.e., an employee brings in someone else's card and attempts to enter that person as being on the premises and therefore to be paid). The system can reject swipes that fall into any number of violation parameters and require the override password of a supervisor in order to record those swipes. This innovation yields a great improvement in a company's control over the timekeeping process. This second innovation yields a second major enhancement, all data swiped into the system requires no further key-punching. All of the data is sent straight into the payroll system where it is reviewed for errors and then used to pay employees. This eliminates the cost of extra data entry, as well as the risk of incurring data-entry errors. However, all of these innovations come at a price, typically in the range of $2,000 to $3,000 per automated time clock. A large facility may require a number of clocks if there are many employees who must use them, so the cost of this addition must be carefully weighed against the added benefits.

A larger volume of data can be obtained by using the just-described computerized time clocks at every workstation in the production area or a modified version thereof. Employees can easily punch in information about which jobs they are working on at any given time without having to walk to a centralized data-entry station to do so. These workstations can be time clocks that are directly linked to the payroll system. However, since these clocks are so expensive, this option is not normally used, especially if many workstations are required.

A more common approach is to purchase a number of "dumb" terminals that have no internal error-checking capacity at all and link them to a central computer that does all of the error-checking for employee and job codes, as well as hours worked. This option is much less expensive, especially for very large facilities. However, it suffers from one significant flaw: if the central computer goes down then the entire system is nonfunctional. This problem does not arise when using automated time clocks since each one is a separately functioning unit that does not depend on the availability of a central computer. This problem is a particular issue in companies that have large amounts of machinery that generate electrical energy. The extra radiation can interfere with the transmission of signals from the workstations to the central computer, usually requiring the installation of either heavily shielded cabling or the use of fiber optics, both of which are expensive options.

An employee uses the dumb terminal to enter his employee number, the start time, and the job number. All time accrued from that point forward will be charged to the entered job number until the employee enters a different job number. This data-entry process may require a large number of entries per day, introducing the risk of a high degree of data inaccuracy. The problem can be reduced by the use of bar-coded or magnetic-stripe employee cards, as previously described, as well as the use of bar-code scanning of all current job numbers.

This last option is clearly much more expensive than any preceding option since the cost of the central computer can be in the range of $10,000 to $250,000 and requires a large number of dumb terminals that cost at least $500 each. Why incur this expense? This system gives a company the ability to track the time worked on specific jobs. This is a very important capability when customers are charged based on the specific number of hours that employees work on their projects, especially when the customer has a right to investigate the underlying hourly records and to protest billings that do not match these detailed records. This is a particularly important issue for government work, where cost-plus contracts are still common and the government has a right to closely review all supporting labor records. It may also be a major concern for any organization where the cost of direct labor is still a relatively large proportion of total costs. Otherwise, managers would have no valid information about how a large proportion of company costs are being incurred. Nonetheless, the data-entry system required to support the collection of this information is very expensive, so one should conduct a cost-benefit analysis to see if the value of the supporting information is worth the cost of the system.

It is also possible to have employees manually track the time they charge to each job on which they are working. This option may seem much less expensive than the use of data-entry terminals that was just described. However, this approach is not recommended unless the number of employees using it is very small. The level of data errors will be extremely high, given the large number of jobs to which labor is charged each day—the time charged to a job may be wrong as well as the job number to which the time is charged. As a result, the cost of the administration time required to track down and correct these problems will greatly exceed the cost of installing an automated time tracking system; this correction cost will be so high for a large facility that the comparable cost of an automated system will be far lower.

A final timekeeping system that is not frequently used is through backflushing. This is not a real timekeeping system at all. Instead, the standard labor hours are stored in the labor routings database for each product and multiplied by the amount of production completed each day. This yields a standard amount of labor that should have been completed for each workstation in order to complete the total amount of production issued. This method is only good for developing approximations of the amount of labor that was needed to complete each step in the production process. It is of no use for spotting labor inefficiencies and cannot be used to derive payroll (since it does not report hours worked at the employee level, nor would these numbers be accurate even if it did so). Thus, the backflushing method, though a simple way to derive approximate labor hours, does not yield accurate information for most purposes to which direct labor information is put.

It should be apparent from the discussion in this section that a higher degree of data accuracy and a lower cost of timekeeping on a per-transaction basis can only be achieved with a high degree of expensive automation—and the more information required from the system, the more expensive it will be to collect it. Accordingly, one must first determine how badly a company needs every possible type of direct labor data, and then structure the type of data collection system based on the level of need. In order to make this decision, it is best to review the following section. It describes the various types of data that can be collected through a timekeeping system.

Information to Collect through Timekeeping

The most obvious item that must be collected through a timekeeping system is the number of hours worked by each employee. This one data element actually involves the collection of two other data items—the employee's name (or identifying number) and the date on which the labor was worked. This most minimal set of information is the smallest set of information required to do nothing more than calculate payroll for direct labor employees.

The next highest level of information that can be collected includes the identifying number of the job on which an employee is working. This additional data allows a company to accumulate information about the cost of each job. In some companies, where employees man a single workstation and perform processing on a multitude of jobs that appear in front of them each day, the amount of data collected may be from five to ten times greater than when only the direct labor hours per day are collected. This level of data collection is most necessary when customer billings are compiled from the number of employee hours charged to their jobs.

A further level of detail that can be collected is the workstation at which an employee is working. This data is collected when a company wants to track the amount of time spent on each of its machines. The company can tell which ones are being utilized the most frequently. This information is most important when a facility has bottleneck operations or very expensive equipment whose utilization is an important factor in the determination of capital efficiency. However, this information can also be obtained by multiplying labor routings by production volumes, which yields an approximate level of machine utilization or simply by a visual examination of the flow of production through a facility. Thus, this additional level of detail will only be worth collecting in selected situations.

Another possibility, in the absence of an identifying workstation, is to track the activity of each employee. For example, an employee could be repairing faulty products, manning a machine as the primary operator, substituting for other workers during their lunch breaks, and sitting in on a quality circle—all in the same day. This added level of detail is quite useful if a company wants to track activities for an activity-based costing system, which in turn can be most useful for activity-based management or the tracking of quality costs. However, this represents a highly detailed level of data tracking that in many situations is not appropriate—picture a large number of employees moving through a facility spending large parts of their day either writing down what they are doing at any given moment or trying to locate a data-entry terminal into which they can enter this information. In many cases, it is more efficient to conduct a study that results in estimates of employee time spent in various activities. It is a much more cost-effective way to collect information.

In short, a timekeeping system can collect information at the following levels of detail:

1. Hours worked.
2. The jobs on which hours were worked.
3. The workstations used to work on jobs.
4. The activities within each workstation that are used to work on jobs.

Each of these levels of data collection represents an increasing level of detail that can overwhelm the timekeeping system. For example, at the first level, there may be just one record per day that identifies the hours worked for one employee. At the next level, an employee may work on five jobs in a day, which increases the number of records to five. For each of those jobs, the employee uses two workstations, which increases the number of records to ten. Finally, there are three activities performed within each workstation, which results in a total of thirty records per employee per day. It is evident that each level of additional detail collected through the timekeeping system results in massive jumps in the amount of data that employees must enter into the system, as well as to be processed by it. One must review the added utility of each level of data collected, compare this benefit to the cost of collecting it, and make a determination of what level of data is sufficient for a company's needs. In many cases, stopping at either the first or second levels of data collection will be more than sufficient.

Timekeeping Reports

The reports issued from a timekeeping system should be directed toward the correction of data that has just been collected, comparisons to budgeted hours, and trends in hours—the reports should not include pay rates or the total dollar cost of direct labor, since this information is more appropriately reported through the payroll system, where all direct labor costs are stored.

A good timekeeping report that is designed to correct data-entry errors should not present the entire (and likely voluminous) list of all employee times recorded in the current period, but rather just those that clearly require correction. These can be times that are too high, any entry with some missing information, overtime, or hours worked during a weekend. A computer program can be created to sift through all direct labor data, pick out possibly incorrect data, and present it in a report format similar to the one shown in Exhibit 2.2.

Exhibit 2.2   *Timekeeping Data Correction Report*

Employee Number	Employee Name	Date Worked	Hours Worked	Job Number Charged	Comments
00417	Smith, J.	04/13/05	10	A-312	Overtime approval needed
00612	Avery, Q.	04/14/05	8	D-040	Invalid job number
00058	Jones, L.	04/13/05	8	—	No job number
01023	Dennison, A.	04/14/05	12	A-312	Overtime approval needed
03048	Grumman, O.	04/15/05	8	D-040	Invalid job number
03401	Smith, J.	04/16/05	8	A-310	Date is for a weekend
02208	Botha, T.L.	04/14/05	25	—	No job number

In addition to error correction, it is also important to devise a report that lists expected direct labor hours for various functions and compare these hours to those actually incurred. By doing so, one can see where operations are being conducted inefficiently or where the underlying standards are incorrect. The budgeted labor information is most easily obtained through a manufacturing resources planning (MRP II) system, which compiles the hours that should be worked each day, by workstation, from labor routings and the production schedule. The budgeted labor information for this report must otherwise be compiled manually. An example of the report is shown in Exhibit 2.3.

Exhibit 2.3   *Comparison of Actual to Budgeted Time Report*

Date	Work Center ID Number	Budgeted Hours	Actual Hours	Variance
04/14/05	PL-42	142	174	−32
04/14/05	PL-45	129	120	+9
04/14/05	RN-28	100	100	0
04/14/05	RN-36	140	145	−5
04/14/05	TS-04	292	305	−7
04/14/05	ZZ-10	81	80	+1
04/14/05	ZZ-12	40	60	−20

There is not normally a budget in the accounting system for the hours worked by each employee since this requires an excessive degree of work in compiling a budget and which must also be recompiled every time employees leave or join the company. Instead, create a trend line report of hours worked by each employee, useful for determining any tendency to work an inordinate amount of overtime or to work less than a normal amount of hours. The example shown in Exhibit 2.4 only covers a few weeks, but this report can be reconfigured in landscape format to show the hours worked by employee for every week of a rolling twelve-week period. Another approach is to report on employee hours by month instead of by week. This allows the hours worked for an entire year to fit into a single report.

As used in Exhibit 2.4, it is also useful to include a column that identifies the department in which an employee works. Overtime utilization frequently varies considerably by department, given the different workloads and capacities under which each one operates. By sorting in this manner, it can readily be determined which departments are consistently under- or over-utilized. In the exhibit, it is readily apparent that the lathe department is being overworked and will require the addition of more equipment, more personnel, or both.

	Exhibit 2.4	*Trend of Hours by Employee Report*			
Department	Employee Name	Hours, Week 1	Hours, Week 2	Hours, Week 3	Hours, Week 4
Drilling	Sanderson, Q.	40	40	40	40
Drilling	Underwood, C.	35	38	37	32
Drilling	Hecheveria, L.	32	32	32 .	32
Lathe	Anderson, B.	48	52	49	58
Lathe	Oblique, M.	47	45	50	52
Sanding	Masters, D.	40	40	40	40
Sanding	Bitters, I.M.	40	40	40	40

Problems with Timekeeping and Payroll

Despite a company's best efforts to create an accurate timekeeping system, there are several errors that will arise from time to time that require special controls to avoid. One error is the charging of time to an incorrect job. This is an easy error to make, involving incorrect data entry by a direct labor person, such as a transposition of numbers or a missing digit. To keep this problem from arising, the timekeeping system can be an interactive one that accesses a database of currently open jobs to see if an entered job number matches anything currently in use. If not, the entry is rejected at once, forcing the employee to reenter the information. This control can be made even more precise by altering the database to associate only particular employees with each job, so that only certain employees are allowed to charge time to specific jobs. However, this greater degree of precision requires additional data entry by the job scheduling staff, who must enter the employee numbers into the database for all people who are scheduled to work on a job. If there are many jobs running through a facility at one time, this extra data entry will not be worth the increase in data accuracy. If the existing data-entry system is only a simple rekeying of data from a paper-based timecard submitted by employees, then the data must be interpreted and then entered by the data-entry staff. This process generally results in the least accurate data of all, for there are now two people entering information (the employee and then the data-entry person), creating two opportunities to make a mistake. In short, the best way to avoid charging time to the wrong job is to have an interactive data-entry system.

Another problem is that vastly inaccurate amounts of hours will sometimes be charged to a job, usually through an inaccurate recording of numbers. For example, an eight-hour shift might be entered incorrectly as 88 hours. To avoid such obvious mistakes, the timekeeping system can be altered to automatically reject any hours that clearly exceed normally boundaries, such as the number of hours in a shift or day. A more sophisticated approach is for the timekeeping system to automatically accumulate the number of hours already charged during the current shift by an employee. This system yields an increasingly small number of hours that can still be worked through the remainder of the shift—any excess can either be rejected or require an override by a supervisor (indicating the presence of overtime being worked). This approach is not possible if employees record their time on paper, since the information is entered after the fact and any correction of an incorrect number will be a guess, sometimes inaccurate, by the data-entry person.

Another possibility is that an employee charges an incorrect employee code to a job resulting in the correct number of hours being charged to the job, but at the labor rate for the employee whose number was used, rather than the rate of the person actually doing the work. To avoid this issue, the timekeeping system should automatically access a list of valid employee numbers to, at least, ensure that any employee code entered corresponds to a currently employed person. Though this is a weak control point, it at least ensures that hours charged to a job will be multiplied by the hourly labor rate of *someone*, rather than zero. A much better control is to require employees to use a bar-coded or magnetically encoded employee number that they carry with them on a card. They are forced to enter the same employee code every time. A lesser control is to post a list of bar-coded or magnetically encoded employee numbers next to each data-entry station—this is a less accurate approach, since an employee can still scan someone else's code into the terminal. If a paper-based system is used, an employee normally writes his or her employee number at the top of a time report, which is then entered by a data-entry person into the computer at a later date. The problem with this approach is that the data-entry person may enter the employee number incorrectly, which will charge all of the data on the entire time report to the wrong employee number. Once again, an interactive timekeeping system is crucial for the correct entry of information.

Yet another problem is that the cost per hour that is used by the timekeeping system may not be the same one used in the payroll system. This problem arises when there is no direct interface between the timekeeping and payroll systems. Costs per hour are only occasionally (and manually) transferred from the payroll system to the timekeeping system. This results in costs per hour on timekeeping reports that are generally too low (on the grounds that employees generally receive pay *increases*, rather than *decreases*, so that any lags in data entry will result in costs per hour that are too low). One way to fix this problem is to create an automated interface between the payroll and timekeeping systems, so that all pay changes are immediately reflected in any timekeeping reports that track labor costs. It is important to use a fully automated interface, rather than one that requires operator intervention, or else there is still a strong chance that the cost data in the timekeeping system will not be updated because of operator inattention.

An alternative approach is to keep all labor costs strictly confined within the payroll system and to import timekeeping data into it, rather than exporting payroll data to the timekeeping system. There are two reasons for taking this approach. First, exporting payroll data anywhere else in a company makes it easier for unauthorized employees to see confidential payroll information. Second, the payroll system cannot generate many meaningful reports without data from the timekeeping system whereas the timekeeping system can generate a number of reports that do not need labor cost data (see the earlier section on timekeeping reports). Thus, it may be better to leave the payroll data where it is and instead to work on an automated interface of timekeeping data into the payroll system.

It is entirely possible that any of the problems described in this section will not only occur, but will also go undetected for a substantial period of time. To avoid this problem, the internal auditing department should be asked to conduct a period review of the controls surrounding the timekeeping and payroll systems, as well as a test of transactions to see if any problems can be spotted. The resulting audit report can be used to further tighten the controls around these data collection systems.

Timekeeping Case Study

A routine analysis of the system costs at a large manufacturing facility discovered that the cost of administering the company's direct labor timekeeping system appeared to be inordinately high. Approximately 50 percent of the entire cost accounting function was devoted to the collection and interpretation of data related to direct labor. The controller asked a cost accountant to investigate the situation and recommend a revised system that will generate usable information, while costing as little as possible to administer.

The cost accountant's plan for this analysis was to first determine the level of detailed information collected by the timekeeping system, calculate the cost of collecting it, and then determine the benefit of using the resulting information. She would then see if costs could be reduced for the existing collection system so that no benefits from the system were lost. If this was not possible or if the costs could only be reduced by a modest amount, then she would investigate the possibility of reducing the level of information gathered, which, in turn, would reduce the cost of data collection.

Her first step was to determine the level of detailed information collected by the timekeeping system. She interviewed the facility's controller, Ms. MacCauley, who said that the timekeeping system required employees to write down on a time sheet the hours they worked each day on specific jobs as well as the work centers within which they worked on each job. The typical time sheet looked like the one shown in Exhibit 2.5.

Exhibit 2.5   *Altanta Facility Time Sheet*

Employee Name: *Mort Dulspice*
Date of Timecard: 4/13/03

Time In	Time Out	Job	Work Center
08:00	08:45	004712	Lithograph
08:46	09:12	004712	Etching
09:13	10:48	004712	Lamination
10:49	12:00	004712	Glue
01:00	02:10	004799	Lithograph
02:11	03:04	004799	Etching
03:05	03:17	004799	Lamination
03:18	04:24	004799	Glue
04:25	05:00	004799	Packaging

It was apparent from the time sheet that each employee must carefully enter a large amount of information during the course of a work shift. Also, the information entered by the employee in the example was not easy to read, making it likely that the data-entry person who entered this information into the computer would have a difficult time entering it all correctly. Further, there were many time sheets submitted each day by the 412 direct labor personnel at the facility, some of which were lost by employees or during the data-entry process—this information had to be recreated, which could only be done through estimates of what work an employee completed during the period. The cost accountant found that these three issues gave rise to three different types of costs.

The first cost was the time required by employees to enter their time worked onto each time sheet and then transport this time sheet to the payroll office for data entry. The second cost was for the data-entry staff to initially enter the data into the computer, while the third cost was to track down and correct any missing information or to correct data that was incorrectly entered. The cost accountant calculated these costs for a typical month in the following manner:

1. *Cost to Initially Record Data.* She estimated that each employee required ten minutes per day to complete and deliver their time sheets. Since the average burdened cost per hour for all 412 employees was $17.92, this resulted in a monthly cost of $25,869 to collect the information, assuming 21 business days per month (412 employees × 21 days × $2.99/day).

2. *Cost to Enter Data into Computer System.* She found that 1.5 employees were required in the accounting department on a full-time basis to enter the information from all 412 time sheets into the computer system. These hourly employees earned a burdened wage of $12.05 per hour. This resulted in a monthly cost of $3,037 per month (1.5 employees × 21 days × 8 hours/day × $12.05/hour).

3. *Cost to Correct Data Errors.* On average, the accounting staff spent three hours per day correcting errors that had been discovered on time sheets or created during data entry. These errors were investigated and corrected by a senior data-entry clerk, whose hourly burdened pay was $15.28 per hour. This resulted in a monthly cost of $963 (3 hours × 21 days × $15.28).

The grand total of all these costs was $29,869 per month, or $358,428 per year.

The cost accountant's next task, that of determining the value of the benefits derived from the timekeeping system, was much more difficult. She found that the daily hours worked were used by the payroll staff to calculate and pay weekly wages to the direct labor employees. She described this function as a mandatory one for which the system must provide sufficient data to calculate the payroll, but she could not ascribe to it a monetary value.

Next, she looked at the benefit of tracking hours by job worked. This information was used by the cost accounting staff to develop an income statement for each job, which the sales staff used to revise its pricing estimates for future jobs, to verify that pricing levels were sufficiently high to ensure a targeted profitability level per job of 30 percent. The proportion of direct labor to all job costs was about one-third, so this was considered a significant cost that must be tracked for this purpose. The pricing staff assured the cost accountant that they frequently altered their pricing strategies in accordance with the information they received through the job income statements. Once again, the cost accountant found herself unable to clearly quantify a benefit associated with the tracking of direct labor hours, this time in relation to job numbers, but it appeared that obtaining the information was mandatory.

Ms. North's last benefits-related task was to quantify the benefit of tracking labor hours by work center within each job. She found that this information was only used by the industrial engineering staff. They summarized the information into a report that listed the total hours worked at each work center, by day, so that it could determine when capacity utilization levels were reaching such heights that new equipment must be purchased or when levels were so low that existing equipment could be sold. A brief discussion with the production scheduling staff revealed that standard capacity amounts per job were already stored in the labor routings of the facility's manufacturing resources planning (MRP II) system, which produced a similar report by multiplying the units in the production schedule by the hours per unit of production listed in the labor routings. This meant that an alternative system could be used to provide the industrial engineering staff with the information it needed, without resorting to additional data entry to provide this information.

The cost accountant then perused a sample of time sheets submitted by employees and noted that an average of three work centers were referenced on each time sheet for each job on which work was performed. If she could convince the management staff to eliminate the tracking of time by work center, she could cut the labor time spent on timekeeping by the direct labor employees by two-thirds, as well as similar amounts by the data-entry clerks who would otherwise have to enter and correct this information, since these additional entries must no longer be made. This worked out to a cost savings of $19,912 per month ($29,869 × 2/3), which was $238,950 per year.

The cost accountant realized that the industrial engineering staff would only agree to this change if it could be proven that the data it received from the MRP II system was sufficiently accurate to replace the work center capacity data it was previously receiving from the timekeeping system. To ensure that the MRP II system maintained a high level of labor routing accuracy (which was the prime driver of the accuracy of capacity information produced by the MRP II system), she added $50,000 back to her estimate of remaining timekeeping system costs, which would pay for an engineer whose sole purpose was to continually review the accuracy of labor routings. This resulted in a timekeeping system cost of $169,478, which still represented a reduction of $188,950 from the earlier timekeeping system, which was a drop in costs of 53 percent.

Summary

The timekeeping function is coming under increasing attack, as cost accountants realize that the cost of administering a detailed timekeeping system is exceeding the value of the resulting information. This issue can be resolved either by reducing the level of timekeeping effort until the effort expended equals the utility of the resulting information (which may result in the complete elimination of the timekeeping function) or by more fully automating the timekeeping and payroll functions, so that the cost of the system administration is reduced to the point where it is once again a cost-effective means of tracking labor activities.

The choice of which direction to take is based not only on the portion of total corporate costs devoted to direct labor but also on how crucial it is to a company to wring out the highest possible profits from operations. Thus, the nature of the timekeeping system is driven not only by the total cost of direct labor, but also by the level of profitability of the business.

3

Payroll Procedures and Controls

Introduction

The payroll function is largely driven by procedures that should be followed every time to ensure that work is completed in a consistent and thorough manner. This also allows a payroll manager to exercise proper control over the function, since anyone following a procedure is also following the control points that have been built into them. In this chapter,[*] we will cover the various types of procedures that should be used to run a payroll department, as well as address many of the control weaknesses and recommended control points that can offset them.

Payroll Procedures

A payroll procedure is a written statement that itemizes the reason for an activity, notes who is responsible for it, and describes exactly how the activity is to be completed. It is highly applicable to the payroll function, which is full of activities that must be completed the same way, every time.

The first step in creating a set of payroll procedures is to construct a flowchart of the overall process to identify all activities. The flowchart ensures that a procedure is written for each one. Also, each box in the flowchart contains an identifying index number for each procedure, which is later listed as the procedure number in the header for each procedure. Thus, one can first refer to a process flowchart for the specific procedure needed and then trace the index number to the detailed procedure. A sample payroll process flowchart is shown in Exhibit 3.1.

The remainder of this section contains six payroll procedures that correspond to the activities just noted on the payroll process flowchart. For consistency, they all have exactly the same format. The header contains a company logo, as well as a notation box on the right side of the header that lists an index (or retrieval) number, the page number, the date on which the procedure was created, and the index number of any procedure that it has replaced. The main body of the procedure is

---

[*] This chapter is derived from Chapter 3 of Bragg, *Essentials of Payroll* (Hoboken, NJ: John Wiley & Sons, 2002).

Exhibit 3.1   Payroll Process Flowchart

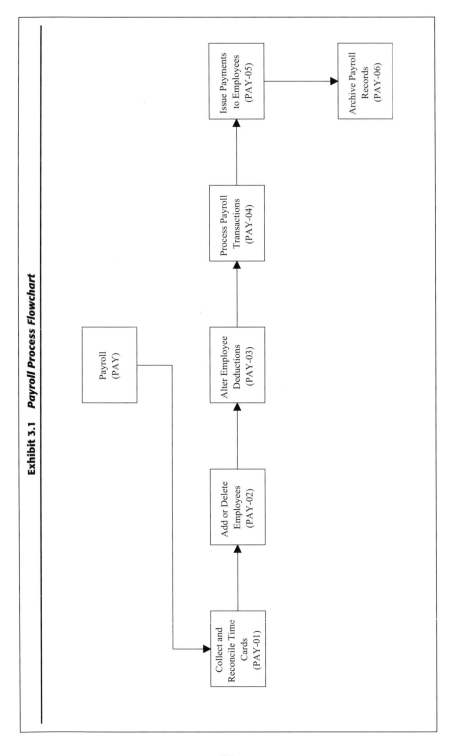

Collect and Reconcile Time Cards (PAY-01)

Add or Delete Employees (PAY-02)

Payroll (PAY)

Alter Employee Deductions (PAY-03)

Process Payroll Transactions (PAY-04)

Issue Payments to Employees (PAY-05)

Archive Payroll Records (PAY-06)

in three sections; the "Purpose and Scope" section summarizes what the procedure is all about, the "Responsibilities" section itemizes what job positions must follow the procedure, and the "Procedures" section lists the exact steps to follow. The exact procedures used here are designed for specific software packages and company procedures, and so, are not meant for exact copying by a user. Instead, it is best to review the general layout and terminology used in each procedure and then use this information to design a customized set of procedures for each company's specific circumstances. Specific payroll procedures, as noted in the preceding flowchart, are:

Policy/Procedure Statement	Retrieval Number	PAY-01
	Page:	1 of 1
	Issue Date	10/28/04
	Supercedes:	N/A
Subject: Collect and Reconcile Timecards		

1. PURPOSE AND SCOPE

This procedure is used by the payroll clerk to assemble timecards for all hourly employees, as well as to locate and resolve timepunching errors.

2. RESPONSIBILITIES

PR CLERK   **Payroll Clerk**

3. PROCEDURES

3.1   PR CLERK   **Obtain Timecards**
                        Obtain timecards from all company locations. Check off the receipts against the standard list of company locations and contact the factory manager of each location from which no cards have been received.

3.2   PR CLERK   **Review Timecards**
                        1. Add up the time on all timecards, circling those time punches that have no clock-ins or clock-outs. Note the total time on all error-free timecards and forward them to the payroll clerk for data entry into the payroll system.
                        2. Any timecard containing overtime hours must also be initialed by a manager; those cards missing this approval must be returned and signed.

3.3   PR CLERK   **Resolve Timecard Discrepancies**
                        1. Review all timecards containing discrepancies with the responsible factory managers. They must initial all timecards for which there is an assumed clock-in or clock-out.
                        2. List the total time worked at the top of these timecards.
                        3. Forward the cards to the payroll clerk for data entry into the payroll system.

Policy/Procedure Statement	Retrieval Number	**PAY-02**
	Page:	1 of 1
	Issue Date	10/28/04
	Supercedes:	N/A

Subject: Add or Delete Employees

1. PURPOSE AND SCOPE

This procedure is used by the payroll clerk to add or delete employees from the payroll system.

2. RESPONSIBILITIES

PR CLERK   **Payroll Clerk**

3. PROCEDURES

3.1 PR CLERK   **Obtain Addition or Deletion Documentation**

1. Receive documentation from the human resources department regarding the addition to or deletion from the payroll database of employees. Review the documentation for correct start or stop dates, extra pay, and (especially) the correct authorization signatures.
2. If any information is missing, return it to the sender for correction.

3.2 PR CLERK   **Update Payroll Database**

1. Go into the payroll software and access the EMPLOYEE menu. Go to the ADD screen if adding an employee. Enter the employee name and social security number, pay rate, and start date. If deleting an employee go into the DELETE screen from the same menu, enter a "Y" in the TERMINATE field, and enter the final pay date, as well as the amount of any bonus payments.
2. Print the Updates Report from the option at the bottom of the screen to verify that the correct entries were made.

3.3 PR CLERK   **File Documentation**

Consult the document destruction policy to determine the date at which the filed documents can be destroyed for any terminated employees. Mark this date on the employee's folder and forward it to the document archiving area.

Policy/Procedure Statement	Retrieval Number	**PAY-03**
	Page:	1 of 1
	Issue Date	10/28/04
	Supercedes:	N/A

Subject: Alter Employee Deductions

1. PURPOSE AND SCOPE

This procedure is used by the payroll clerk to alter employee deductions in the payroll system.

2. RESPONSIBILITIES

PR CLERK   **Payroll Clerk**

3. PROCEDURES

3.1 PR CLERK   **Obtain Deduction Information**
1. Obtain employee payroll deduction information from the human resources department.
2. Verify that all information on the deduction forms are clear and that each one is authorized by the employee.

3.2 PR CLERK   **Update Payroll Database**
1. Go into the payroll software and access the EMPLOYEE menu. Go to the DEDUCT screen and enter the deduction code and the amount of the deduction for each documented deduction. Be sure to enter a deduction termination code for those that are of limited duration.
2. Verify that deductions are correctly allocated to each payroll period, so that the total amount of each deduction is accurate on a monthly or annual basis.
3. Print the Updates Report from the option at the bottom of the screen to verify that the correct entries were made.

3.3 PR CLERK   **File Documentation**
Return all employee documentation to the human resources department, so that they can file it in employee folders.

Policy/Procedure Statement	Retrieval Number	PAY-04
	Page:	1 of 1
	Issue Date	10/28/04
	Supercedes:	N/A

Subject: Process Payroll Transactions

1. PURPOSE AND SCOPE

This procedure is used to guide the human resources coordinator or accounting staff through the payroll process.

2. RESPONSIBILITIES

HR COORD   **Human Resources Coordinator**

3. PROCEDURES

3.1 HR COORD   **Processing Steps**

1. Review all "Request for Time Off" forms that have been submitted during the most recent pay period.
2. Compare time-off requests to the accrued amounts for each employee, as noted in the payroll detail report for the last pay period. Notify employees if they do not have enough accrued vacation time available to fulfill their requests. Then process the portion of time they DO have available into the payroll.
3. Collect all requests for employee transfers to different departments and enter this information into the payroll software.
4. Enter all manual check payments for the current period into the payroll software.
5. Collect all requests for pay changes. Verify that there are authorized signatures on the pay change forms. Then enter the changes into the payroll software.
6. Collect all information regarding terminated employees. Calculate final payments due (if they have not already been paid with manual checks) and enter these final amounts into the payroll software.
7. Compare the garnishments file to the detailed payroll records from the last payroll period to see if any changes are needed to current employee deductions. If so, make those changes in payroll software.

8. On the Friday before the next payroll, clear out all old records from the electronic time clocks that relate back to the previous pay period. Review all electronic timecards for the current period and notify employees if they have incomplete timecards (such as having clocked in but never clocked out).
9. Manually transfer the totals from the electronic time clocks to the payroll processing software. To do this, enter the grand totals of regular and overtime hours into the "Hourly Pay by Employee" screen.
10. Verify all data entry by printing the "Payroll Audit Report" and comparing all entered data to the source documents. If there are problems, go back and make the changes, and then print this report again to ensure that all payroll data is correct.
11. Go to the "Process Payroll" screen and process all employee pay. Be sure to match the check number on the check stock to the check number appearing in the computer.
12. Use a signature stamp to sign the checks. Then stuff them into envelopes, along with any special employee notices, and sort them by department.
13. Back up the payroll database twice. Leave one copy on-site and send the other copy to the off-site storage location.
14. Reset the software to begin processing the payroll for the next pay period.
15. For any off-site locations, send payroll checks by guaranteed overnight delivery.
16. Retrieve the check register from the data center and review it for possible errors. Then file it in the payroll data storage area.

3.2 HR COORD

Process Deductions
1. Move the cafeteria plan amount noted on the payroll summary from the corporate checking account to the cafeteria plan account.
2. Move the 401k amount noted on the payroll summary to the 401k fund management firm from the corporate checking account.
3. Update the corporate life insurance payment by adjusting it for the total number of employees now on the payroll, as noted in the payroll summary.
4. Issue a check to the United Way based on the amount shown on the payroll summary as having been deducted from employee paychecks.
5. Pay garnishments to the various court authorities. Verify that the amounts paid out match the deductions shown on the payroll summary.

Policy/Procedure Statement	Retrieval Number	PAY-05
	Page:	1 of 1
	Issue Date	10/28/04
	Supercedes:	N/A

Subject: Issue Payments to Employees

1. PURPOSE AND SCOPE

This procedure is used by the payroll clerk to determine the locations of all employees in the company, and to issue paychecks or deposit advices to them.

2. RESPONSIBILITIES

PR CLERK   **Payroll Clerk**

3. PROCEDURES

3.1 PR CLERK   **Print Payroll Checks**
1. Go to the the payroll software and access the PRINT option from the PAYMENTS menu.
2. Print the payroll test register and review it to ensure that all paychecks have been correctly calculated.
3. Insert check stock into the printer.
4. Use the TEST option to print a sample check and verify that the line spacing is correct. Repeat as necessary.
5. Print the entire batch of checks.
6. Reset the printer and print all deposit advices for those employees using direct deposit.
7. Print the check register.
8. Review the file of direct deposits and export it to tape.

3.2 PR CLERK   **Issue Direct Deposit Data to Bank**
1. Include the direct deposits tape in a courier package to the bank.
2. Verify that the bank has received the tape and that there are no errors in it.

3.3 PR CLERK   **Distribute Payment Notifications**
1. Have all checks signed by an authorized check signer.
2. Stuff all paychecks and deposit advices in envelopes.
3. Batch the envelopes by supervisor and deliver them to supervisors for delivery to employees.

Policy/Procedure Statement	Retrieval Number	PAY-06
	Page:	1 of 1
	Issue Date	10/28/04
	Supercedes:	N/A

Subject: Archive Payroll Records

1. PURPOSE AND SCOPE

This procedure is used by the payroll clerk to properly label and archive all payroll records once they have been processed through the payroll system.

2. RESPONSIBILITIES

PR CLERK   **Payroll Clerk**

3. PROCEDURES

3.1 PR CLERK   **Index Payroll Records**

1. Extract the personnel folders from the on-site files for all inactive employees.
2. Batch all the timecards for prior work weeks.
3. Referring to the corporate document destruction policy, mark each item with the legally mandated earliest destruction date.

3.2 PR CLERK   **Archive Payroll Records**

1. Box the records by destruction date, mark each box with an index number, and record the index number in the master index, along with the contents of each box.
2. Send the boxes to the archiving center for storage.

After a procedure has been completed, give it to the most junior or least experienced person in the accounting department, with the task of walking through each step to ensure that the described steps are clear, logically flow from one step to the next, and result in correct payroll outputs. Almost always, this person will find missing instructions in a procedure. This occurs because the person writing a procedure is the most experienced at completing a specific task, and therefore makes assumptions about completing steps that a more junior person must have clearly written down.

The Need for Control Systems

The most common situation in which a control point is needed is when an innocent error is made in the processing of a transaction. For example, a payroll clerk incorrectly calculates the number of hours worked by a nonexempt employee, resulting in a paycheck that is substantially larger than would normally be the case. This type of action may occur because of poor employee training, inattention, or the combination of a special set of circumstances that were unforeseen when the accounting processes were originally constructed. There can be an extraordinary number of reasons why a transactional error arises. This can result in errors that are not caught and that, in turn, lead to the loss of corporate assets.

Controls act as review points at those places in a process where these types of errors have a habit of arising. The potential for some errors will be evident when a process flow expert reviews a flowchart that describes a process, simply based on his or her knowledge of where errors in similar processes have a habit of arising. Other errors will be specific to a certain industry—for example, the casino industry deals with enormous quantities of cash and so has a potential for much higher monetary loss through its cash handling processes than do similar processes in other industries. Also, highly specific circumstances within a company may generate errors in unlikely places. For example a manufacturing company that employs mostly foreign workers who do not speak English will experience extra errors in any processes where these people are required to fill out paperwork, simply due to a reduced level of comprehension of what they are writing. Consequently, the typical process can be laced with areas in which a company has the potential for loss of assets.

Many potential areas of asset loss will involve such minor or infrequent errors that accountants can safely ignore them and avoid the construction of any offsetting controls. Others have the potential for very high risk of loss, and so are shored up with not only one control point but a whole series of multilayered cross-checks that are designed to keep all but the most unusual problems from arising or being spotted at once.

The need for controls is also driven by the impact of their cost and interference in the smooth functioning of a process. If a control requires the hiring of an extra person, then a careful analysis of the resulting risk mitigation is likely to occur. Similarly, if a highly efficient process is about to have a large and labor-intensive control point plunked down into the middle of it, it is quite likely that an alternative approach should be found that provides a similar level of control, but from outside the process.

The controls installed can be preventive, designed to spot problems as they are occurring (such as flagging excessive hourly amounts for the payroll data entry staff), or detective, spotting problems after they occur, so that the accounting staff can research the associated problems and fix them after the fact (such as a bank reconciliation). The former type of control is the best, since it prevents errors from ever being completed, whereas the second type results in much more labor by the accounting staff to research each error and correct it. Consequently, the type of control point installed should be evaluated based on its cost of subsequent error correction.

All of these factors—perceived risk, cost, and efficiency—will have an impact on a company's need for control systems, as well as the preventive or detective type of each control that is contemplated.

Key Payroll Controls

The types of payroll controls that should be considered for implementation will vary by the type and size of a business, as well as whether the payroll is processed internally or by a supplier. Because the control risk will vary so much by a company's individual circumstances, it is best to review the following list of controls and then select only those that will improve the control environment. The controls are:

- *Employee Advances.* Employees may ask for advances on their next paycheck or to cover the cost of their next trip on the company's behalf. In either case, it is easy to lose track of the advance. The following controls are needed to ensure that an advance is eventually paid back:
  - *Continually review all outstanding advances.* When advances are paid to employees, it is necessary to continually review and follow up on the status of these advances. Employees who require advances are sometimes in precarious financial positions and must be issued constant reminders to ensure that the funds are paid back in a timely manner. A simple control point is to have a policy that requires the company to automatically deduct all advances from the next employee paycheck, thereby greatly reducing the work of tracking advances.
  - *Require approval of all advance payments to employees.* When employees request an advance for any reason—as a draw on the next paycheck or as funding for a company trip—this should always require formal signed approval from their immediate supervisors. The reason is that an advance is essentially a small short-term loan, which would also require management approval. The accounts payable supervisor or staff should only be allowed to authorize advances when they are in very small amounts.

- *Payroll Checks*. The storage, printing, and distribution problems associated with checks of all types certainly apply to payroll checks. The following list of controls is particularly applicable to those companies that process their payrolls in-house, since they handle check stock. However, even companies that outsource their payroll should consider the controls related to bank reconciliations, uncashed checks, and signature cards. If employees are paid solely through direct deposits, then these controls do not apply. Payroll check controls are as follows:

  - *Control check stock*. The check stock cannot be stored in the supply closet along with the pencils and paper, because anyone can remove a check from the stack, and then is only a forged signature away from stealing funds from the company. Instead, the check stock should be locked in a secure cabinet to which only authorized personnel have access.

  - *Add security features to check stock*. Checks can be successfully modified or copied with today's advanced technologies. To counteract this, purchase check stock with such security features as a "Void" logo that appears when a check is copied, microprinting that is difficult to copy, and holograms that are difficult to reproduce. A particularly effective method is to print a small lock icon on the face of a check, which warns a bank teller that the check contains security features that are listed on the back. The teller can then check the list of features and verify that they exist.

  - *Control signature plates*. If anyone can access the company's signature plates, then it is not only possible to forge checks, but also to stamp authorized signatures on all sorts of legal documents. Accordingly, these plates should always be kept in the company safe.

  - *Fill in empty spaces on checks*. If the line on a check that lists the amount of cash to be paid is left partially blank, a forger can insert extra numbers or words that will result in a much larger check payment. This can be avoided by having the software that prints checks insert a line or series of characters in the spaces.

  - *Mutilate voided checks*. A voided check can be retrieved and cashed. To keep this from happening, a stamping device that cuts the word "void" into the surface of the check should be used, thereby sufficiently mutilating it so that it cannot be used again.

  - *Perform bank reconciliations*. This is one of the most important controls anywhere in a company, for it reveals all possible cash inflows and outflows. The bank statement's list of checks cashed should be carefully compared to the company's internal records to ensure that checks have not been altered once they leave the company, or that the books have not been altered to disguise the amount of the checks. It is also necessary to compare the bank's deposit records to the books to see if there are discrepancies that may be caused by someone taking checks or cash out of the batched bank deposits. Further, one should compare the records of all company bank accounts to see if any check kiting is taking place. In addition, it is absolutely fundamental that the bank reconciliation be completed by someone who is completed unassociated with the payroll function, so that there is no way for anyone to conceal their wrongdoings by altering the bank reconciliation. Finally, it is now possible to call up online bank records through the Internet, so that a reconciliation procedure can be conducted every day. This is a useful approach, since irregularities can be spotted and corrected much more quickly.

- *Review uncashed checks.* If checks have not been cashed, it is possible that they were created through some flaw in the payroll system that sent a check to a nonexistent employee. An attempt should be made to contact these employees to see if there is a problem.

- *Update signature cards.* A company's bank will have on file a list of check signatories that it has authorized to sign checks. If one of these people leaves the company for any reason, he or she still has the ability to sign company checks. To void this control problem, the bank's signature card should be updated as soon as a check signer leaves the company.

- **Payroll Expenses.** The controls used for payroll cover two areas—the avoidance of excessive amounts of pay to employees, and the avoidance of fraud related to the creation of paychecks for nonexistent employees. Both types of controls are addressed here.

  - *Verify hours worked.* Employees may pad their time sheets with extra hours, hoping to be paid for these amounts. Alternatively, they may have fellow employees clock them in and out on days when they are not working. These actions can be difficult to spot, especially when there are many employees for a supervisor to track, or if employees work in outlying locations. Problems in this area can be difficult to find. Supervisors should review and initial all time sheets to ensure that hours have been worked, though they may not remember what happened several days earlier in the reporting period. As noted in Chapter 2, an automated time clock can be used to block out the hours when an employee is allowed to clock in or out, and can be used to quickly create reports for managers that highlight timekeeping irregularities. Finally, review the employee hours loaded into the payroll software to the amounts listed on employee time sheets to ensure that there have been no errors in the rekeying of hours data.

  - *Require approval of all overtime hours worked by hourly personnel.* One of the simplest forms of fraud is to come back to the company after hours and clock out at a later time, or have another employee do it on one's behalf, thereby creating false overtime hours. This can be resolved by requiring supervisory approval of all overtime hours worked. A more advanced approach is to use a computerized time clock that categorizes each employee by a specific work period, so that any hours worked after his or her standard time period will be automatically flagged by the computer for supervisory approval. They may not even allow an employee to clock out after a specific time of day without a supervisory code first being entered into the computer.

- *Require approval of all pay changes.* Pay changes can be made quite easily through the payroll system if there is collusion between a payroll clerk and any other employee. This can be spotted through regular comparisons of pay rates *paid* to the approved pay rates *stored* in employee folders. It is best to require the approval of a high-level manager for all pay changes, which should include that person's signature on a standard pay change form. It is also useful to audit the deductions taken from employee paychecks, since these can be altered downwards to effectively yield an increased rate of pay. This audit should include a review of the amount and timing of garnishment payments, to ensure that these deductions are being made as required by court orders.

- *Require approval of all negative deductions.* A negative deduction from a paycheck is essentially a cash payment to an employee. Though this type of deduction is needed to offset prior deductions that may have been too high, it can be abused by artificially increasing a person's pay. Consequently, all negative deductions should be reviewed by a manager.

- *Obtain computer-generated exception reports.* If the payroll software is sufficiently sophisticated, the programming staff can create exception reports that tell one if payments are being made to terminated employees, the amount of payments to new employees, whether negative deductions are being processed, or when unusually high base pay or overtime amounts are being processed. Any of these situations may call for a more detailed review of the flagged items to ensure that any intentional or unintentional errors will not result in incorrect payments.

- *Issue checks directly to recipients.* A common type of fraud is for the payroll staff to either create employees in the payroll system, or to carry on the pay of employees who have left the company, and then pocket the resulting paychecks. This practice can be stopped by ensuring that every paycheck is handed to an employee who can prove his or her identity. The only exception should be those cases where, due to disability or absence, an employee is unable to collect a check, and so gives written authorization for it be to given to someone else, who brings it to the absent employee.

  In cases where there are outlying locations for which it is impossible to physically hand a paycheck to an employee, a reasonable alternative is to have the internal audit staff periodically travel to these locations with the checks on an unannounced basis, and require physical identification of each recipient before handing over a check.

- *Issue lists of paychecks issued to department supervisors.* It is quite useful to give supervisors a list of paychecks issued to everyone in their departments from time to time, because they may be able to spot payments being made to employees who are no longer working there. This is a particular problem in larger companies, where any delay in processing termination paperwork can result in continuing payments to ex-employees. It is also a good control over any payroll clerk who may be trying to defraud the company by delaying termination paperwork and then pocketing the paychecks produced in the interim.

- *Compare the addresses on employee paychecks.* If the payroll staff is creating additional fake employees and having the resulting paychecks mailed to their home addresses, then a simple comparison of addresses for all check recipients will reveal duplicate addresses (though employees can get around this problem by having checks sent to post office boxes—this control issue can be stopped by creating a policy to prohibit payments to post office boxes).

The preceding set of recommended controls only encompasses the most common ones. These should be supplemented by reviewing the process flows used by a company to see if there is a need for additional (or fewer) controls, depending upon how the processes are structured. Thus, these controls should only be considered the foundation for a comprehensive set of controls that must be tailored to each company's specific needs

When to Eliminate Controls

Despite the lengthy list of controls noted in the last section, there are times when one can safely take controls away. By doing so, one can frequently eliminate extra clerical costs or at least streamline the various accounting processes. To see if a control is eligible for removal, the following steps should be used:

1. *Flowchart the process.* The first step is to create a picture of every step in the entire process in which a control fits by creating a flowchart. This is needed in order to determine where other controls are located in the process flow. With a knowledge of redundant control points or evidence that there are no other controls available, one can then make a rational decision regarding the need for a specific control.

2. *Determine the cost of a control point.* Having used a flowchart to find controls that may no longer be needed, we must then determine their cost. This can be a complex calculation, for it may not just involve a certain amount of labor, material, or overhead costs that will be reduced. It is also possible that the control is situated in the midst of a bottleneck operation, so that the presence of the control is directly decreasing the capacity of the process, thereby resulting in reduced profits. In this instance, the incremental drop in profits must be added to the incremental cost of operating the control in order to determine its total cost.

3. *Determine the criticality of the control.* If a control point is merely a supporting one that backs up another control, then taking it away may not have a significant impact on the ability of the company to retain control over its assets. However, if its removal can only be counteracted by a number of weaker controls, it may be better to keep it in operation.

4. *Calculate the control's cost/benefit.* The preceding two points can be compared to see if a control point's cost is outweighed by its criticality, or if the current mix of controls will allow it to be eliminated with no significant change in risk, while stopping the incurrence of its cost.

5. *Verify the use of controls targeted for elimination.* Even when there is a clearcut case for the elimination of a control point, it is useful to notify everyone who is involved with the process in which it is imbedded, in order to ascertain if there is some other use for which it is being used. For example, a control that measures the cycle time of a manufacturing machine may no longer be needed as a control point, but may be an excellent source of information for someone who is tracking the percentage utilization of the equipment. In these cases, it is best to determine the value of the control to the alternate user of the control before eliminating it. It may be necessary to work around the alternate use before the control point can be removed.

This control evaluation process should be repeated whenever there is a significant change to a process flow. Even if there has not been a clear change for some time, it is likely that a large number of small changes have been made to a process, whose cumulative impact will necessitate a controls review. The period of time between these reviews will vary by industry, since some have seen little process change in many years, while others are constantly shifting their business models, which inherently requires changes to their supporting processes.

If there are any significant changes to a business model, such as the addition of any kind of technology, different types of employment models, the addition of new company locations, or a shift to outsourcing or contracting out various types of labor, a complete review of all associated process flows should be conducted both prior to and immediately after the changes, so that unneeded controls can be promptly removed or weak controls enhanced.

Summary

Procedures and controls are critical components of the payroll process. Procedures are designed to increase the efficiency of the department by standardizing work steps, while controls can have the opposite effect by increasing the number of tasks in the procedures in order to ensure that there is no loss of assets. The payroll manager must reconcile the conflicting goals of procedures and controls—efficiency versus asset control—by balancing the need for additional streamlining with any resultant loss of control. There is no perfect solution to this balancing act, since it will be based on the number of company locations, the skill level of the staff, the department's organizational structure, and other intangible factors. Also, once the payroll manager strikes a balance between the efficiency and control objectives, this issue must be revisited time and again, since the manner in which the payroll department operates will change over time; these changes must be incorporated into procedures and evaluated in terms of their impact on the control environment.

4

Payroll Best Practices

Introduction

Though anyone can cobble together a payroll system that operates moderately well, there are a number of steps that can be taken to greatly increase the efficiency of this operation. The steps, discussed in this chapter,[*] are called "best practices," and are indicative of the work practices used by the operators of highly efficient payroll operations. Though some payroll best practices are clearly designed for larger companies with a multitude of employees, others can be used to improve the operations of companies of any size.

The following sections briefly describe a number of payroll best practices including the pros and cons of their use, any problems with their implementation, and a graphical representation of their cost and installation time. The best practices are generally clustered, in order, by those relating to the gathering of payroll data, the processing of that data, and finally its distribution.

Implementation Issues for Payroll Best Practices

For the reader to understand which of these best practices is the right one for a specific situation, it is useful to review the table shown in Exhibit 4.1. This table lists a number of key implementation issues for each best practice. It notes the likely cost and duration of implementation, which is of concern to those companies that may have a short time and cost budget for improvements. The table is an effective approach for quickly determining which projects to work on and which ones to avoid.

A danger of using the table in Exhibit 4.1 to pick only the easiest best practices is that these are primarily "quick hits" that will generally have a relatively small impact on the overall level of efficiency of the payroll function. Accordingly, it is important to insert changes that require greater implementation effort and that have a correspondingly higher payback. For example, adding direct deposit is an easy and popular improvement, but a more fundamental change that requires

---

[*] This chapter is largely adapted with permission from Chapter 17, "Payroll Best Practices," in *Accounting Best Practices, 3rd Edition*, by Bragg (Hoboken, NJ: John Wiley & Sons, 2004).

Exhibit 4.1 *Summary of Payroll Best Practices*

Best Practice	Cost	Install Time
Employee Deductions		
Disallow prepayments	💵	🕐
Give employees direct access to deduction data	💵💵💵	🕐🕐🕐
Minimize payroll deductions	💵	🕐
Prohibit deductions for employee purchases	💵	🕐
Employee Forms		
Automatic fax-back of payroll forms	💵💵💵	🕐🕐🕐
Post forms on an intranet site	💵	🕐🕐
Employee Time Tracking		
Avoid job costing through the payroll system	💵	🕐
Switch to salaried positions	💵	🕐🕐
Use bar-coded time clocks	💵💵	🕐🕐
Use biometric time clocks	💵💵	🕐🕐
Use honor system to track vacation and sick time	💵	🕐
Payments to Employees		
Issue electronic W-2 forms to employees	💵	🕐🕐
Offer clear cards to employees	💵	🕐🕐
Post commission payments on the company intranet	💵💵	🕐🕐
Transfer payroll to credit card balances	💵	🕐🕐
Use direct deposit	💵	🕐
Payroll Management		
Automate vacation accruals	💵	🕐
Consolidate payroll systems	💵💵💵	🕐🕐🕐
Eliminate personal leave days	💵	🕐
Link payroll changes to employee events	💵💵💵	🕐🕐🕐
Link the 401k plan to the payroll system	💵	🕐🕐🕐
Link the payroll and human resources databases	💵💵💵	🕐🕐🕐
Minimize payroll cycles	💵	🕐🕐🕐
Use a forms/rates data warehouse for automated tax filings	💵💵💵	🕐🕐🕐

much persuasion and more time to implement is reducing the number of payroll cycles. Creating a mix of both easy and difficult projects is key to showing continuing successes, while working towards greater levels of efficiency over the longer term.

Disallow Prepayments

Many employees do not have the monetary resources to see them through until the next payday. Their solution is to request a pay advance, which is deducted from their next paycheck. It is a humane gesture on the part of the payroll manager to comply with such requests but it plays havoc with the efficiency of the payroll department. Whenever such a request is made, the payroll staff must manually calculate the taxes to take out of the payment, then manually cut a check and have it signed. However, the inefficiencies are not yet over! In addition, the staff must manually enter the pay advance in the computer system so that the amount is properly deducted from the next paycheck. For larger advances, it may be necessary to make deductions over several paychecks, which requires even more work. Furthermore, if an employee quits work before earning back the amount of the advance, the company has just incurred a loss. Clearly, paycheck prepayments do not help the efficiency of the payroll department. This is a particularly significant problem in organizations where the average pay level is near the minimum wage, since the recipients may not have enough money to meet their needs.

The best practice that solves this problem seems simple, but can be quite difficult to implement. Create a rule that no paycheck prepayments will be issued, which effectively ends the extra processing required of the payroll staff.

The trouble with this rule is that a needy employee can usually present such a good case for a pay advance that exceptions will be made; this grinds away at the rule over time, until it is completely ignored. Other managers will assist in tearing down the rule by claiming that they will lose good employees if advances are not provided to them. The best way to support this rule is to form an association with a local lending institution that specializes in short-term loans. Then, if an employee requests an advance, he can be directed to the lending institution, which will arrange for an interest-bearing loan to the employee. When this arrangement exists, it is common for employees to tighten their budgets rather than pay the extra interest charged for use of the lender's money. This improves employee finances while increasing the processing efficiency of the payroll staff.

Be sure to arrange for alternative employee financing *before* setting up a no-advance rule in order to be certain that alternative financing will be available to employees. Then go over the rule with all employees several weeks before it is to be implemented, so that employees will have fair warning of the change. Also, have brochures available in the payroll department that describe the services of the lending institution, as well as contact information and directions for reaching it.

Cost: *Installation time:*

Give Employees Direct Access to Deduction Data

A major task for the payroll staff is to meet with employees to go over the effect of any deduction changes they wish to make, calculate the changes, and enter them into the payroll database. This can be a particularly time-consuming task if the number of possible deduction options is large, if employees are allowed to make deduction changes at any time, or if employees are not well educated in the impact of deduction changes on their net pay.

A particularly elegant best practice that resolves this problem is to give employees direct access to the deduction data so they can determine the impact of deduction changes themselves and enter the changes directly into the payroll database. To do so, one must construct an interface to the payroll database that lists all deductions taken from employee paychecks (with the exception of garnishments, which are set by law). However, this is not enough, for most deductions are usually tied to a benefit of some sort. For example, a deduction for a medical plan can only be changed if the underlying medical plan option is changed. Accordingly, an employee needs access to a "split screen" of information, with one side showing benefit options and the other side showing the employee's gross pay, all deductions, and net pay. This view allows one to modify deductions and watch the impact on net pay. Examples of deductions for which this data view will work are federal and state tax deductions, medical and dental plan coverage, life and disability insurance coverage, and pension plan deductions.

Though the primary emphasis of this best practice is on allowing employees to alter their own deduction information, it can be used in other ways, too. For example, employees can alter the bank routing and account numbers used for the direct deposit of their pay into bank accounts, or change the amounts split between deposits to their savings and checking accounts. They could also use this approach to process requests for additional W-2 forms or to download files containing the employee manual or other relevant personnel information.

An example of this approach is the dental plan. On one side of the computer screen, an employee is presented with five dental plan options, all with different costs. The employee can scroll through the list and select any option, while watching the selection automatically change the payroll calculation on the other side of the screen. Once the employee finds the selection that works best, he presses a button to enter the change into the payroll system. Such a system should include some selection blocks so that employees cannot constantly change deductions; for example, the software may limit employees to one health plan change per year.

This approach completely eliminates all work by the payroll staff to enter deduction changes into the computer. An added benefit is that employees are responsible for their own data-entry mistakes. If they make an incorrect entry, they can go into the system themselves to correct it. The system can also be expanded to include other data items, such as employee names, addresses, and phone numbers. In addition, the deduction modeling system just noted allows employees to determine precisely what their net pay will be, eliminating any surprises. In a more traditional system, an employee might make a deduction change without realizing the full impact of the change on her net pay and end up back in the payroll office, demanding a reversion back to the old deduction level. By using the modeling system, the payroll staff can eliminate such multiple visits from employees.

This system will only work if the company is willing to invest a significant amount of software development effort to design an employee interface, as well as to provide either individual computers or central kiosks to employees so that they can use the system. Given its high cost, this system is usually only found in larger organizations with many employees, where the cost-benefit trade-off is obvious.

The software development effort required for this best practice is substantial, so it must be budgeted for well in advance, and must gain the approval of whatever committee schedules the order in which development projects will be completed. Also, be sure to carefully document all benefit plan rules related to changes in the plans, so that employees are not caught unawares; for example, many dental insurance plans only cover the costs of participants for major dental surgery if they have already been in the plan for at least one year—the computer system must warn employees of this requirement before they switch to a different plan.

Cost: 💵 💵 💵   Installation time: 🕒 🕒 🕒

Minimize Payroll Deductions

A company can offer a large number of benefits to its employees, many of which require some sort of deduction from payroll. For example, a company can set up deductions for employee medical, dental, life, and supplemental life insurance, as well as cafeteria plan deductions for medical insurance or child care payments, as well as 401k deductions and 401k loan deductions. If there are many employees and many deduction types, the payroll staff can be snowed under at payroll processing time by the volume of changes continually occurring in this area. Also, whenever there is a change in the underlying cost of insurance provided to the company, the company commonly passes along some portion of these costs to the employees, resulting in a massive updating of deductions for all employees who take that particular type of insurance. This not only takes time away from other, more value-added accounting tasks, but also is subject to error, so that adjustments must later be made to correct the errors, which requires even more staff time.

There are several ways to address this problem. One is to eliminate the employee-paid portion of some types of insurance. For example, if the cost to the company for monthly dental insurance is $20 per employee and the related deduction is only $2 per person, management can elect to pay for the entire cost, rather than burden the accounting staff with the tracking of this trivial sum. Another alternative is to eliminate certain types of benefits, such as supplemental life insurance or 401k loans, in order to eliminate the related deductions. Yet another alternative is to create a policy that limits employee changes to any benefit plans, so they can only make a small number of changes per year. This eliminates the continual changing of deduction amounts in favor of just a few large bursts of activity at prescheduled times during the year. A very good alternative is to create a benefit package for all employees that requires a single deduction of the same amount for everyone, or for a group (such as one deduction for single employees and another for employees with families); employees can then pick and choose the exact amount of each type of benefit they want within the boundaries of each benefit package, without altering the amount of the underlying deduction. This last alternative has the unique advantage of consolidating all deductions into a single item, which is much simpler to administer. Any of these approaches to the problem will reduce the number or timing of deduction changes, thereby reducing the workload of the payroll staff.

Cost: 💵   *Installation time:* ●

Prohibit Deductions for Employee Purchases

Many companies allow their employees to use corporate discounts to buy products through them. For example, a company may have obtained a large discount on furniture from a supplier. Its employees buy at the discounted rate and then have the deductions subtracted from their paychecks in convenient installments. Some employees make excessive use of this benefit, purchasing all kinds of supplies through the company; accordingly, it is common to see a small minority of employees comprising the bulk of these purchases. The problem for the payroll staff is that it must keep track of the total amount that each employee owes the organization and gradually deduct the amount owed from successive paychecks. If an employee has multiple purchases, the payroll staff must constantly recalculate the amount to be deducted. Depending on the number of employees taking advantage of purchases through the company, this can have a measurable impact on the efficiency of the payroll department.

The solution to this problem is to prohibit employee purchases through the organization. By doing so, all the extra paperwork associated with employee purchases is immediately swept away.

Though this is a good best practice for most companies to implement, this one should first be cleared with senior management. The reason is that some employees may be so accustomed to purchasing through the company that they will be rudely surprised by the change, a condition that management may want to avoid (especially if valuable employees will be bothered by the change). Also, some companies have valid reasons for allowing employee purchases, such as steel-toed boots or safety clothing that is necessary for performing their jobs.

As just noted, this best practice should be reviewed with all key department managers and senior management before being made public. Also, any employees who are currently having deductions taken from their paychecks for past purchases should be "grandfathered" into the new rule, so that they are not forced to suddenly pay off the remaining amounts due.

Cost: 💵   *Installation time:* ●

Automate Fax-Back of Payroll Forms

A payroll clerk is the unofficial keeper of the payroll and human resources forms. Employees come to this person to collect these sheets, which can vary from a request to change a payroll deduction to a request to change a pension deduction amount. If a company has many employees, or if it has many locations (which necessitates mailing forms to recipients), the chore of handing out forms can take up a large amount of staff time.

To avoid distributing forms to employees, one can set up an automated fax-back system. This best practice requires employees to contact a computer, either using a touch-tone phone or through the computer system, and request that the appropriate form be sent to a fax number close to the employee. If the employee has computer access, they can also download the form directly and either fill it out on his or her computer or print it, fill it out, and mail it back.

The computer has all of the forms digitized and stored in its memory and can make the transmission with no human intervention. For example, an employee accesses the system through a computer, scrolls through a list of available forms, highlights the needed item, enters the send-to fax number, and logs off. The form arrives a few moments later.

Under a manual distribution system, it is common practice to issue large quantities of forms to outlying locations, so that the payroll staff is not constantly sending out small numbers of additional forms; however, these forms end up being used for a long time, frequently past the date when they become obsolete. An automated fax-back system eliminates this problem by only having the most recent version available for transmission. This is a boon to the payroll staff, who might otherwise receive old forms that do not contain key information, requiring them to contact employees to gather the missing data, or even forcing employees to resubmit their requests on the latest forms.

In addition, the system can automatically send along an extra instruction sheet with each distributed form so that employees can easily fill out forms without having to call the payroll staff for assistance.

An automated fax-back system can be expensive, so one should determine all costs before beginning an implementation. The system includes a separate file server linked to one or more phone lines (for receiving touch-tone phone requests, as well as for sending forms out to recipient fax machines), plus a scanner for digitizing payroll forms. The best way to justify these added costs is if there are a large number of employees to be serviced, which saves a large amount of staff time. Without enough employees to create a valid justification, the system should not be installed.

Be sure to leave enough time in the implementation schedule to review the variety of fax-back systems on the market prior to making a purchase, as well as for configuring the system and testing it with employees. If the system has an option for document requests both by phone and computer, then implement one at a time to ensure that each variation is properly set up.

Cost: 💾 💾 💾   Installation time: 🕐 🕐 🕐

Post Forms on an Intranet Site

Employees frequently come to the accounting department to ask for any of the variety of forms required for changes to their payroll status, such as the IRS's W-4 form, address changes, cafeteria plan sign-up or change forms, and so on. These constant interruptions interfere with the orderly flow of accounting work, especially when the department runs out of a form and must scramble to replenish its supplies.

This problem is neatly solved by converting all forms to Adobe Acrobat's PDF format and posting them on a company intranet site for downloading by all employees. By using this approach, no one ever has to approach the accounting staff for the latest copy of a form. Also, employees can download the required form from anywhere, rather than having to wait until they are near the accounting location to physically pick one up. Further, the accounting staff can regularly update the PDF forms on the intranet site, so there is no risk of someone using an old and outmoded form.

Converting a regular form to PDF format is simple. First, purchase the Acrobat software from Adobe's website and install it. Then access a form in whatever software package it was originally constructed, and print it to "Distiller," which will now appear on the list of printers. There are no other steps—your PDF format is complete! The IRS also uses the PDF format for its forms, which can be downloaded from the *www.irs.gov* site and posted to the company intranet site.

Cost: 💰   *Installation time:* 🔋 🔋

Avoid Job Costing through the Payroll System

Some controllers have elaborate cost accounting systems set up that accumulate a variety of costs from many sources, sometimes to be used for activity-based costing and more frequently for job costing. One of these costs is labor, which is sometimes accumulated through the payroll system. When this is done, employees use lengthy timecards on which they record the time spent on many activities during the day, resulting in vastly longer payroll records than would otherwise be the case. This is a problem when the payroll staff is asked to sort through and add up all of the job-costing records, since this process increases the workload of the payroll personnel by an order of magnitude. In addition, the payroll staff may be asked to enter the job-costing information that it has compiled into the job-costing database, which is yet another task that gets in the way of processing the payroll.

The obvious solution is to not allow job costing to be merged into the payroll function, thereby allowing the payroll staff to vastly reduce the amount of work it must complete, as well as shrink the number of opportunities for calculation errors. However, this step may meet with opposition from those people who need the job-costing records. There are several ways to avoid conflict over the issue. One is to analyze who is charging time to various projects or activities and see if the proportions to time charged vary significantly over time; if they do not, there is no reason to continue tracking job-costing information for hours worked. Another possibility is to split the functions so that the payroll staff collects its payroll data independently of the job-costing data collection, which can be handled by someone else. Either possibility will keep the job-costing function from interfering with the orderly collection of payroll information.

Cost: *Installation time:*

Switch to Salaried Positions

When processing payroll, it is evident that the labor required to process the payroll for a salaried person is significantly lower than for an hourly employee; there is no change in the payroll data from period to period for a salaried person, whereas the number of hours worked must be recomputed for an hourly employee every time the payroll is processed. Therefore, it is reasonable to shift as many employees as possible over to salaried positions from hourly ones in order to reduce the labor of calculating payroll.

Implementing this best practice can be a significant problem; it is not under the control of the accounting department, since it is up to the managers of other departments to switch people over to salaried positions, so the controller must persuade others to make the concept a reality. Another problem is that this best practice is generally opposed by unions, who prefer to give their members the option to earn extra overtime pay. Finally, there may be government regulations that prohibit converting employees to salaried positions, with the main determining criterion being that a salaried person must act with minimal supervision. This situation will vary by state, depending on local laws.

Given the number of issues just noted, it may seem impossible to implement this best practice. However, it is quite possible in some industries. The main factor for success is that the industry have few hourly workers to begin with. For example, a company with many highly educated employees or one that performs limited manufacturing, may already have so many salaried employees that it becomes a minor cleanup issue to convert over the few remaining hourly employees to salaried positions.

Cost: *Installation time:*

Use Bar-Coded Time Clock

The most labor-intensive task in the payroll area is calculating hours worked for hourly employees. To do so, a payroll clerk must collect all of the employee timecards for the most recently completed payroll period, manually accumulate the hours listed on the cards, and discuss missing or excessive hours with supervisors. This is a lengthy process with a high error rate, due to the large percentage of missing start or stop times on timecards. Any errors are usually found by employees as soon as they are paid, resulting in possibly confrontational visits to the payroll staff, demanding an immediate adjustment to their pay with a manual check. These changes disrupt the payroll department and introduce additional inefficiencies to the process.

The solution is to install a computerized time clock. This clock requires an employee to swipe a uniquely identified card through a reader on its side. The card is encoded with either a magnetic strip or a bar code that contains the employee's identification number. Once the swipe occurs, the clock automatically stores the date and time, and downloads this information upon request to the payroll department's computer, where special software automatically calculates the hours worked and also highlights any problems for additional research (such as missed card swipes). Many of these clocks can be installed through a large facility or at outlying locations so that employees can conveniently record their time, no matter where they may be. More advanced clocks also track the time periods when employees are supposed to arrive and leave, and require a supervisor's password for card swipes outside of that time period; this feature allows for greater control over employee work hours. Many of these systems also issue absence reports, so that supervisors can tell who has not shown up for work. Thus, an automated time clock eliminates much low-end clerical work, while at the same time providing new management tools for supervisors.

Before purchasing such a clock, one should recognize its limitations. The most important one is cost. This type of clock costs $2,000 to $3,000 each, or can be leased for several hundred dollars per month. If several clocks are needed, this can add up to a substantial investment. In addition, outlying time clocks that must download their information to a computer at a distant location require their own phone lines, incurring an additional monthly payment to the phone company. There may also be a fee for using the software on the central computer that summarizes all the incoming payroll information. Given these costs, it is most common for bar-coded time clocks to be used only in those situations where there are so many hourly employees that there is a significant savings in the payroll department resulting from their installation.

Also, employees will lose their swipe cards. To encourage them to keep their cards in a safe place, the company can charge a small fee for replacing them.

Prior to the use of this type of clock, hourly employees will have gotten used to paper-based timecards that have their start and stop times punched onto them. When a bar-coded time clock is installed, they lose the security of seeing this record of their hours worked. Instead, they swipe a card through the clock and never see any evidence of time worked. To overcome the loss of security that comes from this changeover, the accounting staff should show the hourly personnel how the new clock works and where the data is stored, so that they can gain some assurance that their time data will not be lost. If there is an option that allows them to look up information on the time clock's LCD display, then they should receive training in how to do this; in addition, a procedure could be posted next to the clock that shows how to obtain this information. It is also useful to install a set of green and red lights next to the scanner, with the green light flashing when a successful scan has been completed (and the red light indicating the reverse).

Cost: 💵 💵   *Installation time:* 🕯 🕯

Use Biometric Time Clock

The bar-coded time clocks noted in the last best practice represent an excellent improvement in the speed and accuracy with which employee time data can be collected. However, it suffers from an integrity flaw—that employees can use each other's badges to enter and exit from the payroll system. This means that some employees may be paid for hours when they were never really on-site at all.

A division of Ingersoll-Rand called Recognition Systems has surmounted this problem with the use of biometric time clocks (which can be seen at *www.handreader.com*). This reader requires an employee to place his or her hand on a sensor, comparing its size and shape to the dimensions already recorded for that person in a central database. The time entered into the terminal will then be recorded against the payroll file of the person whose hand was just measured. Thus, only employees who are on-site can have payroll hours credited to them. The company sells a variation on the same machine, called the HandKey®, which is used to control access to secure areas. These systems have a secondary benefit; no one needs an employee badge or pass key as these tend to be lost or damaged over time, and so represent a minor headache for the accounting or human resources staffs, who must track them. In a biometric monitoring environment, all an employee needs is a hand.

These monitoring devices are expensive and require significant evidence of "buddy punching" to justify their cost. If these clocks are intended to replace bar-coded time clocks, then there is no projected labor savings from reducing the manual labor of the payroll personnel (since this advantage was already covered by the bar-coded clocks), leaving only the savings from buddy punching to justify their purchase.

The same lack of time punched data exists in this case as was noted earlier for the bar-coded time clock. Again, it can be resolved by meeting with the hourly personnel to show them how their time data is collected, stored, and summarized, and how to access this information on the time clock if the device has such data available.

Cost: 💵 💵   *Installation time:* 🕯 🕯

Use the Honor System to Track Vacation and Sick Time

It is common for the payroll staff to be in charge of tracking the vacation and sick time used by employees. This involves sending out forms for employees to fill out whenever they take time off, usually requiring their supervisor's signature. Upon receipt, the payroll staff logs the used time in the payroll system and files the forms away in the employee personnel folders. If the payroll staff does not account for this information correctly in the payroll system, employees will probably spot the problem on their remittance advices the next time they are paid and will go to the payroll office to look into the matter—these inquiries take up accounting staff time, as does the paperwork tracking effort.

When used with some control features, it is possible to completely eliminate the tracking of vacation and sick time by the payroll staff. Under this scenario, employees are placed on the honor system of tracking their own vacation and sick time. Though this system keeps the payroll staff from having to do any tracking of this information, there is also a strong possibility that some employees will abuse the situation and take extra time. There are two ways to avoid this problem. One is to institute a company-wide policy that automatically wipes out all earned vacation and sick time at the end of each calendar year. This policy has the advantage of limiting the amount of vacation and sick time to which an employee can claim that he is entitled. It mitigates a company's losses if a dishonest employee leaves the company and claims payment for many hours of vacation and sick time that may go back for years. The other way to avoid the problem is to switch the tracking role to employee supervisors. These people are in the best position to see when employees are taking time off and can track their time off much more easily than can the payroll staff. In short, with some relatively minor control changes, it is possible to use an honor system for the tracking of employee vacation and sick time.

Cost: 💵   *Installation time:* 🍖

Issue Electronic W-2 Forms to Employees

A large company can experience some difficulty in issuing W-2 forms to its employees if they are distributed over a wide area. The mailing cost of this distribution can also be quite expensive, especially if the employer wants proof of receipt, which calls for the use of more expensive overnight delivery services. This problem can be avoided by issuing electronic W-2 forms to employees, thereby avoiding all related postage costs.

The IRS has issued specific regulations for the use of electronic W-2 forms. First, employees must give their consent to the receipt of an electronic W-2 form, and do so electronically, thereby showing proof that they are capable of receiving the electronic format in which the W-2 form will be sent. Second, the W-2 forms must contain all standard information that would normally be found on a paper W-2 form. Third, employees must be notified that the forms have been posted on a website for their access, and given instructions on how to access the information. Finally, the access must be maintained through October 15th of the year following the calendar year to which they relate.

These regulations are not difficult to meet, and the use of a central website for storage of the information also allows the employer to determine precisely which W-2 forms have been accessed. However, it is likely that some employees who either have minimal access to computers or who are not computer literate will not access their W-2 forms in this manner, requiring a last-minute distribution of W-2 forms to anyone who has not accessed their electronic copies. Also, paper-based W-2 forms must still be issued to any employees who left the company prior to the end of the calendar year. Thus, this best practice will likely result in only a partial electronic distribution of W-2 forms.

Cost: 🖎   *Installation time:* 🎯🎯

Offer Clear Cards to Employees

Employees can find themselves in credit trouble from time to time, frequently resulting in requests for payroll advances to their employers in order to meet pressing bill payments. A payroll advance is a time-consuming item to handle, because it involves the creation of a manual check, clearing the check on the next bank reconciliation, and offsetting the advance on the next paycheck.

An alternative to the payroll advance is to offer a "Clear Card" to employees. Under this approach, an employee pays for something with a Mastercard® and then has the payment automatically deducted from his or per paycheck over the next two months, with no interest or late fees charged on the payment. Employees pay $29 per year for this service, while the employer pays no fee at all. The credit card provider installs the automatic linkage through the corporate payroll system to process payroll deductions, and does so free of charge. The card is only available to employees earning at least $20,000 per year, and who have worked for a company at least six months. The credit limit on the card is 2.5 percent for those earning less than $75,000 per year, with a 4 percent limit for those earning above this amount.

Though the card has the clear advantage of offering a ready source of credit to employees who may otherwise not have available funds, it can also reduce their ready income if they constantly buy the maximum amount available to them, which may send them back to the company once again to ask for a payroll advance.

Cost: 🖎   *Installation time:* 🎯🎯

Post Commission Payments on the Company Intranet

A sales staff whose pay structure is heavily skewed in favor of commission payments, rather than salaries, will probably hound the accounting staff at month-end to see what their commission payments will be. This comes at the time of the month when the accounting staff is trying to close the accounting books, and so increases its workload at the worst possible time of the month. However, by creating a linkage between the accounting database and a company's Internet site, it is now possible to shift this information directly to the webpage where the sales staff can view it at any time, and without involving the valuable time of the accounting staff.

There are two ways to post the commission information. One is to wait until all commission-related calculations have been completed at month-end, and then either manually dump the data into an HTML (HyperText Markup Language) format for posting to a webpage, or else run a batch program that does so automatically. Either approach will give the sales staff a complete set of information about their commissions. However, this approach still requires some manual effort at month-end (even if only for a few minutes while a batch program runs).

An alternative approach is to create a direct interface between the accounting database and the webpage, so that commissions are updated constantly, including grand totals for each commission payment period. By using this approach, the accounting staff has virtually no work to do in conveying information to the sales staff. In addition, sales personnel can check their commissions at any time of the month and call the accounting staff with their concerns right away—this is a great improvement, since problems can be spotted and fixed at once, rather than waiting until the crucial month-end closing period to correct them.

No matter which method is used for posting commission information, a password system will be needed, since this is highly personal payroll-related information. There should be a reminder program built into the system, so that the sales staff is forced to alter its passwords on a regular basis, thereby reducing the risk of outside access to this information.

Cost: 💵 💵   *Installation time:* 🔔 🔔

Transfer Payroll to Credit Card Balances

Some companies employ people who, for whatever reason, either are unable to set up personal bank accounts or do not choose to. In these cases, they must take their paychecks to a check-cashing service that charges them a high fee to convert the check into cash. Not only is it expensive, but the check-cashing service can have a long approval process. Also, employees will be carrying large amounts of cash just after cashing their checks, which increases their risk of theft. They also run the risk of losing their paychecks prior to cashing them. Thus, the lack of a bank account poses serious problems for a company's employees.

A good solution to this problem is to set up a Visa® debit card, called the Visa Paycard®, for any employees requesting one, and then shift payroll funds directly into the card. This allows employees to pull any amount of cash they need from an ATM, rather than the entire amount at one time from a check-cashing service. The card can also be used like a credit card, so that there is little need to make purchases with cash. Further, the fee to convert to cash at an ATM is much lower than the fee charged by a check cashing service. There is also less risk of theft through the card, since it is protected by a personal identification number (PIN). Employees will also receive a monthly statement showing their account activity, which they can use to get a better idea of their spending habits.

Using this card can be difficult for anyone who speaks English as a second language, or who cannot understand ATM instructions. However, Visa offers multilingual customer service personnel, which reduces the severity of this problem.

The Paycard has only recently been rolled out by Visa, and is only available through a few banks. One must contact the company's bank to see if it has this option available. If not, an alternative is to switch the payroll function to the Paymaxx Internet site (found at *www.paymaxx.com*), which offers the Paycard option.

Cost: *Installation time:*

Use Direct Deposit

A major task for the payroll staff is to issue paychecks to employees. This task can be subdivided into several steps. First, the checks must be printed—though it seems easy, it is all too common for the check run to fail, resulting in the manual cancellation of the first batch of checks, followed by a new print run. Next, the checks must be signed by an authorized check signer, who may have questions about payment amounts which may require additional investigation. After that, the checks must be stuffed into envelopes and then sorted by supervisor (since supervisors generally hand out paychecks to their employees). The checks are then distributed, usually with the exception of a few checks that will be held for those employees who are not currently on-site for later pick-up. If checks are stolen or lost, the payroll staff must cancel them and manually issue replacements. Finally, the person in charge of the bank reconciliation must track those checks that have not been cashed and follow up with employees to get them to cash their checks—there are usually a few employees who prefer to cash checks only when they need the money, surprising though this may seem. In short, there are a startlingly large number of steps involved in issuing payroll checks to employees. How can we eliminate this work?

We can eliminate the printing and distribution of paychecks by using direct deposit. This best practice involves issuing payments directly to employee bank accounts. Besides avoiding some of the steps involved with issuing paychecks, it carries the additional advantage of putting money in employee bank accounts at once, so that those employees who are off-site on payday do not have to worry about how they will receive their money—it will appear in their checking accounts automatically, with no effort on their part. Also, there is no longer a problem with asking employees to cash their checks, since it is done automatically.

It can be difficult to get employees to switch over to direct deposit. Though the benefits to employees may seem obvious, there will be some proportion of the employees who prefer to cash their own checks, or who do not have bank accounts.

To get around this problem, an organization can either force all employees to accept direct deposit, or only do so with new employees (while existing employees are allowed to continue taking paychecks). If employees are forced to accept direct deposit, the company can either arrange with a local bank to give them bank accounts, or issue the funds to a debit card (see the preceding best practice).

Another problem is the cost of this service. A typical charge by the bank is one dollar for each transfer made, which can add up to a considerable amount if there are many employees and/or many pay periods per year. This problem can be reduced by shrinking the number of pay periods per year.

Implementing direct deposit requires one to transfer payment information to the company's bank in the correct direct deposit format, which the bank uses to shift money to employee bank accounts. This information transfer can be accomplished either by purchasing an add-on to a company's in-house payroll software, or by paying extra to a payroll outsourcing company to provide the service—either way, there is an expense associated with starting up the service. If there is some trouble with finding an intermediary to make direct deposits, this can also be done through a website that specializes in direct deposits. For example, *www.directdeposit.com* provides this service, and even has upload links from a number of popular accounting packages, such as ACCPAC, DacEasy, and Great Plains.

Also, some paper-based form of notification should still be sent to employees, so that they know the details of what they have been paid. This means that using direct deposit will not eliminate the steps of printing a deposit advice, stuffing it in an envelope, or distributing it (though it can be mailed instead of handed out in person). An alternative is to send e-mails to employees that contain this information, though some employees may not have e-mail, and there may be concerns that other people can access the e-mail messages.

Cost: 🖅   *Installation time:* 🌑

Automate Vacation Accruals

The accounting topic that is of the most interest to the most employees is how much vacation time they have left. In most companies, this information is kept manually by the payroll staff, so employees troop down to the payroll department once a month (and more frequently during the prime summer vacation months!) to see how much vacation time they have left to use. When employees are constantly coming in to find out this information, it is a major interruption to the payroll staff because it happens at all times of the day, never allowing them to settle down into a comfortable work routine. If there are many employees who want to know about their vacation time, it can be a considerable loss of efficiency for the payroll staff.

A simple way to keep employees from bothering the payroll staff is to include the vacation accrual in employee paychecks. The information appears on the payroll stub, showing the annual amount of accrued vacation, net of any used time. By feeding this information to employees in every paycheck, there is no need for them to inquire about it in the payroll office, eliminating a major hindrance.

There are several points to consider before implementing this best practice. First, the payroll system must be equipped with a vacation accrual option. If not, the software must be customized to allow for the calculation and presentation of this information, which may cost more to implement than the projected efficiency savings. Another problem is that the accrual system must be set up properly for each employee when it is originally installed, or else there will be a number of outraged employees crowding into the payroll office, causing more disruption than was the case before. This startup problem is caused by employees with different numbers of allowed vacation days per year, as well as some with unused vacation time from the previous year that must be carried forward into the next year. If this information is not accurately reflected in the automated vacation accrual system when it is implemented, employees will hasten to the payroll department to have this information corrected at once. Another problem is that the accruals must be adjusted over time to reflect changes. Otherwise, once again, employees will interrupt the staff to notify them of changes, thereby offsetting the value of the entire system. For example, an employee may switch from two to three weeks of allowed vacation at the fifth anniversary of his hiring. The payroll department must have a schedule of when this person's vacation accrual amount changes to the three-week level or the employee will come in and complain about it. If these problems can be overcome, using vacation accruals becomes a relatively simple means of improving the efficiency of the payroll department.

Have a schedule available in the payroll department that itemizes the dates on which employees with sufficient seniority are scheduled to have increases in their allowed vacation amounts; include a review of this document in the monthly departmental schedule of activities, so that accrual changes can be made in a timely manner. Also, train the payroll staff in the proper data entry into the payroll system for any vacation hours taken by employees. Finally, create a procedure for making changes to the data in the automated vacation accrual system, so that the staff can correct errors in the system.

Cost: 🖘   *Installation time:* 🌑

Consolidate Payroll Systems

A company that grows by acquisition is likely to have a number of payroll systems—one for each company it has acquired. This situation may also arise for highly decentralized organizations that allow each location to set up its own payroll system. Though this approach does allow each location to process payroll in accordance with its own rules and payment periods while also allowing for local maintenance of employee records, there are several serious problems that can be solved by the consolidation of all these systems into a single, centralized payroll system.

One problem with multiple payroll systems is that employee payroll records cannot be shifted through a company when an employee is transferred to a new location. Instead, the employee is listed as having been terminated in the payroll system of the location he is leaving and is then listed as a new hire in the payroll system of the new location. By constantly reentering an employee as a new hire, it is impossible to track the dates and amounts of pay raises; the same problem arises for the human resources staff, who cannot track eligibility dates for medical insurance or vesting periods for pension plans. In addition, every time employee data is reentered into a different payroll system, there is a risk of data inaccuracies that may result from such embarrassments as wrong pay rates or mailing checks to the wrong address. Also, a company cannot easily group data for company-wide payroll reporting purposes. For all these reasons, it is common practice to consolidate payroll systems into a single, centralized location that operates with a single payroll database.

Before embarking on such a consolidation, one must consider the costs of implementation. One is that a consolidation of many payroll systems can require an expensive new software package that must run on a larger computer, which entails extra capital and software maintenance costs. In addition, there is probably a significant cost associated with converting the data from the disparate databases into the new consolidated one. In addition, there may be extra time needed to test the tax rate for all company locations in order to avoid penalties for improper tax withholdings and submissions. Finally, the timing of the implementation is of some importance. Many companies prefer to make the conversion on the first day of the new year, so there is no need to enter detailed pay information into the system for the prior year in order to issue year-end payroll tax reports to the government. The cost of consolidating payroll systems is considerable and must be carefully analyzed before the decision to convert is reached.

Cost: 💵 💵 💵   *Installation time:* 🕐 🕐 🕐

Eliminate Personal Leave Days

A common task for the payroll staff is to either manually or automatically track the vacation time employees earn and use. Depending on the level of automation, this task can require some portion of staff time every week on an ongoing basis. Some companies then take the additional step of accruing and tracking the usage of personal leave days, which are essentially the same thing as vacation time, but tracked under a different name. By having both vacation and personal leave days, the payroll staff is reduced to tracking data in both categories, which doubles the work required to simply track vacation time.

A reasonable, and easily implemented, best practice is to convert personal leave days into vacation days and eliminate the extra category of time off. By doing so, the payroll staff can cut in half the time it devotes to analyzing employee vacation time. The only resistance to this change usually comes from the human resources department, which likes to offer a variety of benefits to match those of-fered by other companies; for example, if a competitor offers personal leave days, then so should the company. Though only a matter of semantics, this can cause a problem with implementing the simpler system.

Cost: 💷   *Installation time:* 🔴

Link Payroll Changes to Employee Events

There are many payroll changes that must be made when certain events occur in an employee file. Many of these changes are never made, because the payroll staff is so busy with the standard, daily processing of information that it has no time to address them or because the payroll staff does not possess enough knowledge to link the payroll changes to the employee events. For example, when an employee is married, this should trigger a change in that person's W-4 form, so that the amount of taxes withheld will reflect those for a married person. Automation can create many of these linkages. Here are some examples:

- As soon as an employee reaches the age of 55, the system issues a notification to the pension manager to calculate the person's potential pension, while also notifying the employee of his or her pension eligibility. These notifications can be by letter, but a linkage between the payroll system and the e-mail system could result in more immediate notification.

- As soon as an employee has been with a company for 90 days, his or her period of probation has been completed. The system should then automatically in-clude the employee in the company's dental, medical, and disability plans, and include deductions for these amounts in the person's paycheck. Similarly, the system can automatically enroll the employee in the company's 401k plan and enter the deductions in the payroll system. Since these pay changes should not come as a surprise to the employee, the system should also generate a message to the employee, detailing the changes made and their net payroll impact.

- When a company is informed of an employee's marriage, the computer system generates a notice to the employee that a new W-4 form should be filled out, while also sending a new benefit enrollment form, in case the employee wishes to add benefits for the spouse or any children. Finally, a notification message can ask the employee if he or she wants to change the beneficiary's name on the pension plan to that of the spouse.

- When an employee notifies the company of an address change, the system au-tomatically notifies all related payroll and benefit suppliers, such as the 401k plan administrator and health insurance provider, of the change.

- When a new employee is hired, the system sends a message to the purchasing department, asking that business cards be ordered for the person. Another mes-sage goes to the information systems department, requesting that the appropri-ate levels of system security be set up for the new hire. Yet another message goes to the training department, asking that a training plan be set up for the new employee.

Many of these workflow features are available on high-end accounting and human resources software packages. However, this software costs more than a million dollars in most cases, and so is well beyond the purchasing capability of many smaller companies. An alternative is to customize an existing software package to include these features, but the work required will be expensive. Accordingly, these changes should only be contemplated if there are many employees, since this would result in a sufficient volume of savings to justify the added expense.

Cost: *Installation time:*

Link the 401k Plan to the Payroll System

A common activity for the payroll staff is to take the 401k deduction information from the payroll records as soon as each payroll cycle is completed, enter it into a separate database for 401k deductions, copy this information onto a diskette, and send it to the company's 401k administration supplier, who uses it to determine the investment levels of all employees, as well as for discrimination testing. This can be a lengthy data-entry process if there are many employees, and it is certainly not a value-added activity when the core task is simply moving data from one database to another.

The best way to avoid retyping 401k payroll deductions is to link the payroll system directly into a 401k plan. This is done by outsourcing the payroll processing function to a supplier who also offers a 401k plan. A good example of this is Automated Data Processing (ADP), which offers linkages to a number of well-known mutual funds through its payroll system. When a company uses ADP's payroll and 401k services, a payroll department can record a 401k payroll deduction for an employee just once and ADP will then take the deduction and automatically move it into a 401k fund, with no additional bookkeeping required from the payroll staff. For those companies with many employees, this can represent a significant reduction in the workload of the payroll staff.

There are two problems with this best practice. One is that a company must first outsource its payroll function to a supplier that offers 401k administration services, which the company controller may not be willing to do. The second problem is converting to the new 401k plan. To do so, all employees in the old plan must be moved to the new plan. The associated paperwork may be great enough to not make the transition worthwhile; also, the 401k administrator may require a separation fee if the company is terminating its services inside of a minimum time interval, which may involve a small penalty payment. These issues should be considered before switching to a centralized payroll and 401k processing system.

Cost: *Installation time:*

Link the Payroll and Human Resources Databases

The payroll database shares many data elements with the human resources database. Unfortunately, these two databases are usually maintained by different departments—accounting for the first and human resources for the second. Consequently, any employee who makes a change to one database, such as an address field in the payroll system, must then walk to the human resources department to have the same information entered again for other purposes, such as benefits administration or a pension plan. Thus, there is an obvious inefficiency for the employee who must go to two departments for changes, while the accounting and human resources staffs also duplicate each other's data-entry efforts.

An alternative is to tie the two databases together. This can be done by purchasing a software package that automatically consolidates the two databases into a single one.

The considerable cost of buying and implementing an entirely new software package will grossly exceed the cost savings obtained by consolidating the data. A less costly approach is to create an interface between the two systems that automatically stores changes made to each database and updates the other one as a daily batch program. Creating this interface can still be expensive, since it involves a reasonable amount of customized programming work. Consequently, this best practice is an expensive proposition and is usually only done when both computer systems are being brought together for more reasons than a simple reduction in data-entry work.

If the two databases are consolidated into a single system, the initial conversion of data from both originating systems into it can be a major operation. Someone must design an automated conversion program that shifts the old data into the format used by the new system, merge the data from both databases, and then import them into the new system. Also, the new system will probably have a number of processing steps, screens, and online forms that differ from the systems being replaced, so both the payroll and human resources staffs will require training just before the "go live" date for the new system.

Cost: 💵 💵 💵   *Installation time:* 🕯 🕯 🕯

Minimize Payroll Cycles

Many payroll departments are fully occupied with processing some kind of payroll every week, and possibly even several times in one week. The latter situation occurs when different groups of employees are paid for different time periods. For example, hourly employees may be paid every week, while salaried employees may be paid twice a month. Processing multiple payroll cycles eats up most of the free time of the payroll staff, leaving it with little room for cleaning up paperwork or researching improvements to its basic operations.

All of the various payroll cycles can be consolidated into a single, company-wide payroll cycle. By doing so, the payroll staff no longer has to spend extra time on additional payroll processing, nor does it have to worry about the different pay rules that may apply to each processing period—instead, everyone is treated exactly the same. To make payroll processing even more efficient, it is useful to lengthen the payroll cycles. For example, a payroll department that processes weekly payrolls must run the payroll 52 times a year, whereas one that processes monthly payrolls only does so 12 times per year, which eliminates 75 percent of the processing that the first department must handle. These changes represent an enormous reduction in the payroll-processing time the accounting staff requires.

Any changes to the payroll cycles may be met with opposition by the organization's employees. The primary complaint is that the employees have structured their spending habits around the timing of the old pay system, and that any change will not give them enough cash to continue those habits. For example, employees who currently receive a paycheck every week may have a great deal of difficulty in adjusting their spending to a paycheck that only arrives once a month. If a company were to switch from a short to a longer pay cycle, it is extremely likely that the payroll staff will be deluged with requests for pay advances well before the next paycheck is due for release, which will require a large amount of payroll staff time to handle. To overcome this problem, one can increase pay cycles incrementally, perhaps to twice a month or once every two weeks, and also tell employees that pay advances will be granted for a limited transition period. By making these incremental changes, one can reduce the associated amount of employee discontent.

Review the prospective change with the rest of the management team to make sure that it is acceptable to them. They must buy into the need for the change, because their employees will also be impacted by the change, and they will receive complaints about it. This best practice requires a long lead time to implement, as well as multiple notifications to the staff about its timing and impact on them. It is also useful to go over the granting of payroll advances with the payroll staff, so that they are prepared for the likely surge in requests for advances.

Cost: 🖸   Installation time: 🔔 🔔 🔔

Use a Forms/Rates Data Warehouse for Automated Tax Filings

Any organization that operates in a number of states will find that an inordinate number of sales and income tax returns must be filed, not to mention a plethora of lesser forms. The traditional way to meet these filing requirements is to either keep a staff of tax preparation personnel on hand, or else to outsource some or all of these chores to a supplier. Either approach represents a significant cost. An alternative worth exploring is to store tax rates and forms in a database that can be used to automatically prepare tax returns in conjunction with other accounting information that is stored in either a general ledger or a data warehouse.

To make this best practice operational, there must first be a common database containing all of the information that would normally be included on a tax return. This may call for some restructuring of the chart of accounts, as well as the centralization of company-wide data into a data warehouse (see the preceding best practice). This is no small task, since the information needed by each state may vary slightly from the requirements of other states, calling for subtle changes in the storage of data throughout the company that will yield the appropriate information for reporting purposes.

The next step is to obtain tax rate information and store it in a central database. This information can be manually located by accessing the tax agency websites of all fifty states, but is more easily obtained in electronic format from any of the national tax reporting services. This information can then be stored in the forms/rates data warehouse. An additional step is to create a separate program for each of the tax reports, so that a computer report is issued that mimics the reporting format used by each state. Then the information can be manually transferred from the computer report to a printout of the PDF (Portable Document Format) file of each state's tax form. For those programming staffs with a large amount of available time, it is also possible to create a report format that exactly mirrors each state tax form, which can be printed out, with all tax information enclosed within it, and immediately mailed out.

The trouble with this best practice is the exceptionally high programming cost associated with obtaining a complete automated solution. There are so many tax forms to be converted to a digital format that the development task is considerable. Accordingly, it is more cost-effective to determine those tax forms that share approximately the same information, and to develop an automated solution for them first. Any remaining tax forms that would require special programming to automate should be reviewed on a case-by-case basis to determine if it is cost-beneficial to complete further programming work, or to leave a few stray reports for the tax preparation staff to complete by hand.

Cost: 💸 💸 💸   *Installation time:* 🕐 🕐 🕐

Summary

If improperly managed, the payroll function can require an inordinate amount of labor to run. However, by using some of the best practices noted in this chapter, one can streamline the function to a considerable extent, requiring far less effort by a smaller staff. Before implementing every change noted in this chapter, be sure to run cost-benefit calculations to ensure that the contemplated changes will indeed result in increased efficiencies; a number of these best practices are expensive to implement, and so are only available to larger organizations with many employees.

5

Payroll Measurements and Internal Reports

Introduction

Payroll is not just a mechanical function that results in the issuance of paychecks to employees at periodic intervals. It can also be used to produce a variety of reports that assist in measuring vacation time available, trends in overtime usage, total compensation by person, and even to predict likely billable hours before a billing period has been completed. In addition, a variety of measurements can be created for tracking the performance of the payroll staff, the cost of the function, and a variety of employee costs. This chapter shows you how to generate these reports and measurements.

Measurement: Payroll Transaction Fees per Employee

A great many companies have found it well worth the effort of outsourcing their payroll processing functions to specialized service providers, thereby eliminating the hassle associated with payroll tax calculations and submissions. However, few companies go to the trouble of determining the annual cost of this processing on a per-person basis. They may be startled to find that the initial cost at which they agreed to the service has ballooned over time, because of extra fees tacked onto the base processing rate for such services as direct deposit, sealing checks in envelopes, calculating special deductions, and tracking garnishments. For these companies, the payroll transaction fee per employee measurement is a valuable tool.[1]

To calculate this measurement, divide the total payroll outsourcing fee by the total number of employees itemized on the payroll. Be sure to exclude from the total fee any charges that cannot be directly related to individual employees, such as special reports or payroll shipping charges. The formula is as follows:

$$\frac{\text{Total payroll outsourcing fee per payroll}}{\text{Total number of employees itemized in payroll}}$$

For example, a new payroll manager has been hired at the Jebson Maintenance Company, which has a large staff of heating and ventilation maintenance technicians. Accordingly, the payroll function is the key accounting activity. The new manager is interested in obtaining the best cost-benefit performance from the payroll function, which is currently outsourced. He compares the cost of the current outsourcing provider and the fees charged by a competitor in the following table where all information is based on the processing of a single biweekly payroll.

Types of Fees	*Current Provider Fees*	*Competitor Fees*
Minimum processing fee	$50.00	$15.00
Processing fee/each	$1.00	$1.25
Envelope stuffing fee/each	$.15	$.25
Delivery fee	$10.00	Free
Direct deposit fee/each	$0.50	$0.65
401k report	$12.00	$5.00
Sick time report	$10.00	$5.00
Garnishment fee/person	$2.50	$3.50

The company has 26 payrolls per year and 120 employees, all of whom take direct deposit payments. The company has requested 401k and sick time reports once a month. There are 10 employees whose wages are garnished. Based on these volume considerations, the total cost of the current provider is:

Variable cost per year = Processing fee of $1.00 × 120 employees × 26 payrolls

= Envelope stuffing fee of $.15 × 120 employees × 26 payrolls

= Direct deposit fee of $.50 × 120 employees × 26 payrolls

= Garnishment fee of $2.50 × 10 employees × 26 payrolls

= $5,148

Fixed cost per year = Minimum processing fee of $50 × 26 payrolls

= Delivery fee of $10 × 26 payrolls

= 401k report charge of $12 × 12 months

= Sick time report charge of $10 × 12 months

= $1,824

Total cost per year = $6,972

Using the same methodology, the total cost of the competitor's offer is as follows:

Variable cost per year	= Processing fee of $1.25 × 120 employees × 26 payrolls
	= Envelope stuffing fee of $.25 × 120 employees × 26 payrolls
	= Direct deposit fee of $.65 × 120 employees × 26 payrolls
	= Garnishment fee of $3.50 × 10 employees × 26 payrolls
	= $7,618
Fixed cost per year	= Minimum processing fee of $15 × 26 payrolls
	= Delivery fee of $0 × 26 payrolls
	= 401k report charge of $5 × 12 months
	= Sick time report charge of $5 × 12 months
	= $510
Total cost per year	= $8,128

This analysis shows that the competitor's bid is $1,156 higher than that of the existing service provider, primarily because the competitor charges higher per-employee fees (despite having lower fixed service costs). In this case, the variable payroll cost per employee is $42.90 if the current supplier is used, and $63.48 if the competitor is used.

As just noted, those charges that have nothing to do with the per-person fees associated with the payroll must be segregated; in the example, these fees would be the minimum processing fee, delivery charge, and the two reports. By separating these costs, it is easier to determine the pricing strategies of payroll suppliers, some of whom advertise low fixed fees to attract new customers, but who have so many extra per-employee fees that the total cost is higher.

Measurement: Payroll Transaction Error Rate

A great deal of data is brought together into the payroll processing function, especially if a company employs a large number of hourly personnel whose pay fluctuates from period to period. If there is an error in the payroll calculations, it generally requires an inordinate amount of time to recalculate pay and issue manual checks that address the problem. Consequently, it is useful to measure the payroll transaction error rate on a trend line in order to tightly control the number of errors generated.

To calculate the payroll transaction error rate, divide the total number of payroll errors for a payroll by the total number of payroll changes made during that payroll. Payroll changes may include changes to addresses, deductions, pay rates, exemptions, or married status. The denominator should *not* be the total number of employees listed in the payroll, since many of them may be salaried (which requires no payroll change), and so do not provide a true picture of the total number of transactional changes made to the payroll. The measurement is:

$$\frac{\text{Number of payroll transaction errors}}{\text{Total number of payroll entries}}$$

For example, the First Alert Company employs a large part-time staff that assembles thousands of first aid kits by hand. Its payroll staff is overwhelmed by the constantly varying number of employees and changing hours to be charged, resulting in a constant stream of payroll adjustments. The controller wants to determine the payroll transaction error rate before she spends a great deal of money to have a consultant review the payroll process and suggest ways to streamline it. She assembles the following information from the last payroll:

Transaction Type	Total Number	Number of Errors
Address entry	9	1
Deductions entry	8	0
Employee addition/deletion	42	7
Exemptions entry	15	0
Hours entry	312	49
Status entry	3	0
Totals	389	57

Based on this information, the transaction error rate is 57/389, or 15 percent. More importantly, a review of the table quickly reveals that the source of nearly all errors is the timekeeping system, which produced 49 errors in the number of hours entered into the system. The controller should focus the consultant's efforts in this area.

This measurement can be misleading when the payroll function is outsourced and a company employee is calling the information in to the payroll supplier, whose data entry clerk is entering the information into a payroll system. In this instance, it is difficult to tell if payroll errors originate with the person calling in the information, or the data entry clerk who is inputting it.

Measurement: Proportion of Payroll Entries to Headcount

A payroll manager may be tracking too much information about employees through the payroll system. This results in maintaining an excessive number of payroll entries leading to reduced efficiency. For example, the payroll staff may be required to make separate deductions for short-term disability insurance, long-term disability insurance, medical insurance, the cafeteria plan, dental insurance, health club charges, meals from the company cafeteria, and so on. By compiling the total number of payroll entries in the system per employee, one can see if this "data load" is excessive. If so, one can appeal to company management to eliminate some deductions entirely, or see if some deductions can be combined (such as a single deduction for all types of insurance), thereby reducing the payroll staff's workload.

The formula is to accumulate the number of all payroll deductions, memo entries, and goal entries and divide this total by the number of full-time equivalents. The formula is:

$$\frac{\text{Total deductions} + \text{Total memo entries} + \text{Total goal entries}}{\text{Total number of full-time equivalents}}$$

The payroll manager of the Crawly Worm Company, purveyor of fine garden worms for fishermen, likes to know everything about her employees and has gradually built up a massive amount of line items in the payroll database to do this. Upon her retirement, the incoming manager decides to calculate the proportion of payroll entries to employee headcount to see if there is too much information being entered into the system. He accumulates the following information:

Information Type	Number of Entries
Medical insurance deduction	50
Dental insurance deduction	45
Long-term disability deduction	40
Short-term disability deduction	8
Cafeteria plan dependent deduction	12
Cafeteria plan medical deduction	10
Cafeteria plan dependent deduction goal	12
Cafeteria plan medical deduction goal	10
Vacation time remaining	50
Sick time remaining	50
Excess cost of life insurance memo entry	32
Total	319

There are 50 employees, so by dividing the total deductions of 319 by 50, the new manager arrives at a proportion of payroll entries to headcount of 6.4 per person.

This measurement can appear to show a small number of payroll entries per person even when there are a great many types of entries, because some of the entries will apply to only a few employees. As was shown in the example, many types of insurance, such as short-term disability, will only be taken by a few employees, so the total number of payroll entries will appear to be relatively low.

From the perspective of determining the proportion of entries for the payroll staff to make, this still results in an accurate proportion, though one may still wish to reduce the overall number of payroll entry types.

Measurement: Annualized Wages per Employee

A typical payroll register will show the hourly rate of pay and year-to-date pay accumulators for those members of the staff who are paid on an hourly basis. This information does not provide the total annualized rate of pay, which is useful when determining pay raises, comparing pay scales, or comparing in-house pay levels to industry or regional standards. The problem also arises for any employees who are paid on a commission basis or whose pay is a mix of fixed base pay and variable incentive pay. For these employees, maintaining an annualized wage calculation can be useful.

This calculation can be derived either for a single employee or a group, such as for everyone having the same job title. If the former, the calculation is to simply summarize all fixed base pay, wages, commissions, bonuses, overtime, and other variable pay. If the latter, then summarize the same calculation for all employees in the group, and divide by the number of employees in the group. The calculation is as follows:

$$\frac{\text{Fixed base pay + Wages + Commissions + Overtime + Bonuses + Total other variable pay}}{\text{Total number of full-time equivalents}}$$

For example, the payroll manager of the All Seasons Generating Company, a regional utility, is trying to determine the annualized wages per employee for the 12-person electrical engineering department. She obtains the following information for the department for the past twelve months:

Compensation Type	Compensation Amount
Total base pay	$0
Total wages	485,000
Total commissions	0
Total overtime	215,000
Total bonuses	42,000
Grand total	$742,000

The annualized wages per employee for this group are $742,000 divided by 12 employees, or $61,833. The manager notes that the overtime compensation for this group is extremely high because they are constantly being called out to repair damaged power transformers at all times of the day. The manager decides to recommend hiring more off-shift personnel in this area to reduce the amount of overtime paid and thereby reduce the total compensation cost in this area.

Measurement: Net Benefits Cost per Employee

A company's managers make a number of small, incremental decisions related to employee benefits over time, frequently resulting in a wide array of benefits whose true cost is much higher than expected. Frequent use of this measurement tends to result in a much more conservative view of suggested additions to the existing benefits pool. Also, knowing the benefit cost per person allows one to make decisions regarding whether it is less expensive to use contractors on a higher per-hour basis or hire new employees at a lower hourly rate, but with benefits.

Benefit costs are best measured on a per-person basis, so the measurement should include all benefit costs in the numerator and the total number of full-time equivalent employees in the denominator. Benefit costs should include time taken off for vacations and sick time, all types of medical insurance (such as medical, dental, life, and disability insurance) net of employee deductions, and miscellaneous benefits, such as club memberships, dry cleaning costs, and company cars. The measurement is:

$$\frac{\text{Total cost of time off} + \text{Insurance} + \text{Other benefits} - \text{Employee deductions}}{\text{Number of full-time equivalent employees}}$$

For example, the Sod Software Company, maker of operating systems for farmers, has assembled a high-powered group of 40 developers who have been attracted by the company and retained in large part by its excellent benefits package. Nonetheless, the company is finding that the package is extremely expensive, and must determine if any further additions to its staff should be outside contractors who require no benefits. The payroll staff assembles the following annualized benefits information:

Benefit Type	Total Cost	Total Deductions	Net Total Cost
Medical insurance	$238,000	–$23,800	$214,200
Dental insurance	29,000	–2,900	26,100
Long-term disability	11,000	0	11,000
Short-term disability	27,000	0	27,000
Vacation time	80,000	0	80,000
Sick time	9,000	0	9,000
Company cars	40,000	0	40,000
Health club memberships	14,000	0	14,000
Totals	$448,000	–$26,700	$421,300

By dividing the net total cost of $421,300 by total headcount of 40 developers, the payroll staff finds that the net benefit cost per employee is $10,532.50.

This measurement can be modified to show benefits as a percentage of total base pay. To continue the last example, if the average developer earned $75,000, then the total base pay would be $3,000,000, which would yield a benefits percentage of 14 percent. This percentage could then be tracked over time to spot changes, or compared to industry standards to see if a company's benefit costs vary from the norm.

Measurement: Revenue per Employee[2]

This is one of the most closely watched of all performance measures. It is based on the assumption that employees are at the core of a company's profitability, and so, high degrees of efficiency in this area are bound to result in strong profitability. It is also a standard benchmark in many industries.

To calculate this measurement, divide revenue for a full year by the total number of full-time equivalents (FTEs) in the company. An FTE is the combination of staffing that equals a 40-hour week. For example, two half-time employees would be counted as one FTE. The formula is:

$$\frac{\text{Annualized revenue}}{\text{Total full-time equivalents}}$$

A variation on this ratio is to only divide annual revenues by those FTEs who can be categorized as direct labor. This measures the productivity of those personnel who are directly connected to the manufacture of a company's products or services. This measure should be used with care, since it is not always easy to determine which employees can be categorized as direct labor and which ones fall into the overhead category instead. The formula is:

$$\frac{\text{Annualized revenue}}{\text{Total direct labor full-time equivalents}}$$

For example, the operations manager of the Twirling Washing Machine Company wants to determine the sales per person for his company, both for all staff and just the direct labor personnel. The company has annual revenues of $4,200,000. Its headcount is:

Department	Headcount
Direct labor department	22
Direct labor part-time staff	6
Production supervisors	2
Material handling department	4
Sales, general & administrative	10
Administrative part-time staff	2
Engineering department	8

In total, the company has 54 employees. However, if we assume that the part-time staff all work half time, then the eight part-time positions can be reduced to four FTEs, which decreases the total headcount to 50 personnel. Another issue is what constitutes direct labor personnel—the company has a group of clearly defined direct labor personnel, as well as a materials handling support staff and two production supervisors. The company can use any combination of these groups for its sales per direct labor measurement, as long as it consistently applies the measurement over time. However, the technically correct approach is to include in the measure any positions that are required for the proper completion of production efforts, which would require the inclusion of all three categories of labor. If this approach were not used, the person doing the measuring might be tempted to artificially inflate the measurement results by shifting direct labor personnel into other labor categories that fall just outside the definition.

The result of these measurements is overall sales per employee of $84,000 ($4,200,000 in revenues, divided by 50 employees) and sales per direct labor employee of $135,484 ($4,200,000 in revenues, divided by 31 employees). The 31 employee figure is derived by adding 22 direct labor personnel to the three FTEs represented by the six part-time direct labor personnel, plus the production supervisors and material handling staff.

This formula is subject to a high degree of variation, depending upon how personnel are counted. For example, shifting away from employees to an outsourced solution or to the in-house use of temporary employees can artificially reduce the number of FTEs, as can the use of overtime by a smaller number of employees. Also, comparing the number of FTEs to revenue has a less direct bearing on profitability than comparing revenues to the total of all salaries and wages expenses; for example, one company with a large headcount but low pay per person may be more profitable than a company having a lesser headcount but a much higher salary per person. Also, some capital-intensive industries have so few employees in relation to the sales volume generated that this measure has much less significance than other measures, such as sales to fixed assets.

Report: Payroll Summary

From the management team's perspective, the single most important payroll report is the payroll summary. This report itemizes the annualized pay rate for each employee, as well as that person's start date, date of last raise, and comparison to a regional payroll survey. The report is used not only as an overview of company-wide pay levels, but also to determine when pay raises should be scheduled, and how they fit into regional pay scales. Job titles should be listed in the report, so that a person's title can be matched more closely to any salary survey results. An example of this report is shown in Exhibit 5.1.

The report can be expanded to include other forms of compensation, such as the number of options granted. Also, if raises are based on budgeted levels, rather than performance, then the budgeted amounts of the raises and the dates on which they

Exhibit 5.1 Payroll Summary Report

Quad Cities Pay Survey

Name	Hourly/ Salary	Annual Base Pay	Annual Anniversary	Date of Last Raise	Job Title	25th Percentile	50th Percentile	75th Percentile
Barlowe, Cindy	Hourly	$32,240	5/14/01	8/14/02	Software Developer I	$ 31,927	$ 43,400	$ 49,815
Bosley, Sandra	Salary	$51,039	9/27/99	4/1/03	Senior Software Developer	$ 72,574	$ 78,459	$ 90,000
Caraway, Lisa	Salary	$200,000	4/26/99	4/1/03	Chief Executive Officer	$ 125,000	$ 161,143	$ 220,000
Chantilly, Edward	Salary	$46,200	10/30/95	6/1/03	Software Developer II	$ 42,567	$ 51,378	$ 59,748
Davis, Humphrey	Hourly	$31,200	8/20/01	8/20/02	Software Developer I	$ 31,927	$ 43,400	$ 49,815
Dunning, Mortimer	Hourly	$33,280	9/4/01	12/1/02	Software Developer I	$ 31,927	$ 43,400	$ 49,815
Dunwiddy, Alexandra	Salary	$42,400	8/13/01	2/1/03	Software Developer II	$ 42,567	$ 51,378	$ 59,748
Greenstreet, James	Salary	$53,000	4/16/01	4/16/03	Quality Review Analyst	$ 27,249	$ 36,198	$ 41,954
Guthrie, James	Hourly	$37,752	5/14/01	5/16/03	Quality Review Analyst	$ 27,249	$ 36,198	$ 41,954
Halverston, Eric	Salary	$80,250	10/27/97	4/1/03	Development Team Leader	$ 62,286	$ 75,752	$ 81,387
Johnson, Noyes	Salary	$76,000	2/14/94	2/1/03	Vice President - Sales	$ 85,180	$ 108,500	$ 130,000
Montrose, Wesley	Salary	$57,500	6/21/99	11/16/02	Quality Review Supervisor	$ 52,936	$ 69,000	$ 88,500
Mortimer, Victoria	Salary	$100,000	11/10/99	4/1/03	Chief Financial Officer	$ 85,000	$ 98,912	$ 131,897
Penway, Alice	Salary	$46,824	8/9/99	5/16/03	Software Developer II	$ 42,567	$ 51,378	$ 59,748
Quarterstaff, Molly	Salary	$80,000	5/6/98	10/11/02	Senior Software Developer	$ 72,574	$ 78,459	$ 90,000
Rosencrantz, Albert	Salary	$50,000	5/22/95	10/16/02	Software Developer I	$ 31,927	$ 43,400	$ 49,815
Saunders, Ricardo	Salary	$49,920	5/29/01	6/1/02	Sales Representative, Sr.	$ 47,997	$ 55,071	$ 63,461
Von Gundle, Gerta	Salary	$60,000	2/14/94	1/14/02	Regional Sales Manager	$ 63,742	$ 75,600	$ 84,600
Zeta, Xavier	Salary	$47,700	9/20/99	9/1/03	Secretary to CEO	$ 41,500	$ 46,026	$ 50,040

are scheduled to occur can be listed in additional columns. It is also useful to include somewhere on the report the date on which it was run, since this information can quickly become inaccurate, rendering a report useless in short order.

Report: Salary History

A useful addition to the payroll summary report is the salary history report, which itemizes the total pay for each employee during each year of employment. This gives one a good view of the total level of compensation during each person's entire employment history with the company. It should include not only the base pay level, but also any overtime, commissions, and bonuses paid. The best source of this information is the year-end W-2 report. An example of this report is shown in Exhibit 5.2.

Exhibit 5.2 *Salary History Report*					
Employee	**2004**	**2003**	**2002**	**2001**	**2000**
Barlowe, Cindy	$32,240	$73,487	$8,885		
Bosley, Sandra	$51,039				
Caraway, Lisa	$200,000	$102,002	$87,603	$61,511	$57,612
Chantilly, Edward	$46,200	$44,623	$10,625		
Davis, Humphrey	$31,200				
Dunning, Mortimer	$33,280	$13,852			
Dunwiddy, Alexandra	$42,400	$38,750	$34,000	$31,005	
Greenstreet, James	$53,000				
Guthrie, James	$37,752				
Halverston, Eric	$80,250				
Johnson, Noyes	$76,000	$64,189	$58,007	$47,308	$7,788
Montrose, Wesley	$57,500	$56,000	$51,500	$24,705	
Mortimer, Victoria	$100,000	$4,880			
Penway, Alice	$46,824	$41,502	$38,139	$30,679	$24,052
Quarterstaff, Molly	$80,000	$77,205	$74,650	$69,575	$67,005
Rosencrantz, Albert	$50,000				
Saunders, Ricardo	$49,920	$43,521			
Von Gundle, Gerta	$60,000	$53,500	$18,058		
Zeta, Xavier	$47,700				

As the report shows for a number of people, the first year of employment will typically reveal a very low level of pay, since most employees will begin work partway through the year. As illustrated in the exhibit, Victoria Mortimer was obviously hired near the end of 2002, since her pay level for that year was only $4,880, followed by $100,000 in the following year.

Exhibit 5.3 *Billing Summary Report*

June '04

Name	Week Ending					Extrapolated Hours	Percent Chargeable	Hourly Rate	Total Billing
	Jun 2	Jun 9	Jun 16	Jun 23	Jun 30				
Barlowe, Cindy	0.0	21.5	8.0	40.0	39.0	108.5	62%	$ 75.75	$8,219
Bosley, Sandra	0.0	0.0	0.0	0.0	8.0	8.0	5%	$ 103.25	$826
Chantilly, Edward	0.0	7.0	23.9	29.6	5.0	65.5	37%	$ 75.75	$4,962
Davis, Humphrey	0.0	7.0	0.0	1.5	0.0	8.5	5%	$ 75.75	$644
Dunning, Mortimer	0.0	0.2	14.0	8.5	9.5	32.2	18%	$ 75.75	$2,439
Dunwiddy, Alexandra	0.0	0.0	0.0	0.0	2.0	2.0	1%	$ 103.25	$207
Penway, Alice	0.0	40.0	25.0	28.0	13.0	106.0	60%	$ 103.25	$10,945
Quarterstaff, Molly	0.0	0.0	0.0	0.0	0.0	0.0	0%	$ 40.40	$0
Rosencrantz, Albert	0.0	0.0	0.0	0.0	0.0	0.0	0%	$ 40.40	$0
	0.0	75.7	70.9	107.6	76.5	330.7	21%		
							Extrapolated Monthly Billing		$28,241
No. Business Days	3	5	5	5	4				

Report: Billing Summary

Payroll information can be used to estimate likely billing levels for chargeable staff by listing actual hours charged by person for each week of a reporting period, plus estimated billable hours for weeks that have not yet occurred. One can also factor expected vacation time into the estimated billable hours, resulting in highly accurate billing estimates well before the end of a month. An example is shown in Exhibit 5.3.

The billing summary shown in Exhibit 5.3 itemizes the hours worked by each employee by week. Note that the number of working days in each week is itemized in the blocks at the bottom of the report, so that one can reduce the number of days in any week that contains a holiday or shares working days with other months. The percentage of total chargeable time is also listed in the report, as well as the average billable time for the entire group. When multiplied by the average billable rate for each person, one can translate the hours worked from the payroll system directly into a billing estimate.

Report: Vacation Summary

Payroll information can also be used to create reports for the human resources department. The most common request received by this department is how many hours of vacation are left for employees to use. A simple spreadsheet, such as the one shown in Exhibit 5.4, can be developed and easily maintained to answer this question.

The report itemizes the beginning date of the year (listed as the last day of the prior year in the example, due to the way in which Excel calculates the number of days) and the date through which vacation information is requested. The calculation for each person in the report uses these dates to determine the number of vacation hours earned, plus any carryover from previous years, less any vacation time already taken (which comes from the payroll system). The report should list the hours of vacation taken by each week of the year (as shown on the right side of the report), so that the human resources staff can tell employees exactly when they took vacation time. The total hours of vacation left to use, which is listed on the bottom row of the report, is useful for calculating accrued vacation time for the financial statements.

The vacation summary report can be used to distribute vacation usage information to employees. If they are presented with this information on a regular basis, they will not bother the human resources staff with informational requests. Also, they can notify the accounting staff of any errors in the underlying vacation information before too much time passes, keeping the timekeeping database as accurate as possible. An easy way to issue this information to employees is to use the Excel "Hide" command to show only the one row of information in the report that applies to a particular employee. Then use the Excel "Copy" command to extract the header and vacation information for that employee, and use the "Paste" com-

Exhibit 5.4 Vacation Summary Report

12/31/03 ← Start
3/3/04 ← Today

	Hire Date	No. Days per Year	Accrued Hours to Date	Carry-forward Hours	Total Hours Earned	Hours Used	Hours Left to Use	Partial 1/6/02	1/13/02	1/20/02	1/27/02	2/3/02	2/10/02	2/17/02	2/24/02	3/3/02
Barlowe, Cindy	5/14/2001	20	27.6	0.0	27.6	12.0	15.6		4			8				
Caraway, Lisa	4/26/1999	15	20.7	38.6	59.3	19.0	40.3				8				3	8
Chantilly, Edward	10/30/1995	15	20.7	0.0	20.7	11.0	9.7			4			4	3		8
Davis, Humphrey	8/20/2001	15	20.7	5.2	25.9	14.5	11.4				7.25					7.25
Dunning, Mortimer	9/4/2001	20	27.6	9.4	37.0	45.0	−8.0					1.5		3.5	40	
Dunwiddy, Alexandra	8/13/2001	15	20.7	6.9	27.6	7.0	20.6					5	2			
Greenstreet, James	4/16/2001	15	20.7	36.9	57.6	16.0	41.6				8					8
Guthrie, James	5/14/2001	15	20.7	20.8	41.5	4.0	37.5							4		
Halverston, Eric	10/27/1997	20	27.6	23.5	51.1	20.0	31.1					8	12			
Johnson, Noyes	2/14/1994	15	20.7	9.2	29.9	16.0	13.9						16			
Montrose, Wesley	6/21/1999	15	20.7	10.0	30.7	10.0	20.7	2					8			
Mortimer, Victoria	11/10/1999	15	20.7	20.5	41.2	70.0	−28.8	24	7		4			8	23	4
Penway, Alice	8/9/1999	15	20.7	23.3	44.0	8.0	36.0						8			
Quarterstaff, Molly	5/6/1998	15	20.7	18.7	39.4	16.0	23.4				8					8
Rosencrantz, Albert	5/22/1995	15	20.7	9.8	30.5	18.0	12.5	2			8					8
Saunders, Ricardo	5/29/2001	15	20.7	0.0	20.7	4.0	16.7							4		
Von Gundle, Gerta	2/14/1994	15	20.7	0.0	20.7	8.0	12.7						8			
Zeta, Xavier	9/20/1999	15	20.7	34.3	55.0	42.5	12.5			2.5					40	
						Total	333.4									

Exhibit 5.5 Overtime Trend Report

	Week Ended								Hourly Rate	Annualized Overtime
	05/12	05/19	05/26	06/02	06/09	06/16	06/23	06/30		
Barlowe, Cindy	0.00	0.00	1.50	0.00	0.00	0.00	0.00	4.50	$15.50	$930.00
Davis, Humphrey	0.75	0.00	8.00	0.00	0.00	0.00	0.00	2.50	$15.00	$1,687.50
Dunning, Mortimer	2.50	0.00	4.50	0.00	0.00	0.00	0.00	1.00	$16.00	$1,280.00
Guthrie, James	0.00	1.50	0.00	4.00	1.50	0.00	0.00	0.00	$18.15	$1,270.50
Hortense, Alice	0.00	0.00	3.00	0.00	0.00	0.00	5.00	14.00	$17.45	$1,396.00
Innsbruck, Ingmar	0.00	0.00	7.00	0.00	0.00	0.00	3.50	11.00	$15.00	$1,575.00
Total Hours	0.0	0.0	1.5	10.0	4.0	1.5	0.0	8.5		

mand to insert it into an e-mail that is sent to that employee. This approach allows one to issue vacation information very rapidly to the entire staff.

Report: Overtime Trend

If employees record a large amount of overtime, it is best to implement a control at the front end of the process requiring them to have supervisors approve overtime in advance, so the company does not incur an unexpectedly large amount of overtime expense. However, if this is a rare event, it may be easier to allow employees to charge the hours without approval, and have the payroll staff report this information to supervisors after the fact. The management team can then decide if overtime use is being abused, and tighten the level of control as needed. An example of such a report is shown in Exhibit 5.5.

This report itemizes the overtime hours worked by employee on a rolling eight-week basis, with any overtime listed in bold. The report also itemizes employee pay levels per hour and the extended full-year overtime cost. This format gives supervisors an easy overview of how much overtime is being charged by each employee. In the exhibit, note that most overtime is being recorded on the last week of each month, when there is presumably a rush to ship products to customers. The one employee whose overtime appears to run contrary to this activity is James Guthrie, whose overtime hours are spread throughout the month; this may call for additional supervisory review to see if the hours are being charged without any work actually being performed.

Summary

A wide array of measurements and reports are available for determining the cost and efficiency level of the payroll function, and which can also be used to assist in determining pay raises, calculating vacation accruals, monitoring overtime usage, and so on. However, it is not necessary to implement everything described in this chapter. Try not to burden the accounting staff with too many measurement calculations or report preparations. Instead, it is better to categorize these items by their usefulness and gradually implement the most important ones. This approach not only allows one to determine the effort needed to prepare the information, but also allows time to set up data collection and distribution systems for each item, and to correct any problems discovered with the underlying data or report formats before proceeding to the next item on the list.

Notes

1. This measurement was adapted with permission from Chapter 9, "Measurements for the Accounting/Finance Department," in *Business Ratios and Formulas*, by Bragg (Hoboken, NJ: John Wiley & Sons, 2002).
2. This measurement was adapted with permission from Chapter 2, "Asset Utilization Measurements,"

6

Compensation

Introduction

This chapter* covers a multitude of issues surrounding employee compensation, with a particular emphasis on what types of compensation are taxable income to employees. The chapter begins with coverage of guidelines for determining if an employer can designate someone as an employee or contractor and proceeds to guidelines for differentiating between salaried and hourly employees. The chapter then covers a number of general compensation-related topics, such as activities for which wages must be paid, the standard work week, and payments made to temporary work agencies. The bulk of the chapter then covers a variety of compensation types, as well as business expenses that can be reported as gross income to employees for tax purposes. The chapter finishes with coverage of several forms used to report employee and supplier income to the government.

Employee or Contractor Status

A key issue is whether someone is an employee or a contractor, since the reporting of income to the IRS varies considerably for each one, as well as the tax withholding requirements of the employer. The defining test of an employee is when the company controls not only the types of work done by the employee, but also *how* the work shall be done. An employer also controls the work of a contractor, but not how the work is done. Other supporting evidence that an individual is a contractor is the presence of a contract between the parties, whether the contractor provides similar services to the public, and whether the contractor is paid based on the completion of specific tasks, rather than on the passage of time.

An employer may be tempted to categorize employees as contractors even when it is evident that this is not the case, since the employer can avoid matching some payroll taxes by doing so. However, taking this approach leaves an employer liable for all the federal income, Social Security, and Medicare taxes that should

---

* This chapter is derived with permission from Chapter 5 of Bragg, *Essentials of Payroll* (Hoboken, NJ: John Wiley & Son, 2003).

have been withheld. Consequently, strict adherence to the rules governing the definition of an employee and contractor should be followed at all times.

Wage Exemption Guidelines

One should be aware of the general rules governing whether an employee is entitled to an hourly wage or a salary, since this can avoid complaints from employees who wish to switch their status from one to the other. The key guidelines for designating a person as being eligible for a salary are:

- *Administrative.* Those in charge of an administrative department, even if they supervise no one, and anyone assisting management with long-term strategy decisions.
- *Executive.* Those who manage more than 50 percent of the time and supervise at least two employees.
- *Professional.* Those who spend at least 50 percent of their time on tasks requiring knowledge obtained through a four-year college degree (including systems analysis, design, and programming work on computer systems, even if a four-year degree was not obtained). The position must also allow for continued independent decision making and minimal close supervision.

Wage Payment Guidelines

There are a number of special activities falling within the standard work day for which an employee earning an hourly wage must be compensated. The most frequently encountered activities are:

- Employer-mandated charitable work.
- Employer-mandated meal times when employees are required to stay in their work locations.
- Employer-mandated training programs.
- Employer-mandated travel between work locations.
- Employer-mandated work activities.
- Rest periods equal to or less than 20 minutes.

Special activities falling outside the standard work day for which an employee earning an hourly wage must be compensated include the following items:

- Attendance at an employer-mandated training session.
- Emergency work for the employer.
- Equipment start-up or shut-down work.
- Maintenance work.
- Overlapping work related to shift-change problems.

Workers Paid by a Temporary Agency

It is common to ask a temporary agency to send workers to a company to complete work on a short-term basis. The temporary agency is considered the employer of these workers if it screens and hires them and can fire them. Under these conditions, the temporary agency is liable for all tax withholdings from their pay. The company paying the temporary agency for these services is only liable for pre-arranged fees paid to the agency, and is not responsible for their payroll taxes.

The Work Week

The work week is a fixed period of 168 consecutive hours that is recurring on a consistent basis. The beginning and ending start and stop times and dates can be anything management desires, but it should be consistently applied. Whatever the work week is defined to be, it should be listed in the employee manual to avoid confusion about which hours worked fall into which work week, not only for payment purposes but also for the calculation of overtime.

It is unwise to alter the stated work week, since it may be construed as avoidance of overtime payments. For example, a company may have a history of experiencing large amounts of overtime at the end of a month in order to make its delivery targets, so company management elects to change the work week from Monday through Sunday to Wednesday through Tuesday right in the middle of the final week in a month, thereby reducing much of the overtime hours that employees would otherwise earn to regular hours. This would be a highly suspect change of work week that might be construed by the government as being intended to avoid wage payments.

However, different work weeks can be used for different departments and locations. This is particularly common when a company is acquired, and elects not to conform the acquiree's work week to its own. If there are many of these acquisitions, a centralized payroll department may find itself tracking every conceivable variation on a work week, all within the same organization.

The Minimum Wage

The minimum wage is the minimum amount of wage per hour that must be paid to all employees, with some restrictions by type of industry. The minimum wage is set by the federal government, though it can be overridden by local law with a higher minimum wage requirement. Consult with the state wage enforcement division to determine the local rate.

To determine if an employer is paying at least the minimum wage, summarize all forms of compensation earned during a work week and divide it by the number of hours worked. The most common forms of compensation include base wages, commissions, shift differentials, piece-rate pay, and performance bonuses. If the calculation results in an average rate that drops below the minimum wage, then the employer must pay the difference between the actual rate paid and the minimum wage.

> *Example:* The Close Call Company, which specializes in making rush deliveries, pays its delivery staff at a rate of $8.00 per delivery made. In the last week, one employee completed 25 deliveries, which entitled him to $200 in wages. However, the minimum wage of $5.15 for the 40 hours worked should have entitled him to a base wage of $206.00, so the company must pay him an additional $6.00 in order to be in compliance with the law.

Computing Pay under the Hourly Rate Plan

The hourly rate plan is by far the most common method for calculating wages for hourly employees. This simply involves multiplying the wage rate per hour times the number of hours worked during the work week. It can be complicated by adding shift differentials, overtime, and other forms of bonus pay to the base wage rate. The overtime calculation is covered in a later section.

> *Example:* Manuel Eversol works the second shift at a manufacturing facility, where he earns an extra $0.25 per hour as a shift differential, as well as a base wage of $12.50 per hour. He works a standard 40 hours in the most recent work week. The calculation of his total wages earned is:
>
> ($12.50 base wage + $0.25 shift differential) × 40 hours = <u>$510.00</u> weekly pay

Computing Pay under the Piece Rate Plan

The piece-rate pay plan is used by companies that pay their employees at least in part based on the number of units of production completed. To calculate wages under this method, multiply the rate paid per unit of production by the number of units completed in the work week. An employer who uses this approach must still pay its staff for overtime hours worked; to calculate this, divide the total piece-rate pay by the hours worked, and then add the overtime premium to the excess hours worked. An employer can avoid this extra calculation by computing wages earned during an overtime period by using a piece rate that is at least 1.5 times the regular piece rate.

> *Example:* The Alice Company makes miniature Alice dolls, and pays its staff a piece rate of $0.75 for each doll completed. One worker completes 320

dolls in a standard 40 hour work week, which entitles her to pay of $240.00 (320 dolls × $0.75 piece rate). The worker then labors an extra five hours, and produces an additional 42 dolls. To calculate her pay for this extra time period, her employer first calculates her regular piece-rate pay, which is $31.50 (40 dolls × $0.75 piece rate). The employer then calculates the overtime due by calculating the standard wage rate during the regular period, which was $6.00 per hour ($240.00 total pay divided by 40 hours), resulting in a premium of $3.00 per hour. The employee's overtime pay is therefore $15.00 ($3.00 overtime premium × five hours).

The employer could also have simply set the piece rate 50 percent higher for work performed during the overtime period, which would have been $1.13 ($0.75 × 1.5). In this example, the higher piece rate would have resulted in a slightly higher payment to the employee, since the person produced slightly more than the standard number of dolls during the period.

Paying Salaries for Partial Periods

Many salaried employees begin or stop work partway through a pay period, so the payroll staff must calculate what proportion of their salary has been earned. This calculation also arises when a pay change has been made that is effective as of a date partway through the person's pay period.

To determine the amount of a partial payment, calculate the salaried employee's hourly rate and then multiply this rate by the number of hours worked. A common approach for determining the hourly rate is to divide the total annual salary by 2,080 hours, which is the total number of work hours in a year.

Example: The Pembrose Company pays its employees on the 15th and last day of each month, which amounts to 24 pay periods per year. One employee, Stephanie Ortiz, has been hired partway through a pay period at an annual salary of $38,500. She starts work on the 20th of the month, and there are seven business days left in the pay period. The payroll staff first determines her hourly rate of pay, which is $38,500 divided by 2,080 hours, or $18.51. They then calculate the number of hours left in the pay period, which is eight hours a day times seven working days, or 56 hours. Consequently, Ms. Ortiz's pay for her first pay period will be $18.51 times 56 hours, or $1,036.56.

Overtime Pay

Overtime is a pay premium of 50 percent of the regular rate of pay that is earned by employees on all hours worked beyond 40 hours in a standard work week. This calculation can vary for individual states, so be sure to check with the local state agency that tracks wage law issues to see if there are variations from the federally mandated rule.

When calculating overtime, the employer does not have to include in the 40 base hours such special hours as vacations, holidays, sick time, or jury duty.

Example: Ahmad Nefret is a welder who works 47 hours during a standard work week at an hourly wage of $22.00 per hour. The overtime premium he will be paid is 50 percent of his hourly wage, or $11.00. The calculation of his total pay is as follows:

47 hours × regular pay rate of $22.00/hour = $1,034.00
7 hours × overtime premium of $11.00/hour = 77.00

Total pay = $1,111.00

Example: Jamie Hildebrandt worked 33 hours during the four-day work week following Labor Day. Though her employer will pay her for 41 hours worked (eight hours of holiday time plus 33 hours worked), there will be no overtime paid out, since eight of the hours were not actually worked.

Commissions

An employee earns a commission when he or she secures a sale on behalf of a business. The commission may be earned at the point when an invoice is issued or when cash is received from the customer. The commission calculation may be quite complex, involving a percentage of the dollar amount sold, a fixed fee per sale, a bonus override for the sale of specific items, or perhaps a commission sharing arrangement with another member of the sales force. In any case, commissions are considered regular wages for tax withholding purposes, so all normal income tax withholdings, as well as taxes for Social Security, Medicare, and Federal Unemployment Tax (FUTA), must be deducted from them.

Example: Mr. Charles Everson is a salesperson for the Screaming Fiddler Company. His basic compensation deal is a six percent commission on all sales at the time they are invoiced, plus $25 each for any fiddle that is currently overstocked. He sells two of the Melodic series fiddles for $600 each, and also sells three of the overstocked Kid's Mini model for $450 each. His compensation is as follows:

2 × $600 Melodic series fiddles = $1,200 × 6% commission = $72.00
3 × $450 Kid's Mini series fiddles = $1,350 × 6% commission = $81.00
Bonus on sales of overstocked Kid's Mini model = $75.00

                                              Total = $228.00

Tips

Tips are paid directly to employees by customers for services performed. Employees who receive tips must report them to the employer by the tenth day of the month after the month in which the tips were received, except when total tips for the month are less than $20. This information should be reported to the employer on Form 4070, "Employee's Report of Tips to Employer."

The employer is required to withhold income, Social Security, and Medicare taxes from employee tips. These deductions are frequently made from employee base wages rather than tips, since employees do not usually contribute their tip income back to the employer so taxes can be withheld from it. If, by the tenth day of the following month, there are not enough employee funds from which to withhold the designated amount of taxes, the employer no longer has to collect it. If there are some employee funds on hand but not enough to cover all taxes to be withheld, then the withholdings should first be for Social Security and Medicare on all regular wages, then for federal income taxes on regular wages, then for Social Security and Medicare taxes on tips, and finally on income taxes for tips. Also, if the employer does not have enough reportable wages for an employee to withhold the full amount of required taxes, the employer must still provide the full amount of matching taxes.

Example: Alice Mane is a waitress at the Bowers Café. In the past month, she reported $390 in tip income, while her employer paid $120 in base wages. The Bowers Café needs to deduct the following amounts from her total pay:

	Tips	*Wages*	*Total Income*
Gross pay	$390.00	$120.00	$510.00
Federal income tax	78.00	24.00	102.00
Social Security	24.18	7.44	31.62
Medicare	5.66	1.74	7.40
Net pay	282.16	86.82	368.98

The employer finds that the total withholdings on both tip and wage income for Ms. Mane is $141.02. However, only $120.00 was paid out as wages, so the entire $120.00 must be deducted. The first types of taxes to be deducted from the $120.00 shall be the Social Security and Medicare taxes on her regular pay, which totals $9.18 and leaves $110.82 available for other taxes. Next in line is the federal income tax on her regular pay, which is for $24.00, leaving $86.82 available for other taxes. Next in order of priority is Social Security and Medicare taxes on her tip income, which totals $29.84 and leaves $56.98 available for the last deduction, which is the federal income tax withholding on her tip income. By allocating the remaining $56.98 to her federal income tax withholding, the company has paid off all her other taxes, leaving her responsible for $21.02 in unpaid federal income taxes.

Back Pay

Back pay is frequently paid to an employee as part of an arbitration award, perhaps related to an unjustified termination or an incorrectly delayed wage increase. Whatever the reason, it should be treated as regular wages for tax withholding purposes. However, some recent court cases have more tightly defined the types of back pay awards that are subject to withholding, so one should consult with a lawyer to determine the correct treatment.

Business Expense Reimbursements

If an employee submits substantiation of all expenses for which reimbursement is requested, then the corresponding payment from the employer to the employee is not considered income to the employee. Substantiation can take the following forms:

- A receipt that clearly indicates the amount of the expense.
- Per diem rates that do not exceed the per diem rates listed in IRS Publication 1542, which itemizes per diems for a variety of locations throughout the country. If an acceptable per diem rate is used, then travel, meals, and entertainment expense receipts for those days do not have to be submitted. If an employee is traveling to or from the home office, then the IRS allows a per diem on travel days of up to three-fourths of the normal rate.

Meals and entertainment present a special situation from the employer's perspective. Only 50 percent of these costs are allowed as tax deductions on the employer's tax return, though all of the expense claimed by employees can be reimbursed to them without it being listed as income to them. Also, meal expenses incurred by the company on behalf of an employee are not wages to the employee if they are incurred for the employer's convenience and are provided on the employer's premises.

Health insurance costs, including expenses incurred for an employee's family, are not considered employee wages, but must be recorded as wages in Subchapter S corporations for those employees who own more than two percent of the business.

If an employee lives away from home for less than one year on company business, the living costs paid to the employee for this period are not considered taxable income. However, once the duration exceeds one year, the employee is considered to have permanently moved to the new location, rendering all such subsequent payments taxable income to the employee.

Such fringe benefits as tickets to entertainment events, free travel, and company cars should be recorded as employee gross income. The amount of incremental gross income added should be the fair market value of the fringe benefit, minus its cost to the employee, minus any deductions allowed by law.

Example: Brad Harvest obtains discounted season tickets to the local baseball team through his company. The market price for the tickets is $2,500, but he only pays his employer $750 for them. The difference of $1,750 is considered income to Mr. Harvest, and should be reported as such to the IRS.

Club Memberships

Club dues are taxable income to the employee, except for that portion of the dues that are business related, which must be substantiated. Clubs that fall into this category are airline and hotel clubs, as well as golf, athletic, and country clubs. The portion of the club dues that are personal income to the employee can be treated as a wage expense to the employer for tax purposes.

Example: Brad Harvest is a member of an airline club, which allows him access to club facilities at a variety of airports around the country. He estimates that he uses these facilities 70 percent of the time while he is traveling on company business. He can substantiate this estimate with travel records. The annual cost of the membership is $400. Accordingly, only 30 percent of the cost, or $120, is recognizable as his personal income.

Education Reimbursement

The reimbursement of an employee's educational expenses by the employer is not income to the employee if the education being reimbursed is related to his or her current job and will either maintain or improve the person's skills for conducting that job. However, the payments *are* income if the education is to promote the person or shift him or her into an unrelated position requiring different skills.

An employer can change the reportable income situation somewhat by creating an educational assistance plan (EAP). This is a written plan that an employer creates on behalf of its employees, who are the only recipients of educational assistance under the plan. The plan is only acceptable to the IRS if it does not favor highly compensated employees or shareholders, does not give employees the option to receive cash instead of educational assistance, and is created with a reasonable amount of notice to employees. For this plan, employees are considered to be current staff, long-term leased staff, former staff who have retired, were laid off, or who left due to disability, or a sole proprietor or business partner. Expenses covered under the plan include school fees, supplies, books, and equipment related to training, but do not include expenses for lodging, meals, and transportation, nor education related to sports or hobbies unless this education is both related to the business and is part of a degree program. If all of these conditions are met, then using an EAP will allow each employee to exclude up to $5,250 per year for educational assistance paid by the employer.

Employee Achievement Awards

Employee achievement awards can be excluded from employee gross income, but only if the awards are tangible property given in recognition of length of service with the business or for safety achievement, and awarded as part of a meaningful presentation. This exclusion is up to $400 per year. A higher limit of $1,600 applies if the awards are made under a written plan that does not favor highly compensated employees. The total exclusion for both types of awards is $1,600, not the combined total of $2,000.

Example: Marion Smith continues to receive achievement awards for every quarter during which she works in a meat packing plant without being injured. Every quarter, she is paid a bonus of $50 during a formal achievement ceremony. This payment is taxable gross income to her, because it is a cash award instead of a tangible award.

Golden Parachute Payments

Golden parachute payments are made to employees or officers as a result of a change in corporate control or ownership. This type of payment is subject to all normal payroll tax withholdings. In addition, if the payment is more than three times a person's average annual compensation for the past five years, the employer must also withhold a 20 percent excise tax for the incremental amount exceeding this limit.

Example: The Golden Egg Company has laid one by being sold to a large international conglomerate. Under the terms of a golden parachute agreement, its president, Jason Fleece, is awarded a payment of $500,000. His average pay for the past five years was $125,000. Three times this amount, or $375,000, is the limit above which a 20 percent excise tax will be imposed. The amount subject to this tax is $125,000, so the company must deduct $25,000 from the total payment, in addition to all normal payroll taxes on the full $500,000 paid.

Life Insurance

The value of group term life insurance paid for by the employer is excluded from income for the first $50,000 of life insurance purchased. The excess value of life insurance coverage over this amount must be included in employee income. This income is only subject to Social Security and Medicare taxes. Use the following IRS table to determine the fair market value of group term life insurance per $1,000 of insurance for a range of age brackets:

Exhibit 6.1   *Fair Market Value Multiplier for Group Term Life Insurance*

Age Bracket	Value per $1,000 per Month
Under Age 25	$0.05
Age 25–29	0.06
Age 30–34	0.08
Age 35–39	0.09
Age 40–44	0.10
Age 45–49	0.15
Age 50–54	0.23
Age 55–59	0.43
Age 60–64	0.66
Age 65–69	1.27
Age 70 and above	2.06

Example: $80,000 of group term life insurance is purchased for a 54-year-old employee, who contributes $2 per month to this benefit. The first $50,000 of this amount is excluded from the employee's gross income. To calculate the value of the remaining $30,000, divide it by 1,000 and multiply the result by $0.23 (as taken from the above table for the 50-54 age bracket), which yields a fair value of $6.90 per month. Then subtract her $2.00 monthly contribution to arrive at a net monthly value received of $4.90. Next, multiply the monthly value of $4.90 by 12 in order to obtain the full-year value of the life insurance, which is $58.80. The $58.80 should be reported as her gross income.

The above scenario does not apply if the employer is the beneficiary of the life insurance. This would not be a benefit to the employee, and therefore its fair value should not be included in his or her gross income.

Meal Breaks

Some organizations will pay employees for a fixed amount of time off for a meal break if they exceed a set number of hours worked in a day. For example, if employees work more than 10 hours in a day, they are awarded an extra half-hour of pay, as long as they turn in a receipt as evidence of having purchased a meal. This extra amount is typically paid at an overtime pay rate.

If an employer gives time off for a meal break partway through a shift, such as lunch, this does not have to be paid time as long as the employees are relieved from all work responsibilities during the time period. If they are required to be on call during this period, then the employer would otherwise have had to pay someone else to take that position, so they should receive compensation for this type of meal break.

Though it may be company policy to automatically deduct some amount of time from the reported working time of its nonexempt employees to account for a lunch break, there should be a system in place that verifies the actual absence of employees from their places of work. This is necessary in case employees claim they had to work through their lunch breaks and were not compensated for this effort. Possible verification techniques are having the employees log themselves in and out of the payroll system at lunch time (though this tends to result in a number of missing card punches), locking down the work area during the lunch break, or having substitutes take their places who can record for whom they were working during the lunch break.

Moving Expenses

Employers may ask employees to move to a different company location. If the employer pays a third party or reimburses the moving employee for actual costs incurred, there is no reportable income to the employee. This only applies if the employee's new workplace is at least 50 miles further from his/her residence than the old workplace, and the employee must work out of the new location for at least 39 weeks during the 12-month period following the move. Otherwise, the move transaction will have the appearance of being a simple compensation by the employer of the employee, who happens to use the funds to move to a new location while still working at the same place of work.

If the employer pays the employee a fixed amount in order to complete the move and if the actual expenses incurred are less than the payment, then the difference is reported as income to the employee.

Example: The Fragrant Perfume Company asks its lead software developer to move to New York, where she can create a new logistics system for herbs being shipped through the New York port facilities. The new location is 250 miles away from her previous position at company headquarters. The company pays her $20,000 to complete the move, against which she can substantiate incurred expenses of $16,000. The difference of $4,000 is gross income, from which the company must deduct payroll taxes.

Outplacement Services

An employer may offer resumé assistance, counseling, and so on to employees it has terminated. The value of these services are not recorded as income for the affected employees, but only if the employer receives a substantial business benefit from providing the services and the services would have been reimbursable business expenses to the employees if they had paid for them directly. These rules will usually apply, since a business can claim a business benefit from the morale of the remaining employees, who can see that terminated employees are being well taken care of. If these rules do not apply, then the employer must withhold taxes on the fair market value of the services.

If the services are provided in exchange for severance pay, then the employer must withhold taxes on them. This latter situation arises when employees ask that the services be provided in an attempt to mask the offsetting compensation, so they can avoid paying payroll taxes.

Personal Use of Company Vehicles

A number of taxation rules apply if an employee drives a company vehicle for personal use. The basic rule is that personal use of this asset is taxable income to the employee. The following rules apply:

- If the vehicle is a specialty one, such as a garbage truck, then there is an assumption that no personal use will occur, so using this type of vehicle will never result in taxable income to the employee.
- If the employer requires the employee to use the vehicle to commute to work; an enforced company policy prohibits the vehicle from all other personal use; and the employee is not a highly compensated employee, director, or officer; then the employee will be charged with $1.50 of taxable income for each commute in each direction.

- If the employee can substantiate the amount of business use to which the vehicle was put, including dates, miles, and the purpose of each trip, all remaining miles are assumed to be for personal use. Under this scenario, one can determine the income charged to the employee by multiplying the IRS-designated rate of 36.0 cents per mile (which is revised annually) by the number of miles of personal use, less 5.5 cents per miles if the employee pays for all fuel. This approach is only allowable if the fair market value of the vehicle is approximately $15,000 or less (also revised annually) and the car is driven at least 10,000 miles per year in total. If the situation exceeds these restrictions, then the alternative approach is to multiply the proportion of personal miles used on the vehicle by its annual lease value (which is a percentage of a vehicle's fair market value, as supplied by the IRS) and record this amount as personal income to the employee.

Example: The president of Hot Rod Custom Modifiers, Inc. drives a company-owned Ferrari. The value of the car is clearly beyond $15,000, so he must record as personal income the proportion of his personal use of the car multiplied by its annual lease value of $28,000. The proportion of his personal use was 78 percent, so the company must record 78 percent of $28,000, or $21,840, as his gross income associated with his use of the car.

Reduced Interest Loans

An employer may loan money to employees. When this happens, if the amount of the loan is greater than $10,000 and is at an interest rate less than the Applicable Federal Rate (AFR), the difference is taxable income to the employee. This income is subject to Social Security and Medicare taxes, but not income tax withholding. The current AFR is available on the IRS website at *www.irs.gov*, or can be obtained by calling 800-829-1040.

Example: An employer loans $1,000,000 to one of its officers so the individual can purchase a new home. The stated interest rate on the loan is 3 percent, while the AFR is 7 percent. The amount of income reportable by the employee is the 4 percent difference between the two rates, or $40,000.

Travel Time

The time spent to travel back and forth from work to home and vice versa is not time for which the employer is liable to pay compensation, unless an employee is called away from home for emergency work and must travel for a significant period of time to reach the requested location.

If an employee is traveling amongst multiple locations as part of his or her job, such as is experienced by a traveling salesperson, then this travel time is paid time. However, the amount of paid time only corresponds to those hours during which an employee works during a regular working day.

> **Example:** Herbert Bailes normally works from 8 a.m. to 4 p.m., Monday through Friday. However, a special project requires him to stay at an off-site location and travel home on Saturday, which occupies him from 7 a.m. to noon. Of the five hours spent traveling on Saturday, the hours in the time period from 8 a.m. to noon can be claimed for wage reimbursement, since they fall within his regularly scheduled work day.

Annual Paperwork Reminders

There are several documents that the payroll department must issue or process at the end of a calendar year. The following paperwork-related items should be placed on the payroll activities calendar so they are not forgotten:

- Remind employees to review their withholding status and submit a new W-4 form if changes are in order.
- Remind employees who claimed total exemption from income tax withholding to submit a new W-4 form by the end of December.
- Give a completed W-2 form to all employees by the end of January.
- Give a completed 1099 form to all qualifying suppliers by the end of January.
- Send Copy A of all completed W-2 forms to the Social Security Administration by the end of January.
- Send a copy of all completed 1099 forms to the IRS with a transmittal Form 1096 by the end of January.
- Verify that all Forms W-2 and W-3 sum up to the totals listed on the Form 941, or be aware of the differences between the two sets of numbers.

The W-2 Form

The W-2 form contains the information needed by employees to file their annual income tax returns with the government. It itemizes the various types of income paid by the employer to the employee during the past calendar year. If an employee works for several employers during a year, then each one must provide a completed W-2 form. Also, if an employer changes payroll systems during the year, it is not uncommon to issue a separate W-2 form from each system for that period of the year during which each payroll system was recording compensation paid to employees.

An employer can send W-2 forms to its employees in either a paper or electronic format. However, if it uses the electronic format, it must first obtain permission from each employee to do so, which may be withdrawn with 30 days notice. No matter what format is used, the W-2 form must be sent to employees no later than January 31 following the year for which the form is being provided. Copies of these completed forms must also be sent to the IRS along with a transmittal form.

An example of the W-2 form is shown in Exhibit 6.2.

Exhibit 6.2   The W-2 Form

a Control number		22222	Void ☐	For Official Use Only ▶ OMB No. 1545-0008		

b Employer identification number				1 Wages, tips, other compensation $	2 Federal income tax withheld $

c Employer's name, address, and ZIP code			3 Social security wages $	4 Social security tax withheld $
			5 Medicare wages and tips $	6 Medicare tax withheld $
			7 Social security tips $	8 Allocated tips $

d Employee's social security number			9 Advance EIC payment $	10 Dependent care benefits $

e Employee's first name and initial	Last name		11 Nonqualified plans $	12a See instructions for box 12 $
		13 Statutory employee ☐ Retirement plan ☐ Third-party sick pay ☐		12b $
		14 Other		12c $
				12d $

f Employee's address and ZIP code					

15 State Employer's state ID number	16 State wages, tips, etc. $	17 State income tax $	18 Local wages, tips, etc. $	19 Local income tax $	20 Locality name
	$	$	$	$	

Form **W-2** Wage and Tax Statement   (99)   **2003**

Department of the Treasury—Internal Revenue Service
For Privacy Act and Paperwork Reduction Act Notice, see separate instructions.

Copy A For Social Security Administration— Send this entire page with Form W-3 to the Social Security Administration; photocopies are not acceptable.   Cat. No. 10134D

Do Not Cut, Fold, or Staple Forms on This Page — Do Not Cut, Fold, or Staple Forms on This Page

---

The employer fills out the form by listing the employer's name, address, and identifying information in the upper left corner of the form, followed by the same information for the employee in the lower left corner. The right side contains many numbered blocks in which the various types of wages paid are listed. Descriptions for the most commonly used boxes in the form are as follows:

Box 1: *Wages, tips, other compensation.* Include in this box the total amount of all wages, salaries, tip income, commissions, bonuses, and other types of compensation paid to the employee.

Box 2: *Federal income tax withheld.* The federal income taxes withheld by the company from the employee's pay are recorded here. *Only* federal taxes should be included here, since state income taxes withheld are listed later in box 17 at the bottom of the report.

Box 3: *Social Security wages.* The total amount of compensation paid that is subject to Social Security taxes should be listed here. This means that anyone's pay that exceeds the statutory limit set for Social Security wages in any given year will only see the statutory limit listed in this box.

Box 4: *Social Security tax withheld.* List the total amount of Social Security taxes withheld for the calendar year in this box.

Box 5: *Medicare wages and tips.* The total amount of all compensation paid during the year should be listed here. Unlike Social Security, there is no upper limit on the wages on which Medicare taxes are paid, so in most cases the number listed in this box will be the same as the one listed earlier in Box 1.

Box 6: *Medicare tax withheld.* List the total amount of Medicare taxes withheld for the calendar year in this box.

Box 12: *Cost of group term life insurance over $50,000.* As was explained earlier in the Life Insurance section, the value of all life insurance purchased by an employer on behalf of its employees in excess of $50,000 must be reported as income. This portion of total compensation is itemized in Box 12 next to a signifying letter "G."

Box 12: *Excise tax on golden parachute payments.* As was explained earlier in the Golden Parachute Payments section, the employer must withhold a 20 percent excise tax on excessively large golden parachute payments. The total excise tax is listed in Box 12 next to a signifying letter "K."

In addition, state and local wage and income tax withholding information is listed across the bottom of the form in Boxes 15 through 20.

The Employer's Annual Tip Income Tax Return

An employer is required to submit a Form 8027, "Employer's Annual Information Return of Tip Income and Allocated Tips," to the IRS no later than February 28 of each year following the reporting calendar year. This form is used by large eating establishments to report tips earned by employees. If an employer runs multiple eating establishments, a separate form must be completed for each one. The form is not used to submit any taxes, but rather to give the IRS an idea of the amount of employee tip income as a proportion of total receipts for an establishment. A sample Form 8027 is shown in Exhibit 6.3.

What the IRS is trying to determine with this form is whether an establishment's tipped employees are not reporting some portion of their tip income to the business. To do this, lines 1 and 2 of the form are used to determine the proportion of tips that customers are charging through their credit cards, which can be easily proven by a review of the underlying charge receipts. This proportion is then compared to the proportion of actual total receipts reported to the business by

Exhibit 6.3 The Employer's Annual Tip Income Return

Form **8027**	Employer's Annual Information Return of Tip Income and Allocated Tips	OMB No. 1545-0714
Department of the Treasury Internal Revenue Service	▶ See separate instructions.	2003

Use IRS label. Make any necessary changes. Otherwise, please type or print.	Name of establishment Number and street (see instructions) Employer identification number City or town, state, and ZIP code	Type of establishment (check only one box) ☐ 1 Evening meals only ☐ 2 Evening and other meals ☐ 3 Meals other than evening meals ☐ 4 Alcoholic beverages

Employer's name (same name as on Form 941)   Establishment number (see instructions)

Number and street (P.O. box, if applicable)   Apt. or suite no.

City, state, and ZIP code (if a foreign address, see instructions)

Does this establishment accept credit cards, debit cards, or other charges?	Yes ☐ (lines 1 and 2 must be completed) No ☐	Check if: Amended Return ☐ Final Return ☐

1	Total charged tips for calendar year 2003	1	
2	Total charge receipts showing charged tips (see instructions)	2	
3	Total amount of service charges of less than 10% paid as wages to employees	3	
4a	Total tips reported by indirectly tipped employees	4a	
b	Total tips reported by directly tipped employees	4b	

Note: Complete the Employer's Optional Worksheet for Tipped Employees   on page 4 of the instructions to determine potential unreported tips of your employees.

c	Total tips reported (add lines 4a and 4b)	4c	
5	Gross receipts from food or beverage operations (not less than line 2—see instructions) .	5	
6	Multiply line 5 by 8% (.08) or the lower rate shown here ▶ _____ granted by the IRS. (Attach a copy of the IRS determination letter to this return.)	6	

Note: If you have allocated tips using other than the calendar year (semimonthly, biweekly, quarterly, etc.), mark an "X" on line 6 and enter the amount of allocated tips from your records on line 7.

7	Allocation of tips. If line 6 is more than line 4c, enter the excess here	7	

▶ This amount must be allocated as tips to tipped employees working in this establishment. Check the box below that shows the method used for the allocation. (Show the portion, if any, attributable to each employee in box 8 of the employee's Form W-2.)

a Allocation based on hours-worked method (see instructions for restriction) . . . . ☐
Note: If you marked the checkbox in line 7a, enter the average number of employee hours worked per business day during the payroll period. (see instructions) _____
b Allocation based on gross receipts method . . . . ☐
c Allocation based on good-faith agreement (Attach a copy of the agreement.) . . . . ☐

8   Enter the total number of directly tipped employees at this establishment during 2003 ▶

Under penalties of perjury, I declare that I have examined this return, including accompanying schedules and statements, and to the best of my knowledge and belief, it is true, correct, and complete.

Signature ▶   Title ▶   Date ▶

For Privacy Act and Paperwork Reduction Act Notice, see page 4 of the separate instructions.   Cat. No. 49989U   Form **8027** (2003)

its employees to the total amount of gross receipts for the business. Ideally, the two percentages should match. If the latter percentage is lower, this indicates that employees are not reporting all of their tip income. If this appears to be a problem, the business owner can call the IRS at 800-829-1040 or search for "Voluntary

Compliance Agreements" on the IRS website at *www.irs.gov*. This program gives assistance in educating employees about their obligations in reporting tip income.

The 1099 Form

The 1099 form is issued to all suppliers to whom a business pays (to quote the IRS):

at least $600 in rents, services (including parts and materials), prizes and awards, other income payments, medical and health care payments, crop insurance proceeds, cash payments for fish (or other aquatic life)[1]

As was the case for the W-2 form, this form must be issued to suppliers no later than January 31 of the year following the reporting year, as well as to the IRS.

This form is not issued if the supplier is a corporation, or if the payments are for rent to real estate agents, telegrams, telephone, freight or storage, wages paid to employees, business travel allowances paid to employees, and payments made to tax-exempt organizations. An example of the 1099 form is shown in Exhibit 6.4.

The 1099 form is similar to the W-2 form, in that the upper left corner of the form contains employer contact information and the lower left corner contains supplier contact information. The right side of the report contains a number of boxes for itemizing the types of payments made to suppliers. The most commonly used box is number seven, "Nonemployee compensation," which is a catchall for the majority of payments made, unless they are specified in one of the other boxes. Box four is also needed if the company cannot obtain a taxpayer identification number (see next paragraph) from a supplier, in which case it must withhold 30% on payments made, and report the withheld amount here.

The key determining factor for the average business is to determine if its suppliers are corporations or not. This is most easily done by issuing a W-9 form, "Request for Taxpayer Identification Number and Certification," in which the supplier states its form of legal organization and identification number, which the company can then use to issue a Form 1099, if necessary. A sample W-9 Form is shown in Exhibit 6.5.

The W-9 is a simple form. The supplier fills out the identification information in the top block, enters an identification number in Part I, and signs the document in Part II. Since suppliers can change their form of legal organization from time to time, a company that wants to be in complete compliance with the law may want to consider making an annual W-9 mailing to all of its suppliers, so it has documentary proof of why it is (or is not) issuing 1099 forms.

Rather than go through the expense of making an annual mailing of W-9 forms to suppliers, one can simply e-mail them a PDF file that contains the form's image. Suppliers can then print the form directly from the e-mail and either mail or fax back the completed form. The only problem is that one must compile a data-

Exhibit 6.4   The 1099 Form

9595 ☐ VOID ☐ CORRECTED		

PAYER'S name, street address, city, state, ZIP code, and telephone no.	1 Rents $	OMB No. 1545-0115	
	2 Royalties $	**2003** Form 1099-MISC	Miscellaneous Income
	3 Other income $	4 Federal income tax withheld $	Copy A
PAYER'S Federal identification number RECIPIENT'S identification number	5 Fishing boat proceeds $	6 Medical and health care payments $	For Internal Revenue Service Center File with Form 1096.
RECIPIENT'S name	7 Nonemployee compensation $	8 Substitute payments in lieu of dividends or interest $	For Privacy Act and Paperwork Reduction Act Notice, see the 2003 General Instructions for Forms 1099, 1098, 5498, and W-2G.
Street address (including apt. no.)	9 Payer made direct sales of $5,000 or more of consumer products to a buyer (recipient) for resale ▶ ☐	10 Crop insurance proceeds $	
City, state, and ZIP code	11	12	
Account number (optional) 2nd TIN not. ☐	13 Excess golden parachute payments $	14 Gross proceeds paid to an attorney $	
15	16 State tax withheld $	17 State/Payer's state no.	18 State income $

Form 1099-MISC   Cat. No. 14425J   Department of the Treasury - Internal Revenue Service

Do Not Cut or Separate Forms on This Page — Do Not Cut or Separate Forms on This Page

base of e-mail addresses for the accounting contacts at all suppliers. If this information is not available for some suppliers, then a supplemental mailing is typically required to account for them.

Summary

The wage rules described in this chapter cover a considerable majority of the situations in which an employer will find itself. However, in those cases where one wishes to be certain of the rules for specific industries or for scenarios that appear to fall outside the ones described here, go to the IRS website at *www.irs.gov* and download its *Publication 15-B, Employer's Tax Guide to Fringe Benefits*. As the name implies, this publication covers a wide range of fringe benefit exclusion rules, ranging from accident and health benefits to working condition benefits. It also addresses fringe benefit valuation rules as well as rules for withholding, depositing, and reporting taxes.

Note

1. IRS, *Internal Revenue Manual*, section 4.6.2.13.2.

Exhibit 6.5 *The W-9 Form*

| Form **W-9** (Rev. January 2003) Department of the Treasury Internal Revenue Service | Request for Taxpayer Identification Number and Certification | Give form to the requester. Do not send to the IRS. |

Print or type
See Specific Instructions on page 2.

Name

Business name, if different from above

Check appropriate box: ☐ Individual/ Sole proprietor ☐ Corporation ☐ Partnership ☐ Other ▶ ....   ☐ Exempt from backup withholding

Address (number, street, and apt. or suite no.)

Requester's name and address (optional)

City, state, and ZIP code

List account number(s) here (optional)

Part I Taxpayer Identification Number (TIN)

Enter your TIN in the appropriate box. For individuals, this is your social security number (SSN). However, for a resident alien, sole proprietor, or disregarded entity, see the Part I instructions on page 3. For other entities, it is your employer identification number (EIN). If you do not have a number, see How to get a TIN on page 3.

Note: If the account is in more than one name, see the chart on page 4 for guidelines on whose number to enter.

Social security number

| | | | | | | | |

or

Employer identification number

| | | | | | | |

Part II Certification

Under penalties of perjury, I certify that:

1. The number shown on this form is my correct taxpayer identification number (or I am waiting for a number to be issued to me), and

2. I am not subject to backup withholding because: (a) I am exempt from backup withholding, or (b) I have not been notified by the Internal Revenue Service (IRS) that I am subject to backup withholding as a result of a failure to report all interest or dividends, or (c) the IRS has notified me that I am no longer subject to backup withholding, and

3. I am a U.S. person (including a U.S. resident alien).

Certification instructions.   You must cross out item 2 above if you have been notified by the IRS that you are currently subject to backup withholding because you have failed to report all interest and dividends on your tax return. For real estate transactions, item 2 does not apply. For mortgage interest paid, acquisition or abandonment of secured property, cancellation of debt, contributions to an individual retirement arrangement (IRA), and generally, payments other than interest and dividends, you are not required to sign the Certification, but you must provide your correct TIN. (See the instructions on page 4.)

| Sign Here | Signature of U.S. person ▶ | Date ▶ |

Purpose of Form

A person who is required to file an information return with the IRS, must obtain your correct taxpayer identification number (TIN) to report, for example, income paid to you, real estate transactions, mortgage interest you paid, acquisition or abandonment of secured property, cancellation of debt, or contributions you made to an IRA.

U.S. person. Use Form W-9 only if you are a U.S. person (including a resident alien), to provide your correct TIN to the person requesting it (the requester) and, when applicable, to:

1. Certify that the TIN you are giving is correct (or you are waiting for a number to be issued),

2. Certify that you are not subject to backup withholding, or

3. Claim exemption from backup withholding if you are a U.S. exempt payee.

Note: If a requester gives you a form other than Form W-9 to request your TIN, you must use the requester's form if it is substantially similar to this Form W-9.

Foreign person. If you are a foreign person, use the appropriate Form W-8 (see Pub. 515, Withholding of Tax on Nonresident Aliens and Foreign Entities).

Nonresident alien who becomes a resident alien. Generally, only a nonresident alien individual may use the terms of a tax treaty to reduce or eliminate U.S. tax on certain types of income. However, most tax treaties contain a provision known as a "saving clause." Exceptions specified in the saving clause may permit an exemption from tax to continue for certain types of income even after the recipient has otherwise become a U.S. resident alien for tax purposes.

If you are a U.S. resident alien who is relying on an exception contained in the saving clause of a tax treaty to claim an exemption from U.S. tax on certain types of income, you must attach a statement that specifies the following five items:

1. The treaty country. Generally, this must be the same treaty under which you claimed exemption from tax as a nonresident alien.

2. The treaty article addressing the income.

3. The article number (or location) in the tax treaty that contains the saving clause and its exceptions.

4. The type and amount of income that qualifies for the exemption from tax.

5. Sufficient facts to justify the exemption from tax under the terms of the treaty article.

Cat. No. 10231X   Form **W-9** (Rev. 1-2003)

7

Payroll Deductions

Introduction

There are many possible payroll deductions, most being at the behest of employees, but some required by court order. This chapter[*] covers several possible payroll deductions, giving an overview of each item, discussing the problems associated with each one, and giving an example of how several might be administered. In addition, deductions related to employee benefits are discussed in Chapter 9.

Asset Purchases

An employer may allow its employees to either purchase assets from the company or through it. In the first case, the company may be liquidating assets and offers to sell them to its employees. In the latter case, employees are allowed to use the company's bulk-purchase discounts in order to obtain items at reduced prices from other suppliers. The company may also sell its own products at reduced prices to employees through a company store.

Whatever the reason for the purchase, some asset purchases are so large that employees are unable to pay back the company immediately for the full amount of the purchase. Instead, the company allows them to pay back the company through a series of payroll deductions. When this happens, an employee should sign an agreement with the company, acknowledging responsibility for paying back the company and also agreeing to a specific payment schedule. Though not common, the company can also charge the employee an interest rate, which may encourage the person to pay back the company somewhat sooner in order to avoid an excessive interest expense.

For long repayment schedules, it may be useful to keep employees apprised of the remaining amount of each loan, so the payroll staff should consider either maintaining a separate schedule of payments or creating a loan goal through its payroll software that tracks the amount of the goal that has not yet been reached.

---

[*] This chapter is derived with permission from Chapter 8 of Bragg, *Essentials of Payroll* (Hoboken, NJ: John Wiley & Sons, 2003).

Charitable Contributions

Many employers encourage their employees to give regular contributions to local or national charities, The United Way is the most common example. Employers typically have employees sign a pledge card that authorizes certain deduction amounts to be withheld from their pay. After payrolls are completed, the accounting staff then creates a single lump-sum check representing the contributions of all employees, matches the amounts withheld if this is part of the deal offered employees, and forwards the payment to the designated charity. Some employees prefer to make a single lump-sum payment to the charity, in which case the company usually forwards their check directly to the charity without creating any deduction through the payroll system.

Employees can renege on a pledge card and ask the payroll department to stop making further deductions from their pay, though this request (as is the case for all deductions) should be made in writing and kept in each employee's personnel or payroll file for future reference. Also, the remittance advice that accompanies each employee's paycheck should itemize both the amount of each deduction and the year-to-date total deduction that has gone to the charity. If there are multiple charities for which deductions are being made, the remittance advice should list each one separately. The employee needs this information when filing his or her income tax return at year-end in order to prove the amount of contributions itemized on the tax return.

The Internal Revenue Code requires employees to have written substantiation from a charity if the amount of a contribution exceeds $250. However, this requirement is for *individual* contributions of $250 or more, which is unlikely to be the case for a single payroll deduction (each of which is considered an individual contribution). Charities are unlikely to have enough information to issue a written substantiation in any case, since they receive a lump-sum payment from the employer and usually have no means for tracking individual contributions within each payment. Consequently, employees who make such large contributions should use the year-end remittance advice attached to their paychecks as proof of the year-to-date amount of the contributions made and should also retain their original pledge cards as proof of the commitment made.

Example: David Anderson and Charles Weymouth both make contributions to The United Way. Mr. Anderson has authorized the company to make regular deductions of $80 from each of his weekly paychecks, which the company will match and forward to The United Way. Because each contribution is less than $250, there is no need to obtain a written substantiation from The United Way. Charles Weymouth has authorized the company to make exactly the same sized annual contribution, but he wants it to be taken only from his month-end paycheck, which increases the individual deduction to $320 ($80 times four weekly paychecks). Because the individual deduction exceeds

$250, Mr. Weymouth must obtain a written substantiation of the contribution from The United Way, or obtain some similar form of evidence for the IRS.

Child Support Payments

The payroll manager will almost certainly see court-ordered child support with-holding orders at some point during his or her career. There are tightly enforced federal laws that help to track down parents who are not making support payments and require employers to withhold various amounts from employees' pay in order to meet mandated child support payments.

The maximum amount of an employee's disposable earnings that is subject to child support withholding is 60 percent of his or her pay, or 50 percent if the employee is already making payments to support other children or spouses. Both percentages increase by 5 percent if an employee is 12 or more weeks in arrears in making support payments. In order to calculate disposable earnings, subtract all legally mandated deductions from an employee's gross pay, such as federal and state income taxes, Social Security and Medicare taxes, and any locally mandated disability or unemployment taxes. Voluntary deductions, such as pension and medical insurance deductions, are not used to calculate disposable earnings.

A good garnishment management technique is to keep a calendar itemizing the amount of each garnishment, the declining balance on each one, and the date on which the last deduction and related payment to a third party is due. Also, there can be some dispute regarding the start date of the deductions, which are frequently tied to the date of receipt of a withholding order. Consequently, mark and initial the date of receipt, as well as the postmark date, on the withholding order.

Example: The Dim Bulb I.Q. Testing Company receives a court order to withhold child support payments from the pay of its employee, Ernest Evans, in the amount of $390 per weekly paycheck. The payroll manager needs to determine how much can actually be withheld from Mr. Evans's pay. Mr. Evans earns $850 per week and does not make support payments to another child or spouse. His typical pay check remittance advice is as follows:

Gross pay	$850
Federal income tax	125
State income tax	35
Social Security tax	53
Medicare tax	12
Medical insurance	62
401k plan deduction	80
Net pay	$483

Of the amounts listed on the remittance advice, the medical insurance and 401k deductions are voluntary, and so cannot be included in the calculation of disposable earnings. This increases Mr. Evans's disposable earnings to $625. The payroll manager then multiplies this amount by 60 percent, which is the maximum amount of disposable earnings that can be remitted for child support. The result is $375, $15 less than the $390 listed on the court order. The payroll manager begins deducting and remitting the $375 per week.

When a child support court order is received, it takes precedence over all other types of garnishment orders, with the exception of tax levies that were received prior to the date of the court order. An employer must begin withholding the maximum allowable amount from an employee's pay no later than the first pay period beginning after 14 working days after the posted date of the court order and must continue to withhold funds until the order is rescinded by the court.

A common point of confusion is where to send child support payments. Contrary to the not uncommon demands of the parent who is designated to receive the payments, the payments typically go to a court-designated person, who then disburses the funds to the parent—payments never go straight to the parent. Instructions for remitting funds will be listed on the court order; the employer should follow these instructions to the letter.

An employer can charge an employee an administrative fee for withholding child support from his or her paycheck. The amount is mandated by state law, and is itemized in Exhibit 7.1. Whichever is the case, the fee can only be taken from an employee's remaining wages after the support payment amount has already been withheld.

If an employee leaves employment before the obligations of a court order are discharged, the employer is obliged to notify the issuing enforcement agency of the employee's last known address, as well as the location of a new employer (if known). The agency needs this information in order to track down the employee and continue to enforce the court order.

If an employer chooses to ignore a court order, it will be liable for the total amount that should have been withheld. This means that an employer must act promptly to begin withholding by the date specified in the court order and must withhold the full required amount, taking into account the rules noted earlier in this section.

Deduction of Prior Pay Advances

Employees who require more cash than they can obtain through their normal paychecks sometimes ask their employers for an advance on their pay. The need may be nonbusiness, such as a sudden medical crisis or a home purchase, or it may be

Exhibit 7.1 *Employer Administrative Fees for Child Support Withholding by State*

Allowable Fee	Applicable States
None	Connecticut, Delaware, Michigan, New York, South Dakota
$1/payment	California, Kentucky, Massachusetts, Minnesota, New Hampshire, New Jersey, New Mexico, Washington, West Virginia
$2/month	Alabama
$2/payment	District of Columbia, Florida, Hawaii, Indiana, Iowa, Maine, Maryland, Mississippi, North Carolina, Ohio, Rhode Island
$2.50/month	Nebraska
$2.50/pay period	Arkansas
$3/month	North Dakota
$3/payment	Georgia, Nevada, South Carolina, Wisconsin
$4/month	Arizona
$5/month	Colorado, Illinois, Montana, Oregon, Tennessee, Vermont
$5/payment	Alaska, Idaho, Oklahoma, Virginia, Wyoming
$5/pay period	Kansas, Louisiana
$6/month	Missouri
$10/month	Texas
Other	
2% of payment	Pennsylvania
$25 once	Utah

to buy something on behalf of the company; the most common example of the latter case is to provide funds for a company trip, for which the employee will be reimbursed once an expense report is submitted. In the latter case, it is most common to reimburse employees through the accounts payable system if there is a shortfall between the amount of expenses incurred and the original advance. However, if an employee neglects to turn in an expense report, then he or she is liable to the company for the amount of the advance that was issued. This is also the case when an employee has obtained an advance prior to his or her normal paycheck.

In either of these last two cases, the payroll staff needs to track the amount of outstanding advances and make deductions from employee paychecks in order to recover the amounts outstanding. This frequently occurs in smaller increments over multiple paychecks, so that employees do not have so much deducted from their pay that there are minimal net funds left for their personal needs. Managing this process properly calls for interaction with the accounts payable staff (who would have paid out the initial advances), as well as the employees (in order to determine the appropriate amount of deductions for each paycheck). There should also be standard policies in place that regulate the amount of advances handed out and the speed with which they must be paid back, so that a company does not turn into a personal bank for its employees and has minimal risk of losing outstanding advances if employees quit work before paying them back.

Example: Andrew Wodehouse, a warehouse worker, has requested an advance of $400 on his next paycheck. Company policy states that advances cannot exceed the net amount of an employee's prior paycheck, which limits the amount to $360. Mr. Wodehouse also requests that the advance be taken out of his pay over the next six paychecks, which would be $60 per paycheck. However company policy requires all advances to be paid back within no more than four paychecks, so the amount deducted from his paychecks is increased to $90. After three paychecks, a garnishment order is sent to the company for a loan repayment that Mr. Wodehouse owes a creditor. He promptly quits work and disappears. However, as a result of the company's strict rules for employee advances, there is only $90 left on the advance that will not be paid back to the company.

Employee Portion of Insurance Expenses

Most businesses offer some form of medical and related insurance to their employees. This can include medical, dental, vision, short-term disability, long-term-disability, life, and supplemental life insurance coverage. An employer may pay for all of this expense, a portion of it, or merely make it available to employees, who must foot the entire bill. It is quite rare for an employer to pay for all of this expense, since insurance is quite expensive; consequently, there will usually be a deduction from payroll to cover some portion of the cost.

The type of deduction calculation used is typically employer reimbursement of a relatively high percentage of the medical insurance for an employee and a lesser percentage for that person's portion of the insurance that covers his or her family members. For example, the employer may pay for 80 percent of an employee's medical insurance and 50 percent of the portion of additional coverage that applies to the employee's family. Additional types of insurance, such as vision or life insurance, are less commonly paid by employers, with employees being given the option to purchase and fully pay for them.

When the payroll department sets up deductions for the various types of insurance, it is better to itemize each one separately on the employee paycheck remittance advice, so there is no question about the amount of each deduction being withheld for each type of insurance. This approach makes it easier for employees to judge whether or not they want to continue to pay for various types of insurance and also makes it easier for the payroll staff to calculate and track deduction levels.

The insurance companies that provide the various types of insurance may enter into contracts that freeze expense levels for up to a year, which makes it a simple once-a-year event to recalculate the amount of employee insurance deductions. However, other insurance providers may alter rates on a more frequent basis, necessitating more frequent reviews and recalculations of employee deduction levels. If this is the case, employees should be warned of upcoming changes in the rates they are paying.

Example: The Doughboy Donut Company pays for 90 percent of its employees' medical insurance, 25 percent of the additional medical insurance for the families of employees, and 90 percent of employee life insurance. It makes short-term, long-term, and dental insurance available to its employees, but employees must pay for these benefits. Ms. Emily Swankart is a single parent and has subscribed to all of these types of insurance. The total amount of deductions for her is calculated:

Type of Insurance	Total Cost	Deduction (%)	Deduction ($)
Medical insurance	$225	90%	$23
Medical insurance, dependent	200	25%	150
Life insurance	35	90%	32
Short-term disability insurance	42	0%	42
Long-term disability insurance	15	0%	15
Dental insurance	28	0%	28
Total			**$290**

As is commonly the case under this type of deduction plan, note that the largest portion of the expense to be paid by the employee is the medical insurance for the dependent.

Employee Purchases through the Company

Some employees can get into the habit of purchasing a large number of items through the company, which can present several problems. First, the payroll staff may find itself tracking multiple repayment schedules for each employee, which is quite time-consuming. Second, if an employee leaves the company, the amount of the outstanding loans to the company for unreimbursed asset purchases may exceed the person's final paycheck by a significant amount, making it difficult for the company to collect on the remaining loans. Several simple rules can be implemented to avoid these problems. First, do not allow an employee to purchase something from or through the company until the last purchase has been fully paid off. Second, do not allow the full amount of such a purchase to exceed the amount of an employee's net pay for one month, or perhaps just a single paycheck. These rules reduce the number of purchase reimbursements to track and also reduce the risk of loss to the company if an employee quits with unpaid loans.

Garnishments for Unpaid Taxes

If an employee does not pay his or her federal or local income taxes, the employer may receive a notification from the IRS to garnish that person's wages in order to repay the taxes. The garnishment will cover not only the original amount of unpaid taxes, but also any penalties and interest expenses added by the government.

A garnishment for unpaid taxes takes priority over all other types of garnishments, except for child support orders that were received prior to the date of the tax garnishment. If a business receives orders from multiple taxing authorities to garnish an employee's wages and there are not enough wages to pay everyone, then the orders are implemented in the order in which they were received.

The Notice of Levy on Wages, Salary, and Other Income, Form 668-W, is the standard form used for notifying a company to garnish an employee's wages. It has the following six parts:

Part 1:   This is for the employer. It states the employer's obligation to withhold and remit the unpaid tax and also states the amount of the unpaid tax.

Part 2:   This is the employee's copy of the notification.

Parts 3–4:   The employee must complete these pages and return them to the employer within three business days, who in turn completes the back side of Part 3 and then returns it to the IRS and retains Part 4.

Part 5:   The employee keeps this page, which includes tax status and exemption information.

Part 6:   The IRS keeps this page for its records.

If an employee fails to remit parts 3 and 4 of Form 668-W to the employer, the employer is required to calculate the employee's exempt amount of wages under the assumption that the person is married filing separately, with one exemption. These assumptions result in the smallest possible amount of exempt wages, so employees should be strongly encouraged to turn in parts 3 and 4 in order to avoid having the maximum amount withheld from their pay.

When a Form 668-W order is received to garnish an employee's wages, the payroll staff must first determine if any wages are not subject to the order. Only 15 percent of the following types of wages are subject to a tax payment order issued by the IRS, and they are completely exempt from an unpaid tax order issued by a *state* government:

- Armed forces disability benefits.
- Pension and annuity payments as specified under the Railroad Retirement Act.
- Unemployment compensation benefits.
- Welfare and Supplemental Social Security payments.
- Workers' compensation benefits.

Once the above types of wages have been accounted for, the payroll staff must determine which deductions can be made from an affected employee's pay before determining the amount of the tax levy. Allowable deductions include:

- Federal and state income taxes.
- Social Security and Medicare taxes.
- Increases in deductions over which an employee has no control, such as a medical insurance increase imposed by a health care provider.
- Deductions required in order to be employed by the company.
- Deductions in effect *prior to* the tax garnishment notice, which can include deductions for medical, life, and disability insurance, as well as cafeteria plan deductions

Once the applicable deductions have been used to reduce an employee's wages to the amount to which the tax levy will be applied, the payroll staff should use an IRS-supplied table to determine the amount of net wages that are exempt from the tax levy. This table is shown in Exhibit 7.2.

Example: Molly Gammon has not been paying her federal income taxes, so her employer, the Red Herring Fish Company, receives a notice from the IRS informing it that she owes the government $10,000 in back taxes. The company is obligated to withhold this amount and remit it to the IRS. The payroll manager must calculate the amount of the tax levy to withhold from each paycheck. He obtains the following information from her pay records:

Weekly salary	$1,000
Federal and state income taxes	192
Social Security and Medicare taxes	77
Medical insurance deductions	40
Stock purchase plan deductions	50
Net Pay	$ 641

To calculate the amount of her net pay that is exempt from the tax levy, the payroll manager turns to the table for figuring exemptions that was listed in Exhibit 9.2. Molly is an unmarried head of household with four exemptions. For a weekly pay period, this gives her an exemption of $363.46 from the tax levy. This means that $277.54 is subject to the tax levy, which is calculated as her net pay of $641, less the exemption of $363.46.

If Molly subsequently asks to have her stock purchase plan deductions increased, the net change will not reduce her tax levy, since this change occurred *after* receipt of the tax levy notice. However, if the company becomes unionized subsequent to the tax levy date and Molly is required to pay union dues as a condition of her employment, then the tax levy will be reduced by the amount of her

Exhibit 7.2 Table for Figuring the Amount Exempt from Levy on Wages

I. Table for Figuring Amount Exempt from Levy on Wages, Pay, and Other Income—Forms 668-W(c) and 668-W(c)(DO)
(NOTE: Amounts are for each pay period.)

2003

Filing Status: Single

Pay Period	Number of Exemptions Claimed on Statement						
	1	2	3	4	5	6	More than 6
Daily	30.00	41.73	53.46	65.19	76.92	88.65	18.27 plus 11.73 for each exemption
Weekly	150.00	208.65	267.31	325.96	384.62	443.27	91.35 plus 58.65 for each exemption
Biweekly	300.00	417.31	534.62	651.92	769.23	886.54	182.69 plus 117.31 for each exemption
Semimonthly	325.00	452.08	579.17	706.25	833.33	960.42	197.92 plus 127.08 for each exemption
Monthly	650.00	904.17	1158.33	1412.50	1666.67	1920.83	395.83 plus 254.16 for each exemption

Filing Status: Married Filing Joint Return (and Qualifying Widow(er)s)

Pay Period	Number of Exemptions Claimed on Statement						
	1	2	3	4	5	6	More than 6
Daily	42.31	54.04	65.77	77.50	89.23	100.96	30.58 plus 11.73 for each exemption
Weekly	211.54	270.19	328.85	387.50	446.15	504.81	152.88 plus 58.65 for each exemption
Biweekly	423.08	540.38	657.69	775.00	892.31	1009.62	305.77 plus 117.31 for each exemption
Semimonthly	458.33	585.42	712.50	839.58	966.67	1093.75	331.25 plus 127.08 for each exemption
Monthly	916.67	1170.83	1425.00	1679.17	1933.33	2187.50	662.50 plus 254.16 for each exemption

Filing Status: Unmarried Head of Household

Pay Period	Number of Exemptions Claimed on Statement						
	1	2	3	4	5	6	More than 6
Daily	38.65	50.38	62.12	73.85	85.58	97.31	26.92 plus 11.73 for each exemption
Weekly	193.27	251.92	310.58	369.23	427.88	486.54	134.62 plus 58.65 for each exemption
Biweekly	386.54	503.85	621.15	738.46	855.77	973.08	269.23 plus 117.31 for each exemption
Semimonthly	418.75	545.83	672.92	800.00	927.08	1054.17	291.67 plus 127.08 for each exemption
Monthly	837.50	1091.67	1345.83	1600.00	1854.17	2108.33	583.33 plus 254.16 for each exemption

Filing Status: Married Filing Separate Return

Pay Period	Number of Exemptions Claimed on Statement						
	1	2	3	4	5	6	More than 6
Daily	27.02	38.75	50.48	62.21	73.94	85.67	15.29 plus 11.73 for each exemption
Weekly	135.10	193.75	252.40	311.06	369.71	428.37	76.44 plus 58.65 for each exemption
Biweekly	270.19	387.50	504.81	622.12	739.42	856.73	152.88 plus 117.31 for each exemption
Semimonthly	292.71	419.79	546.88	673.96	801.04	928.13	165.62 plus 127.08 for each exemption
Monthly	585.42	839.58	1093.75	1347.92	1602.08	1856.25	331.25 plus 254.16 for each exemption

II. Table for Figuring Additional Exempt Amount for Taxpayers at Least 65 Years Old and / or Blind

Filing Status	*	Additional Exempt Amount				
		Daily	Weekly	Biweekly	Semimonthly	Monthly
Single or Head of Household	1	4.42	22.12	44.23	47.92	95.83
	2	8.85	44.23	88.46	95.83	191.67
Any other Filing Status	1	3.65	18.27	36.54	39.58	79.17
	2	7.31	36.54	73.08	79.17	158.33
	3	10.96	54.81	109.62	118.75	237.50
	4	14.62	73.08	146.15	158.33	316.67

* ADDITIONAL STANDARD DEDUCTION claimed on Parts 3, 4, and 5 of levy

Examples

These tables show the amount exempt from a levy on wages, salary, and other income. For example:

1. A single taxpayer who is paid weekly and claims three exemptions (including one for the taxpayer) has $267.31 exempt from levy.
2. If the taxpayer in number 1 is over 65 and writes 1 in the ADDITIONAL STANDARD DEDUCTION space on Parts 3, 4, and 5 of the levy, $289.43 is exempt from this levy ($267.31 plus $22.12).
3. A taxpayer who is married, files jointly, is paid biweekly, and claims two exemptions (including one for the taxpayer) has $540.38 exempt from levy.
4. If the taxpayer in number 3 is over 65 and has a spouse who is blind, this taxpayer should write 2 in the ADDITIONAL STANDARD DEDUCTION space on Parts 3, 4, and 5 of the levy. Then, $613.46 is exempt from this levy ($540.38 plus $73.08).

Publication **1494** (Rev. 1-2003)   www.irs.gov   Catalog Number 11439T   Department of the Treasury – Internal Revenue Service dues. Finally, if her medical insurance deduction increases, the tax levy will also be reduced by this amount.

Once the Form 668-W is received, the company is obligated to begin withholding the mandated amount of taxes from an employee's next paycheck, even if the applicable wages were earned prior to receipt of the form. The company should forward the withheld amount to the IRS, with the employee's name and social security number noted on the check.

The calculation of a government-imposed tax levy is complex and can change whenever an employee's circumstances are altered. For example, the amount of the tax levy will change as a result of a change in employee pay, changes in medical insurance deductions, and the addition of union dues as a new deduction. If an employer does not adjust for these changes, it can be subject to penalties imposed by the IRS for the amount of any tax levies that should have been withheld from the employee's pay. To avoid this problem, the payroll staff should maintain a "tickler list" for all employees subject to tax levies. This list should be incorporated into the processing procedure for every payroll, so the payroll staff is reminded to verify any changes to the targeted employees' pay, and to alter the amount of their tax levies as necessary.

If the employee leaves the company while this tax levy is still being deducted, the employer must notify the IRS of this event, and if possible forward the name and address of the new employer to the IRS. If the employee continues to work for the company, then IRS will inform the company when to stop making these deductions with Form 668-D.

If an employer for any reason does not withhold and forward to the IRS the periodic garnishments required by Form 668-W, then the company is liable for the amounts that it should have withheld, as well as a stiff penalty.

Loan Repayments

Employees may either have loans payable to the company or the company may have obtained loans on their behalf. For example, a corporate officer may have been extended a loan in order to move to a different company location and purchase a larger house. Alternatively, a company may have a computer purchasing arrangement with a local bank, whereby employees buy computers for their personal use and the company both guarantees payment to the bank and collects periodic payments from employees and remits them to the bank. In either case, the payroll staff must create a loan payback schedule for each employee and use it to set up deductions from their paychecks. If the loan is through a local bank, then the bank will likely provide a payback schedule to the payroll department. If the loan is internal, then the payroll staff must create a payback schedule in accordance with the terms of the loan agreement.

If there is a standard loan program for asset purchases with the company guaranteeing payment of the loans, then it behooves the company to require relatively short payback intervals, such as one to three years, to ensure that its risk of paying back loans in the absence of employees is minimized. Part of the agreement with employees should be their written understanding that if they leave the company prior to paying off the loan, as much as is legally allowable shall be deducted from their final paychecks in order to pay down the remainder of any outstanding loans.

Pensions and Other Savings Plans

An employer may offer several types of savings plans to its employees. In its simplest form, a business may arrange to make regular deductions from employee paychecks and deposit these funds in any number of pension plans. A slightly more complex arrangement is for the company to match some portion of the contributed funds and deposit them alongside the employee funds. These contributions may vest immediately or at some point in the future; vesting gives ownership in the company-contributed amount to the employee. The company may also retain the contributed funds and pay back employees with company stock.

If funds are being matched by the company, there will be an upper limit on the amount of matching, as well as a matching percentage. For example, a company may contribute 50 percent of the amounts contributed by its employees, up to a maximum of 6 percent of an employee's total pay.

This topic is covered in considerable detail under the "Pension Plan Benefits" section in Chapter 9, "Benefits."

Student Loans

The government can mandate the garnishment of an employee's wages in order to pay back the overdue portion of an outstanding student loan. Garnishment orders can be issued by either the Department of Education or a state guarantee agency, depending upon who is guaranteeing the loan. Upon receipt of the order, the employer must give an employee 30 days notice prior to making deductions from his or her wages. An employee cannot be fired from work because of the garnishment order and an employer who does so is liable for the employee's lost wages. Also, if an employer neglects to withhold the authorized garnishment amount, it is liable for the amount that was not withheld.

Union Dues

If an employer has entered into a collective bargaining agreement with a union, it is generally required to deduct union dues from employee wages, as per the terms of the agreement, and forward them to the union. It can stop doing this as of the date when the collective bargaining agreement terminates. The requirement to make this deduction will vary by agreement and may in some cases not be required at all, with the union instead obtaining dues directly from its members.

Timing of Payroll Deductions

When an employer has multiple pay periods in a month, it has the choice of making payroll deductions all in one pay period or of spreading them equally throughout the month. The preferred approach is to spread them throughout the month. By doing so, employees do not suffer a significant decline in their take-home pay for one of their paychecks. Also, by setting up deductions to occur in the same amounts in all pay periods, the payroll staff does not have to constantly delete deductions from the payroll system and then reenter them for one payroll per month. Instead, the deductions stay in the payroll database as active deductions for all pay periods, which requires much less maintenance.

Summary

A key item to remember for all of the voluntary deductions discussed in this chapter is that an employee's written approval must be obtained for all of them, so there is no subsequent issue with employees claiming that they never authorized a deduction, possibly resulting in the company not being compensated for an expenditure (such as medical insurance) that it has already made on behalf of the employee. For this reason, one should *not* use the approach of automatically signing up employees for various benefits and having them only decline the benefit in writing, since employees can state that they were never properly informed of the nature of the benefit.

8

Payroll Taxes and Remittances

Introduction

Calculating and remitting a variety of payroll taxes is a function central to the payroll department. In this chapter,[*] we will cover the purpose and instructions for filling out several tax-related IRS forms as well as the calculation methodologies and remittance instructions for federal and state income taxes, Medicare taxes, and Social Security taxes. The discussion also includes how to register with the federal government to remit taxes and specialized issues related to the withholding of payroll taxes for aliens or employees working abroad.

The Definition of an Employee

The definition of an employee is extremely important to a business since it directly impacts whether or not taxes are to be withheld from a person's pay, which also must be matched in some cases by the business. The basic rule is that a person doing work for a company is an employee if the employer not only controls the person's work output but also the manner in which the work is performed. The second part of the definition is crucial, since the first part essentially defines a contractor, who can choose to create a deliverable for a company in any manner he or she chooses. This definition results in the following two classes of workers:

- *Employee.* An employee is paid through the payroll system; the employing business is responsible for withholding taxes and paying matching tax amounts where applicable.

- *Contractor.* A contractor is paid through the accounts payable system; the business that uses its services is only responsible for issuing a Form 1099 to the contractor at the end of the calendar year to both the IRS and contractor, stat-

---

[*] This chapter is derived with permission from Chapter 7 of Bragg, *Essentials of Payroll* (Hoboken, NJ: John Wiley & Sons, 2003).

ing the total amount paid to the contractor during the year. The contractor is liable for remitting all payroll taxes to the government.

If a company incorrectly defines an employee as a contractor, it may be liable for all payroll taxes that should have been withheld from that person's pay. Consequently, when in doubt as to the proper definition of a worker, it is safer from a payroll tax law perspective to assume that the person is an employee.

The W-4 Form

When an employee is hired, he or she is required by law to fill out a W-4 form, which can be done on paper or in an electronic format. An employee uses this form to notify the payroll staff of single or married status and the number of allowances to be taken; this information has a direct impact on the amount of income taxes withheld from one's pay. The form is readily available in Adobe Acrobat form through the Internal Revenue Service's website. An example is shown in Exhibit 8.1.

There are two pages associated with the Form W-4. The first contains a personal allowances worksheet in the middle of the page and the actual form at the bottom, while the second page is used only by those taxpayers who plan to itemize their deductions, claim certain credits, or claim adjustments to income on their next tax return.

On the first page of the form, an employee generally should accumulate one allowance for him or herself, another for a working spouse, and one for each dependent. Additional allowances can be taken for "head of household" status or for certain amounts of child or dependent care expenses. The total of these allowances is then entered in Line 5 of the form at the bottom of the page, as well as any *additional* amounts that an employee may want to withhold from his or her paycheck. (Note: Employees cannot base withholdings on a fixed dollar amount or percentage, but they *can* add fixed withholding amounts to withholdings that are based on their marital status and number of allowances.) An employee can also claim exemption from tax withholding on Line 7 of the form. This lower portion of the form should be filled out, signed, and kept on file every time an employee wants to change the amount of an allowance or additional withholding, so there is a clear and indisputable record of changes to the employee's withholdings.

If an employee has claimed exemption from all income taxes on Line 7 of the form, this claim is only good for one calendar year, after which a new claim must be made on a new W-4 form. If an employee making this claim has not filed a new W-4 by February 15 of the next year, the payroll staff is required to begin withholding income taxes on the assumption that the person is single and has no withholding allowances.

The second page of the form is a considerably more complex variation on the top portion of the first page and is intended to assist employees who itemize their tax returns in determining the correct amount of their projected withholdings. The page is split into thirds. The top third is for the use of single filers, while the mid-

Exhibit 8.1 *Form W-4*

Form W-4 (2003)

Purpose. Complete Form W-4 so that your employer can withhold the correct Federal income tax from your pay. Because your tax situation may change, you may want to refigure your withholding each year.

Exemption from withholding. If you are exempt, complete only lines 1, 2, 3, 4, and 7 and sign the form to validate it. Your exemption for 2003 expires February 16, 2004. See Pub. 505, Tax Withholding and Estimated Tax.

Note: You cannot claim exemption from withholding if: (a) your income exceeds $750 and includes more than $250 of unearned income (e.g., interest and dividends) and (b) another person can claim you as a dependent on their tax return.

Basic instructions. If you are not exempt, complete the Personal Allowances Worksheet below. The worksheets on page 2 adjust your withholding allowances based on itemized deductions, certain credits, adjustments to income, or two-earner/two-job situations. Complete all worksheets that apply. However, you may claim fewer (or zero) allowances.

Head of household. Generally, you may claim head of household filing status on your tax return only if you are unmarried and pay more than 50% of the costs of keeping up a home for yourself and your dependent(s) or other qualifying individuals. See line E below.

Tax credits. You can take projected tax credits into account in figuring your allowable number of withholding allowances. Credits for child or dependent care expenses and the child tax credit may be claimed using the Personal Allowances Worksheet below. See Pub. 919, How Do I Adjust My Tax Withholding? for information on converting your other credits into withholding allowances.

Nonwage income. If you have a large amount of nonwage income, such as interest or dividends, consider making estimated tax payments using Form 1040-ES, Estimated Tax for Individuals. Otherwise, you may owe additional tax.

Two earners/two jobs. If you have a working spouse or more than one job, figure the total number of allowances you are entitled to claim on all jobs using worksheets from only one Form W-4. Your withholding usually will be most accurate when all allowances are claimed on the Form W-4 for the highest paying job and zero allowances are claimed on the others.

Nonresident alien. If you are a nonresident alien, see the Instructions for Form 8233 before completing this Form W-4.

Check your withholding. After your Form W-4 takes effect, use Pub. 919 to see how the dollar amount you are having withheld compares to your projected total tax for 2003. See Pub. 919, especially if your earnings exceed $125,000 (Single) or $175,000 (Married).

Recent name change? If your name on line 1 differs from that shown on your social security card, call 1-800-772-1213 for a new social security card.

Personal Allowances Worksheet (Keep for your records.)

A   Enter "1" for yourself if no one else can claim you as a dependent . . . . A _____

B   Enter "1" if:
- You are single and have only one job; or
- You are married, have only one job, and your spouse does not work; or
- Your wages from a second job or your spouse's wages (or the total of both) are $1,000 or less.
. . B _____

C   Enter "1" for your spouse. But, you may choose to enter "-0-" if you are married and have either a working spouse or more than one job. (Entering "-0-" may help you avoid having too little tax withheld.) . . . . C _____

D   Enter number of dependents (other than your spouse or yourself) you will claim on your tax return . . . . D _____

E   Enter "1" if you will file as head of household on your tax return (see conditions under Head of household above) . E _____

F   Enter "1" if you have at least $1,500 of child or dependent care expenses for which you plan to claim a credit . . F _____
(Note: Do not include child support payments. See Pub. 503, Child and Dependent Care Expenses, for details.)

G   Child Tax Credit (including additional child tax credit):
- If your total income will be between $15,000 and $42,000 ($20,000 and $65,000 if married), enter "1" for each eligible child plus **1** additional if you have three to five eligible children or **2** additional if you have six or more eligible children.
- If your total income will be between $42,000 and $80,000 ($65,000 and $115,000 if married), enter "1" if you have one or two eligi ble children, "2" if you have three eligible children, "3" if you have four eligible children, or "4" if you have five or more eligible children. . . . G _____

H   Add lines A through G and enter total here. Note: This may be different from the number of exemptions you claim on your tax return. ▶ H _____

For accuracy, complete all worksheets that apply.
- If you plan to itemize or claim adjustments to income   and want to reduce your withholding, see the Deductions and Adjustments Worksheet   on page 2.
- If you have more than one job   or are married and you and your spouse both work   and the combined earnings from all jobs exceed $35,000, see the Two-Earner/Two-Job Worksheet   on page 2 to avoid having too little tax withheld.
- If neither of the above situations applies, stop here and enter the number from line H on line 5 of Form W-4 below.

- - - - - - - - - - - - - - - -   Cut here and give Form W-4 to your employer. Keep the top part for your records.   - - - - - - - - - -

Form W-4
Department of the Treasury
Internal Revenue Service

Employee's Withholding Allowance Certificate

▶ For Privacy Act and Paperwork Reduction Act Notice, see page 2.

OMB No. 1545-0010

2003

1 Type or print your first name and middle initial	Last name	2 Your social security number

Home address (number and street or rural route)	3 ☐ Single ☐ Married ☐ Married, but withhold at higher Single rate. Note: If married, but legally separated, or spouse is a nonresident alien, check the "Single" box.
City or town, state, and ZIP code	4 If your last name differs from that shown on your social security card, check here. You must call 1-800-772-1213 for a new card. ▶ ☐

5   Total number of allowances you are claiming (from line H above or from the applicable worksheet on page 2)   **5** _____

6   Additional amount, if any, you want withheld from each paycheck . . . . **6** $ _____

7   I claim exemption from withholding for 2003, and I certify that I meet both of the following conditions for exemption:
- Last year I had a right to a refund of all Federal income tax withheld because I had no tax liability and
- This year I expect a refund of all Federal income tax withheld because I expect to have no tax liability.
If you meet both conditions, write "Exempt" here . . . . ▶ **7**

Under penalties of perjury, I certify that I am entitled to the number of withholding allowances claimed on this certificate, or I am entitled to claim exempt status.

Employee's signature
(Form is not valid
unless you sign it.) ▶   Date ▶

8 Employer's name and address (Employer: Complete lines 8 and 10 only if sending to the IRS.)	9 Office code (optional)	10 Employer identification number

Cat. No. 10220Q

Exhibit 8.1 (Continued)

Form W-4 (2003)   Page 2

Deductions and Adjustments Worksheet

Note: Use this worksheet only if you plan to itemize deductions, claim certain credits, or claim adjustments to income on your 2003 tax return.

1   Enter an estimate of your 2003 itemized deductions. These include qualifying home mortgage interest, charitable contributions, state and local taxes, medical expenses in excess of 7.5% of your income, and miscellaneous deductions. (For 2003, you may have to reduce your itemized deductions if your income is over $139,500 ($69,750 if married filing separately). See Worksheet 3 in Pub. 919 for details.) . . . **1** $ _____

2   Enter: { $7,950 if married filing jointly or qualifying widow(er)
            $7,000 if head of household
            $4,750 if single
            $3,975 if married filing separately }   . . . . **2** $ _____

3   Subtract line 2 from line 1. If line 2 is greater than line 1, enter "-0-" . . . . **3** $ _____
4   Enter an estimate of your 2003 adjustments to income, including alimony, deductible IRA contributions, and student loan interes t **4** $ _____
5   Add lines 3 and 4 and enter the total. Include any amount for credits from Worksheet 7 in Pub. 919 . **5** $ _____
6   Enter an estimate of your 2003 nonwage income (such as dividends or interest) . . . . **6** $ _____
7   Subtract line 6 from line 5. Enter the result, but not less than "-0-" . . . . **7** $ _____
8   Divide the amount on line 7 by $3,000 and enter the result here. Drop any fraction . . . . **8** _____
9   Enter the number from the Personal Allowances Worksheet, line H, page 1 . . . . **9** _____
10 Add lines 8 and 9 and enter the total here. If you plan to use the Two-Earner/Two-Job Worksheet, also enter this total on line 1 below. Otherwise, stop here and enter this total on Form W-4, line 5, page 1 . **10** _____

Two-Earner/Two-Job Worksheet

Note: Use this worksheet only if the instructions under line H on page 1 direct you here.

1   Enter the number from line H, page 1 (or from line 10 above if you used the Deductions and Adjustments Worksheet) **1** _____
2   Find the number in Table 1 below that applies to the lowest paying job and enter it here . . . . . **2** _____
3   If line 1 is more than or equal to line 2, subtract line 2 from line 1. Enter the result here (if zero, enter "-0-") and on Form W-4, line 5, page 1. Do not use the rest of this worksheet . . . . **3** _____

Note: If line 1 is less than line 2, enter "-0-" on Form W-4, line 5, page 1. Complete lines 4–9 below to calculate the additional withholding amount necessary to avoid a year-end tax bill.

4   Enter the number from line 2 of this worksheet . . . . **4** _____
5   Enter the number from line 1 of this worksheet . . . . **5** _____
6   Subtract line 5 from line 4 . . . . **6** _____
7   Find the amount in Table 2 below that applies to the highest paying job and enter it here . . . . . **7** $ _____
8   Multiply line 7 by line 6 and enter the result here. This is the additional annual withholding needed . . **8** $ _____
9   Divide line 8 by the number of pay periods remaining in 2003. For example, divide by 26 if you are paid every two weeks and you complete this form in December 2002. Enter the result here and on Form W-4, line 6, page 1. This is the additional amount to be withheld from each paycheck . . . . **9** $ _____

Table 1: Two-Earner/Two-Job Worksheet

Married Filing Jointly				All Others			
If wages from LOWEST paying job are—	Enter on line 2 above	If wages from LOWEST paying job are—	Enter on line 2 above	If wages from LOWEST paying job are—	Enter on line 2 above	If wages from LOWEST paying job are—	Enter on line 2 above
$0 - $4,000	0	44,001 - 50,000	8	$0 - $6,000	0	75,001 - 100,000	8
4,001 - 9,000	1	50,001 - 60,000	9	6,001 - 11,000	1	100,001 - 110,000	9
9,001 - 15,000	2	60,001 - 70,000	10	11,001 - 18,000	2	110,001 and over	10
15,001 - 20,000	3	70,001 - 90,000	11	18,001 - 25,000	3		
20,001 - 25,000	4	90,001 - 100,000	12	25,001 - 29,000	4		
25,001 - 33,000	5	100,001 - 115,000	13	29,001 - 40,000	5		
33,001 - 38,000	6	115,001 - 125,000	14	40,001 - 55,000	6		
38,001 - 44,000	7	125,001 and over	15	55,001 - 75,000	7		

Table 2: Two-Earner/Two-Job Worksheet

Married Filing Jointly		All Others	
If wages from HIGHEST paying job are—	Enter on line 7 above	If wages from HIGHEST paying job are—	Enter on line 7 above
$0 - $50,000	$450	$0 - $30,000	$450
50,001 - 100,000	800	30,001 - 70,000	800
100,001 - 150,000	900	70,001 - 140,000	900
150,001 - 270,000	1,050	140,001 - 300,000	1,050
270,001 and over	1,200	300,001 and over	1,200

dle third is intended for a household of two wage earners and the bottom third is a wage table to be used by households of two wage earners.

If for some reason the payroll staff has not received a W-4 form from a new employee as of the date when payroll must be calculated, then the IRS requires one to assume the person to be single, with no withholding allowances. This is the most conservative way to calculate someone's income taxes and will result in the largest possible amount of taxes withheld.

A little-known rule is that the IRS requires an employer to send to it any W-4 forms for employees who may be taking an excessive number of allowances or who are claiming exemption from withholdings. This is the case when an existing employee claims more than ten withholdings, or claims full exemption from withholding despite earning more than $200 per week. The W-4 form should only be sent to the IRS if the employees submitting the forms are still in employment at the end of the quarter. The forms should be sent to the same IRS office where the corporate form 941 is filed, along with a cover letter that identifies the business and notes its Employer Identification Number.

Employees will probably not know about this refiling requirement, so the payroll department should assist them with periodic reminders. This can be difficult, since W-4 forms are usually buried in an employee's payroll file and are not reviewed regularly. One approach is to create a "tickler" file containing copies of just those W-4 forms that must be replaced regularly and make a notation on the departmental activities calendar to review the tickler file on specific dates. Another alternative is to set up a meeting date in an electronic planner (such as Microsoft Outlook) that will issue a warning on the user's computer to review this issue on specific dates. The meeting date warning can even be sent automatically to those people who are required to complete new W-4 forms, though they must have ready access to a computer in order to receive this warning.

Federal Income Taxes

An employer is required by law to deduct income taxes from employee pay. If it uses a payroll supplier, then the calculation of the appropriate income tax amounts is completely invisible to it, since the supplier handles this task. If it calculates income taxes through a software package, then the software supplier will issue new tax tables each year to accompany the software. Once again, there is little need for an employer to know how the tax tables function. However, if a business calculates its payroll internally and manually, then it needs the wage bracket tax tables published by the IRS. They are contained within Publications 15 and 15-A, which can be downloaded from the IRS website at *www.irs.gov*. These tables are published for a variety of scenarios, such as for single or married employees, a variety of payroll periods, and for withholding allowances numbering from zero to ten. An example is shown in Exhibit 8.2, which is taken from page 35 of the 2003 Publication 15-A. It lists the amount of income, Social Security, and Medicare taxes to be withheld for a single person. The exhibit is incomplete, only showing taxes due for wages in a small range and for zero through five withholding allowances.

Exhibit 8.2   Tax Table for a Single Filer on a Weekly Payroll Period

| | | Number of Withholding Allowances | | | | | |
Pay at least	But less than	0	1	2	3	4	5
$400	$410	77.98	69.98	60.98	51.98	42.98	36.98
410	420	80.75	71.75	62.75	54.75	45.75	38.75
420	430	82.51	74.51	65.51	56.51	47.51	40.51
430	440	85.28	76.28	67.28	59.28	50.28	42.28
440	450	87.04	79.04	70.04	61.04	52.04	44.04
450	460	89.81	80.81	71.81	63.81	54.81	45.81
460	470	91.57	83.57	74.57	65.57	56.57	47.57
470	480	94.34	85.34	76.34	68.34	59.34	50.34
480	490	96.10	88.10	79.10	70.10	61.10	52.10
490	500	98.87	89.87	80.87	72.87	63.87	54.87

Example: Ms. Storm Dunaway works in the Humble Pie Company's baking division, which pays its employees once a week. She earned $462 in the past week, and has claimed three withholding allowances. Using the wage bracket table in Exhibit 8.2, we can find the correct wage bracket that contains her pay range (of at least $460 but less than $470), and then shift horizontally across the table from that wage bracket to the column for three withholding allowances, which shows that her total taxes should be $65.57.

An alternative calculation is shown in Exhibit 8.3, which shows the underlying formulas that were used to derive the wage bracket tax table in Exhibit 8.2. Under Alternative One in Exhibit 8.3, we subtract a dollar amount from an employee's base wage that corresponds to the number of withholding allowances taken, then multiply by a base tax rate, and then reduce the tax rate by a fixed amount to arrive at the income tax. Please note that these tables *do not* include the Social Security or Medicare taxes, as was the case in Exhibit 8.2. Under Alternative 2 in Exhibit 8.3, we subtract a dollar amount from an employee's base wage that corresponds to the number of withholding allowances taken, then reduce the taxable wage by a fixed amount, and then multiply by a base tax rate to arrive at the income tax. Either method results in an identical income tax.

Example: The Humble Pie Company's baking division is switching to an in-house computer-based payroll processing system, and wants to ensure that both IRS formula tables contained within it are correctly calculating income tax withholdings. As a baseline, they use the $65.57 withholding that was calculated for Ms. Storm Dunaway in the last example. By netting out the 6.2

Exhibit 8.3 *Alternative Formulas for Calculating Income Tax*

(For Wages Paid in 2003)

Alternative 1.—Tables for Percentage Method Withholding Computations

Table A(1)—WEEKLY PAYROLL PERIOD (Amount for each allowance claimed is $58.65)

Single Person				Married Person			
If the wage in excess of allowance amount is:		The income tax to be withheld is:		If the wage in excess of allowance amount is:		The income tax to be withheld is:	
Over—	But not over—	Of such wage—	From product	Over—	But not over—	Of such wage—	From product
$0	—$51	0%	$0	$0	—$124	0%	$0
$51	—$164	10% less	$5.10	$124	—$355	10% less	$12.40
$164	—$579	15% less	$13.30	$355	—$1,007	15% less	$30.15
$579	—$1,268	27% less	$82.78	$1,007	—$2,150	27% less	$150.99
$1,268	—$2,792	30% less	$120.82	$2,150	—$3,454	30% less	$215.49
$2,792	—$6,032	35% less	$260.42	$3,454	—$6,093	35% less	$388.19
$6,032	—	38.6% less	$477.57	$6,093	—	38.6% less	$607.54

Table B(1)—BIWEEKLY PAYROLL PERIOD (Amount for each allowance claimed is $117.31)

Single Person				Married Person			
If the wage in excess of allowance amount is:		The income tax to be withheld is:		If the wage in excess of allowance amount is:		The income tax to be withheld is:	
Over—	But not over—	Of such wage—	From product	Over—	But not over—	Of such wage—	From product
$0	—$102	0%	$0	$0	—$248	0%	$0
$102	—$329	10% less	$10.20	$248	—$710	10% less	$24.80
$329	—$1,158	15% less	$26.65	$710	—$2,013	15% less	$60.30
$1,158	—$2,535	27% less	$165.61	$2,013	—$4,300	27% less	$301.86
$2,535	—$5,585	30% less	$241.66	$4,300	—$6,908	30% less	$430.86
$5,585	—$12,063	35% less	$520.91	$6,908	—$12,187	35% less	$776.26
$12,063	—	38.6% less	$955.18	$12,187	—	38.6% less	$1,214.99

Table C(1)—SEMIMONTHLY PAYROLL PERIOD (Amount for each allowance claimed is $127.08)

Single Person				Married Person			
If the wage in excess of allowance amount is:		The income tax to be withheld is:		If the wage in excess of allowance amount is:		The income tax to be withheld is:	
Over—	But not over—	Of such wage—	From product	Over—	But not over—	Of such wage—	From product
$0	—$110	0%	$0	$0	—$269	0%	$0
$110	—$356	10% less	$11.00	$269	—$769	10% less	$26.90
$356	—$1,254	15% less	$28.80	$769	—$2,181	15% less	$65.35
$1,254	—$2,747	27% less	$179.28	$2,181	—$4,658	27% less	$327.07
$2,747	—$6,050	30% less	$261.50	$4,658	—$7,483	30% less	$466.81
$6,050	—$13,069	35% less	$564.19	$7,483	—$13,202	35% less	$840.96
$13,069	—	38.6% less	$1,034.67	$13,202	—	38.6% less	$1,316.23

Table D(1)—MONTHLY PAYROLL PERIOD (Amount for each allowance claimed is $254.17)

Single Person				Married Person			
If the wage in excess of allowance amount is:		The income tax to be withheld is:		If the wage in excess of allowance amount is:		The income tax to be withheld is:	
Over—	But not over—	Of such wage—	From product	Over—	But not over—	Of such wage—	From product
$0	—$221	0%	$0	$0	—$538	0%	$0
$221	—$713	10% less	$22.10	$538	—$1,538	10% less	$53.80
$713	—$2,508	15% less	$57.75	$1,538	—$4,363	15% less	$130.70
$2,508	—$5,493	27% less	$358.71	$4,363	—$9,317	27% less	$654.26
$5,493	—$12,100	30% less	$523.50	$9,317	—$14,967	30% less	$933.77
$12,100	—$26,138	35% less	$1,128.50	$14,967	—$26,404	35% less	$1,682.12
$26,138	—	38.6% less	$2,069.47	$26,404	—	38.6% less	$2,632.66

Table E(1)—DAILY OR MISCELLANEOUS PAYROLL PERIOD
(Amount for each allowance claimed per day for such period is $11.73)

Single Person				Married Person			
If the wage in excess of allowance amount divided by the number of days in the pay period is:		The income tax to be withheld multiplied by the number of days in such period is:		If the wage in excess of allowance amount divided by the number of days in the pay period is:		The income tax to be withheld multiplied by the number of days in such period is:	
Over—	But not over—	Of such wage—	From product	Over—	But not over—	Of such wage—	From product
$0.00	—$10.20	0%	$0	$0.00	—$24.80	0%	$0
$10.20	—$32.90	10% less	$1.02	$24.80	—$71.00	10% less	$2.48
$32.90	—$115.80	15% less	$2.66	$71.00	—$201.30	15% less	$6.03
$115.80	—$253.50	27% less	$16.56	$201.30	—$430.00	27% less	$30.18
$253.50	—$558.50	30% less	$24.16	$430.00	—$690.80	30% less	$43.08
$558.50	—$1,206.30	35% less	$52.09	$690.80	—$1,218.70	35% less	$77.62
$1,206.30	—	38.6% less	$95.51	$1,218.70	—	38.6% less	$121.49

Note.—The adjustment factors may be reduced by one-half cent (e.g., 7.50 to 7.495; 69.38 to 69.375) to eliminate separate half rounding operations.

The first two brackets of these tables may be combined, provided zero withholding is used to credit withholding amounts computed by the combined bracket rates, e.g., $0 to $51 and $51 to $164 combined to read, Over $0, But not over $164.

The employee's excess wage (gross wage less amount for allowances claimed) is used with the applicable percentage rates and subtraction factors to calculate the amount of income tax withheld.

Exhibit 8.3 *(Continued)*

(For Wages Paid in 2003)

Alternative 2.—Tables for Percentage Method Withholding Computations

Table A(2)—WEEKLY PAYROLL PERIOD (Amount for each allowance claimed is $58.65)

Single Person				Married Person			
If the wage in excess of allowance amount is:		The income tax to be withheld is:		If the wage in excess of allowance amount is:		The income tax to be withheld is:	
Over—	But not over—	Such wage—	Times	Over—	But not over—	Such wage—	Times
$0	—$51	minus $0.00	0%	$0	—$124	minus $0.00	0%
$51	—$164	minus $51.00	10%	$124	—$355	minus $124.00	10%
$164	—$579	minus $88.67	15%	$355	—$1,007	minus $201.00	15%
$579	—$1,268	minus $306.59	27%	$1,007	—$2,150	minus $559.22	27%
$1,268	—$2,792	minus $402.73	30%	$2,150	—$3,454	minus $718.30	30%
$2,792	—$6,032	minus $744.06	35%	$3,454	—$6,093	minus $1,109.11	35%
$6,032	—	minus $1,237.23	38.6%	$6,093	—	minus $1,573.93	38.6%

Table B(2)—BIWEEKLY PAYROLL PERIOD (Amount for each allowance claimed is $117.31)

Single Person				Married Person			
If the wage in excess of allowance amount is:		The income tax to be withheld is:		If the wage in excess of allowance amount is:		The income tax to be withheld is:	
Over—	But not over—	Such wage—	Times	Over—	But not over—	Such wage—	Times
$0	—$102	minus $0.00	0%	$0	—$248	minus $0.00	0%
$102	—$329	minus $102.00	10%	$248	—$710	minus $248.00	10%
$329	—$1,158	minus $177.67	15%	$710	—$2,013	minus $402.00	15%
$1,158	—$2,535	minus $613.37	27%	$2,013	—$4,300	minus $1,118.33	27%
$2,535	—$5,585	minus $805.53	30%	$4,300	—$6,908	minus $1,436.20	30%
$5,585	—$12,063	minus $1,488.31	35%	$6,908	—$12,187	minus $2,217.89	35%
$12,063	—	minus $2,474.55	38.6%	$12,187	—	minus $3,147.65	38.6%

Table C(2)—SEMIMONTHLY PAYROLL PERIOD (Amount for each allowance claimed is $127.08)

Single Person				Married Person			
If the wage in excess of allowance amount is:		The income tax to be withheld is:		If the wage in excess of allowance amount is:		The income tax to be withheld is:	
Over—	But not over—	Such wage—	Times	Over—	But not over—	Such wage—	Times
$0	—$110	minus $0.00	0%	$0	—$269	minus $0.00	0%
$110	—$356	minus $110.00	10%	$269	—$769	minus $269.00	10%
$356	—$1,254	minus $192.00	15%	$769	—$2,181	minus $435.67	15%
$1,254	—$2,747	minus $664.00	27%	$2,181	—$4,658	minus $1,211.37	27%
$2,747	—$6,050	minus $872.30	30%	$4,658	—$7,483	minus $1,556.03	30%
$6,050	—$13,069	minus $1,611.97	35%	$7,483	—$13,202	minus $2,402.74	35%
$13,069	—	minus $2,680.50	38.6%	$13,202	—	minus $3,409.93	38.6%

Table D(2)—MONTHLY PAYROLL PERIOD (Amount for each allowance claimed is $254.17)

Single Person				Married Person			
If the wage in excess of allowance amount is:		The income tax to be withheld is:		If the wage in excess of allowance amount is:		The income tax to be withheld is:	
Over—	But not over—	Such wage—	Times	Over—	But not over—	Such wage—	Times
$0	—$221	minus $0.00	0%	$0	—$538	minus $0.00	0%
$221	—$713	minus $221.00	10%	$538	—$1,538	minus $538.00	10%
$713	—$2,508	minus $385.00	15%	$1,538	—$4,363	minus $871.33	15%
$2,508	—$5,493	minus $1,328.56	27%	$4,363	—$9,317	minus $2,423.19	27%
$5,493	—$12,100	minus $1,745.00	30%	$9,317	—$14,967	minus $3,112.57	30%
$12,100	—$26,138	minus $3,224.29	35%	$14,967	—$26,404	minus $4,806.06	35%
$26,138	—	minus $5,361.32	38.6%	$26,404	—	minus $6,820.37	38.6%

Table E(2)—DAILY OR MISCELLANEOUS PAYROLL PERIOD
(Amount for each allowance claimed per day for such period is $11.73)

Single Person				Married Person			
If the wage in excess of allowance amount divided by the number of days in the pay period is:		The income tax to be withheld multiplied by the number of days in such period is:		If the wage in excess of allowance amount divided by the number of days in the pay period is:		The income tax to be withheld multiplied by the number of days in such period is:	
Over—	But not over—	Such wage—	Times	Over—	But not over—	Such wage—	Times
$0.00	—$10.20	minus $0.00	0%	$0.00	—$24.80	minus $0.00	0%
$10.20	—$32.90	minus $10.20	10%	$24.80	—$71.00	minus $24.80	10%
$32.90	—$115.80	minus $17.77	15%	$71.00	—$201.30	minus $40.20	15%
$115.80	—$253.50	minus $61.32	27%	$201.30	—$430.00	minus $111.78	27%
$253.50	—$558.50	minus $80.53	30%	$430.00	—$690.80	minus $143.60	30%
$558.50	—$1,206.30	minus $148.81	35%	$690.80	—$1,218.70	minus $221.77	35%
$1,206.30	—	minus $247.44	38.6%	$1,218.70	—	minus $314.74	38.6%

Note.—The first two brackets of these tables may be combined, provided zero withholding is used to credit withholding amounts computed by the combined bracket rates, e.g., $0 to $51 and $51 to $164 combined to read, Over $0, But not over $164.

The employee's excess wage (gross wage less amount for allowances claimed) is used with the applicable percentage rates and subtraction factors to calculate the amount of income tax withheld.

percent Social Security and 1.45 percent Medicare taxes that were included in that figure, they arrive at a baseline income tax of $30.23.

Using the formulas listed under Alternative 1 for a weekly pay period for a single person in Exhibit 8.3, they first subtract $58.65 from Ms. Dunaway's gross pay for each withholding allowance claimed, which reduces her gross income for calculation purposes to $286.05. They then multiply this amount by 15 percent and then subtract $13.30 from it, as specified in the table. This process results in a calculated income tax of $29.61, which is substantially the same figure found under the wage bracket method.

They then switch to the formulas listed under Alternative 2 for a weekly pay period for a single person in Exhibit 8.3, which requires the same deduction of $58.65 from Ms. Dunaway's gross pay for each withholding allowance claimed, once again resulting in gross pay of $286.05. Under this approach, they subtract $88.67 from the gross pay to arrive at $197.38, and then multiply by 15 percent to arrive at the same income tax of $29.61.

There are several other, less-used methods for calculating tax withholding amounts that require the override of one's computerized withholding calculation system with manual calculations. They are:

- *Basis is annualized wages.* Under this approach, calculate an employee's annual pay rate and then determine the annual withholding amount in the IRS's Annual Payroll Period tax table. Then divide this amount by the number of pay periods in the year to determine the deduction for an individual paycheck.

- *Basis is partial-year employment.* This method can only be used at an employee's written request, which must state the last day of work with any prior employer, that the employee uses the calendar year accounting method, and that the employee does not expect to work during the year for more than 245 days. The company then compiles all wages paid to the employee during his or her current term of employment, including the current pay period. Next, determine the number of pay periods from the date of the employee's last employment, through and including the current pay period, and divide this amount into the total wages figure, resulting in an average wage per pay period. Use the correct tax table to arrive at a withholding amount for the average wage, and multiply this amount by the total number of pay periods, as already calculated. Finally, subtract the total amount of withholdings already made, resulting in the withholding to be made in the current pay period.

  This approach is requested by employees, such as part-time students or seasonal workers, who expect to be out of work so much during the calendar year that their full-year pay will drop them into a lower tax bracket, resulting in smaller income tax withholdings.

- *Basis is year-to-date cumulative wages.* This method can only be used at an employee's written request. To calculate it, compile all wages paid to the employee for the year-to-date through and including the current pay period and divide the sum by the total number of year-to-date pay periods, including the current period. Then use the percentage method to calculate the withholding on this average wage. Multiply the withholding amount by the total number of year-to-date payroll periods, and subtract the actual amount of withholdings made year-to-date. The remainder is the amount to withhold from the employee's wages during the current pay period.

This complicated approach is requested by employees who may have had an excessive amount of taxes withheld from their pay earlier in the year, perhaps due to a large commission or bonus payment that bumped them into a higher income tax bracket. By using the cumulative wages calculation, these excessive withholdings may sometimes result in a one-time withholding on the payroll in which this calculation is requested that is much smaller than usual.

Supplemental Pay

Several of the alternative tax calculation methods just noted are used because the amount withheld from employee pay for the year-to-date is higher than will be needed by the end of the calendar year. This may be caused by a large payment to an employee earlier in the year, perhaps a commission or bonus; when this happens, the extra payment is typically lumped into the person's regular pay, which bumps the person into a higher tax bracket on the assumption that he or she always receives this amount of money during every pay period. As a result, there will be an excessively large withholding at the end of the year, and the employee will receive a tax refund.

One approach for avoiding the excessive amount of tax withholdings is to separate the supplemental pay from the base pay and issue two separate payments to an employee. Under this approach, the percentage withheld will likely be smaller than if the pay had been combined into a single paycheck. Another approach that is acceptable to the IRS is to combine the payments together, and then withhold a flat 27 percent rate from it. Under most computerized payroll systems, it is easier to implement the first approach.

Sick Pay

In general, sick pay made to employees requires all of the Social Security, Medicare, and income tax withholdings that one calculates for normal wages. However, there are a few exceptions. For example, if an employee dies and sick pay is made to his or her estate in the following calendar year, this amount is not subject to any of the usual payroll withholdings or taxes. The same rules apply if sick payments are made to an employee who has been absent from work for at least six months.

If employees contribute to a sick pay plan with after-tax dollars, then any payments made to them from that plan will not require any withholdings or payroll taxes, on the grounds that the employee already paid those taxes on the initial cash used to fund the plan. Alternatively, if the sick pay plan is funded with pretax dollars (as can occur through a cafeteria plan), then any pay from the sick pay plan will require income tax withholdings and all other normal payroll taxes, on the grounds that the employee would otherwise never pay taxes on the wages paid.

If employees are paid sick pay through a third party, such as an independent insurance company, the third party has no obligation to withhold income taxes, though it can do so if an employee submits to it a form W-4S that states how much is to be withheld. The *minimum* amount that can be withheld in this manner is $20 per week.

Social Security Taxes

Employers are required to withhold 6.2 percent of each employee's pay, which is forwarded to the government Social Security fund. The employer must also match this amount, so the total remittance to the government is 12.4 percent. This withholding applies to the first $87,000 of employee pay in each calendar year, though this number increases regularly by act of Congress.

Example: The President of the Humble Pie Company is Ms. Elinor Plump. She earned $185,000 in calendar year 2002. She expects to be paid the same amount in 2003, and wants to know how much Social Security tax will be deducted from her pay in that year, so she can budget her cash flow. The calculation is:

Total annual pay	$185,000
Total annual pay subject to the Social Security tax	$ 87,000
Tax rate	6.2%
Social Security taxes to be withheld	$5,394.00

If a company takes over another business or purchases its assets, the buying entity can include the year-to-date wages paid to the acquiree's employees in determining the amount of Social Security taxes withheld. This reduces the amount of withholdings for those employees who earn more than $87,000 per year, and also reduces the amount of matching taxes paid by the business.

Medicare Taxes

Employers are required to withhold 1.45 percent of each employee's pay, which is forwarded to the government Medicare fund. The employer must also match this amount, so the total remittance to the government is 2.9 percent. This withholding applies to all employee earnings during the year, with no upper limit.

Example: The Humble Pie Company's most productive salesperson is Mrs. Elma Soders, whose annual base pay is $25,000. The total of her commissions and performance bonuses for the past year was $147,000, giving her a total compensation of $171,000. What will both Mrs. Soders and the company pay to the government for her Medicare taxes?

Total annual pay	$171,000
Total annual pay subject to the Medicare tax	$171,000
Tax rate	2.9%
Medicare taxes to be remitted	$4,959.00

State Income Taxes

All states require state income tax withholding, with the exceptions of Alaska, Connecticut, Florida, Nevada, New Hampshire, South Dakota, Tennessee, Texas, Washington, and Wyoming. Those states requiring a business to withhold state income taxes from its employees all have different methods and forms for doing so, which requires a detailed knowledge of the withholding and remittance requirements of each state. If an organization calculates its own payroll, then it will likely be sent this information on a regular basis through the mail by each state government with which it has registered. It can also access this information for most states by accessing their official websites. A much easier approach is to outsource the payroll processing function, which gives the payroll supplier responsibility for making the correct withholdings and remittances (if the employer chooses this service).

Unlike the federal government, which allows most payroll tax payments to be remitted with a single remittance document, states may require employers to use a variety of forms, perhaps one for income taxes, another for unemployment insurance, and another for disability insurance (though this is only required by a small number of states). Given the amount of paperwork involved, a company that remits its own state taxes should construct a calendar of remittances, which the payroll manager can use to ensure that payments are always made, thereby avoiding late payment penalties and interest charges.

If an employer has nonresident employees and the state in which it does business has an income tax, the employer will usually withhold income for each employee's state of residence. Alternatively, an employer can withhold income on behalf of the state in which it does business and let the employee claim a credit on his or her state tax return to avoid double taxation. The ability to do this will vary by individual state law.

Payroll Taxes for Aliens

An employer is required to withhold all types of taxes for resident aliens. Holders of the I-551 Permanent Resident Card (Green Card) fall into this category. However, do not withhold Social Security or Medicare taxes if someone is an alien agricultural worker, or holds a variety of nonimmigrant visas, such as F-1 (students), H-1B (professionals and technical workers), or Q (cultural exchange visitors).

A nonresident alien is required to complete a W-4 form. When doing so, the person cannot claim exemption from withholding, must state his or her marital status as being single, and in most cases can only claim one allowance.

Registering with the Government for Tax Remittances

When a company sends payroll tax remittances to the federal government, the government needs to identify the company, so it can give the company proper credit for the remittances. This is done with an employer identification number (EIN). One applies for an EIN number with the Application for Employer Identification Number, Form SS-4, which is shown in Exhibit 8.4. Once the Form SS-4 is sent to the IRS, it takes four weeks to receive an EIN number back in the mail. If the first payroll deposit is due before the receipt of the EIN, one can call the IRS's Tele-TIN or Fax-TIN numbers in order to obtain the number more quickly. The Tele-TIN number is 1-866-816-2065. Before calling, fill out the Form SS-4, since most of the information on it will be needed for the call. You will be given an EIN over the phone. If you'd like to accelerate the processing of the regular Form SS-4, then fax it to the regional Fax-TIN number, which will result in the fax-back of an EIN number in about four business days. One problem with this approach is that the IRS does not use a cover sheet when sending a response back through a company's fax machine, so the transmitted document containing the new EIN number may be lost. The Fax-TIN numbers for all regions are listed in Exhibit 8.5.

Instructions for filling out the Form SS-4 are as follows:

Line 1:   Enter the legal name of the entity (not its doing-business-as name). If the business is a person or sole proprietorship, then enter person's first, middle, and last names.

Line 2:   If there is a doing-business-as (dba) or "trade" name, enter it on this line.

Line 3:   If there is an executor or trustee of a trust, enter that person's first, middle, and last name here.

Lines 4–6: Enter the complete mailing address, including the county name. The EIN will be sent to this location.

Line 7:   Enter the first, middle, and last name of the principal officer, general partner, or sole proprietor, depending on the type of business entity.

Exhibit 8.4 *Application for Employee Identification Number*

Form **SS-4**	Application for Employer Identification Number	EIN
(Rev. December 2001)	(For use by employers, corporations, partnerships, trusts, estates, churches, government agencies, Indian tribal entities, certain individuals, and others.)	OMB No. 1545-0003
Department of the Treasury Internal Revenue Service	▶ See separate instructions for each line. ▶ Keep a copy for your records.	

Type or print clearly.

1 Legal name of entity (or individual) for whom the EIN is being requested

2 Trade name of business (if different from name on line 1)	3 Executor, trustee, "care of" name
4a Mailing address (room, apt., suite no. and street, or P.O. box)	5a Street address (if different) (Do not enter a P.O. box.)
4b City, state, and ZIP code	5b City, state, and ZIP code

6 County and state where principal business is located

7a Name of principal officer, general partner, grantor, owner, or trustor	7b SSN, ITIN, or EIN

8a Type of entity (check only one box)
- ☐ Sole proprietor (SSN) _____
- ☐ Partnership
- ☐ Corporation (enter form number to be filed) ▶ _____
- ☐ Personal service corp.
- ☐ Church or church-controlled organization
- ☐ Other nonprofit organization (specify) ▶ _____
- ☐ Other (specify) ▶

- ☐ Estate (SSN of decedent) _____
- ☐ Plan administrator (SSN) _____
- ☐ Trust (SSN of grantor) _____
- ☐ National Guard   ☐ State/local government
- ☐ Farmers' cooperative   ☐ Federal government/military
- ☐ REMIC   ☐ Indian tribal governments/enterprises
- Group Exemption Number (GEN) ▶ _____

8b If a corporation, name the state or foreign country (if applicable) where incorporated	State	Foreign country

9 Reason for applying (check only one box)
- ☐ Started new business (specify type) ▶ _____
- ☐ Hired employees (Check the box and see line 12.)
- ☐ Compliance with IRS withholding regulations
- ☐ Other (specify) ▶

- ☐ Banking purpose (specify purpose) ▶ _____
- ☐ Changed type of organization (specify new type) ▶ _____
- ☐ Purchased going business
- ☐ Created a trust (specify type) ▶ _____
- ☐ Created a pension plan (specify type) ▶ _____

10 Date business started or acquired (month, day, year)	11 Closing month of accounting year

12 First date wages or annuities were paid or will be paid (month, day, year). Note: If applicant is a withholding agent, enter date income will first be paid to nonresident alien. (month, day, year) . . . . ▶

13 Highest number of employees expected in the next 12 months. Note: If the applicant does not expect to have any employees during the period, enter "-0-." . . . . ▶	Agricultural	Household	Other

14 Check one box that best describes the principal activity of your business.   ☐ Health care & social assistance   ☐ Wholesale–agent/broker
- ☐ Construction   ☐ Rental & leasing   ☐ Transportation & warehousing   ☐ Accommodation & food service   ☐ Wholesale–other   ☐ Retail
- ☐ Real estate   ☐ Manufacturing   ☐ Finance & insurance   ☐ Other (specify)

15 Indicate principal line of merchandise sold; specific construction work done; products produced; or services provided.

16a Has the applicant ever applied for an employer identification number for this or any other business?   . . . . ☐ Yes   ☐ No
Note: If "Yes," please complete lines 16b and 16c.

16b If you checked "Yes" on line 16a, give applicant's legal name and trade name shown on prior application if different from line 1 or 2 above.
Legal name ▶   Trade name ▶

16c Approximate date when, and city and state where, the application was filed. Enter previous employer identification number if known.

Approximate date when filed (mo., day, year)	City and state where filed	Previous EIN

	Complete this section only if you want to authorize the named individual to receive the entity's EIN and answer questions about the completion of this form.	
Third Party Designee	Designee's name	Designee's telephone number (include area code) ( )
	Address and ZIP code	Designee's fax number (include area code) ( )

Under penalties of perjury, I declare that I have examined this application, and to the best of my knowledge and belief, it is true, correct, and complete.

Applicant's telephone number (include area code) ( )

Name and title (type or print clearly) ▶

Applicant's fax number (include area code) ( )

Signature ▶   Date ▶

For Privacy Act and Paperwork Reduction Act Notice, see separate instructions.   Cat. No. 16055N   Form **SS-4** (Rev. 12-2001)

Exhibit 8.5 *Fax-TIN Numbers by State*	
Fax-TIN Number	**Applicable State**
631-447-8960	Connecticut, Delaware, District of Columbia, Florida, Georgia, Maine, Maryland, Massachusetts, New Hampshire, New Jersey, New York, North Carolina, Ohio, Pennsylvania, Rhode Island, South Carolina, Vermont, Virginia, West Virginia
859-669-5760	Illinois, Indiana, Kentucky, Michigan
215-516-3990	Alabama, Alaska, Arizona, Arkansas, California, Colorado, Hawaii, Idaho, Iowa, Kansas, Louisiana, Minnesota, Mississippi, Missouri, Montana, Nebraska, Nevada, New Mexico, North Dakota, Oklahoma, Oregon, Puerto Rico, South Dakota, Tennessee, Texas, Utah, Washington, Wisconsin, Wyoming
215-516-3990	No legal residence or principal place of business

Line 8: Check off the type of business entity under which the business is legally organized. If it is a sole proprietorship, also enter the Social Security number. If it is a corporation, enter the state or foreign country in which it is organized.

Line 9: Check off just one of the listed options as a reason for applying for the EIN. You should not be applying for an EIN if you are simply hiring additional employees, since you should already have obtained an EIN for the existing entity. If you have created a pension plan, it must have a separate EIN from that of the business entity.

Line 10: If the business was just started, enter its start date. If you purchased an existing business, enter the purchase date.

Line 11: Enter the last month of the business's accounting year. For an individual, this is usually the calendar year-end, though it can vary for other types of business entities.

Line 12: Enter the date when wages were first paid or are expected to be paid. If there is no prospective date, enter "N/A" in this space.

Line 13: Enter in each space provided the maximum number of employees expected to be on the payroll during the next twelve months. There are spaces for agricultural, household, and other employees.

Line 14: Check off just *one* box next to the industry group that best describes your business's main area of operations. If none apply, check the "Other" box and briefly describe the principal activity.

Line 15: Describe the business entity's principal activities in somewhat more detail, noting specific types of products or services sold.

Line 16: Indicate if the business has ever applied for an EIN before. If it has, list the legal and trade names of the business used on the prior application, as well as the date and location where it was filed.

If you have no EIN number by the time a deposit is due to the government, send the payment in anyway, noting the business's legal name, address, type of tax, period covered, and the date on which you applied for the EIN. If the EIN has not yet been received by the time a return is due, write "Applied For" in the space on the form where the EIN would normally go, and also the date when the EIN was applied for.

Remitting Federal Taxes

Once Social Security, income tax, and Medicare taxes have been withheld from an employee's pay, they are essentially the property of the federal government and the company is merely holding them in escrow until the next required remittance date. Depending upon the size of the remittances, a company may periodically cut a check for the remittance amount and deliver it to a local bank or Federal Reserve Bank that is authorized to forward the funds to the IRS. Alternatively, companies with larger remittances are required to make electronic funds transfers directly to the IRS. If a company uses a payroll supplier, then this process is invisible to the company, since the supplier will handle remittances.

Assuming that a company processes its own payroll, it must then determine the frequency with which it remits tax deposits to the federal government. A business can make deposits in the following three ways:

- *On a monthly basis.* Under this approach, a business must deposit its payroll taxes no later than the 15th day of the month following the reporting month. This method can only be used if the total amount of deposits during the "lookback period" is less than $50,000. The lookback period is the four previous quarters during which deposits were reported on the Form 941, beginning July 1 and ending on June 30 of the next year. When making this determination, include all Social Security, Federal Income, and Medicare taxes withheld during the lookback period. A new employer will generally fall into this category, because the amount of the lookback period (which does not yet exist) is assumed to be zero.

- *On a semi-weekly basis.* The government will force one to use the semi-weekly deposit schedule if the dollar volume of taxes during the annual lookback period exceeded $50,000. If not, deposits can be made on a monthly basis. The "semi-weekly" refers to two possible dates in each week by which deposits must be made if a payroll payment date falls within that week. If a payment date falls on a weekend, Monday, or Tuesday, then the deposit must be made by the following Friday. If the payment date falls on a Wednesday, Thursday, or Friday, then the deposit must be made by Wednesday of the following week. One additional business day is added to this schedule if the day by which a deposit is required falls on a banking holiday.

- *Using electronic funds transfers.* The minimum threshold for this approach is $200,000 in deposits during the lookback period, or if the company was required to use it in the previous year. Once a company is required to use this method but does not do so, it will be subject to a 10 percent penalty. Payments are made using the Electronic Federal Tax Payment System (EFTPS). Under this approach, a business notifies its bank of the amount to be deposited with the government; the bank then electronically shifts the funds from the business's account to the government's. This approach gives the government more immediate access to the funds. No deposit coupon is required if this approach is used since it is only required to identify an accompanying check and this method requires no check. The payment intervals are the same as those used for semi-weekly depositors, except that any company accumulating $100,000 of taxes for any payroll must deposit it on the business day immediately following the payroll payment date. A business can enroll in the EFTPS by completing the EFTPS Business Enrollment Form (Form 9779).

There is one special case that overrides all of the preceding depositing scenarios. If a company accumulates a payroll tax liability of $100,000 or more as a result of a payroll, the amount must be deposited no later than the next business day, irrespective of the company's status as determined through the lookback method. This special case does not continue to apply if a company's subsequent payroll tax liabilities drop below $100,000; however, if a company had previously been a monthly depositor, this situation will result in the company immediately converting to a semi-weekly deposit schedule.

Example: The Red Light Company, maker of lighting fixtures for traffic intersections, reported the following deposit totals:

1st Quarter 2003	$ 8,500
2nd Quarter 2003	$ 9,000
3rd Quarter 2003	$10,000
4th Quarter 2003	$11,000
1st Quarter 2004	$15,000
2nd Quarter 2004	$16,000

The controller wants to know if the company will have to make semi-weekly or monthly deposits for the calendar year 2004. Though the total deposits made during 2003 only totaled $38,500, the lookback period is for just the last two quarters of 2003 and the first two quarters of 2004, when tax deposits were somewhat higher. The official lookback period contains deposits of $52,000, which is higher than the government-mandated threshold of $50,000. Consequently, the company must deposit on a semi-weekly basis.

Example: The Red Light Company's payroll manager wants to know when deposits must be made to the government, now that the company is required to remit deposits on a semi-weekly basis. The company pays its employees on Tuesday of each week, based on hours worked during the preceding calendar week. Since the company always pays its employees on a Tuesday, it has until the following Friday to deposit its taxes.

If remittances are to be made to the local bank, then the check must be accompanied by a Form 8109, which is a standard remittance coupon that is used for a variety of tax remittances. In order to obtain a booklet of blank Form 8109s, one must file for an Employee Identification Number (EIN), which was described earlier in the "Registering with the Government for Tax Remittances" section. The EIN is required because the IRS preprints an organization's EIN, name, and address on each form in the booklet. Filling out the form is simple enough—just enter the dollar amount being remitted, the company's contact phone number, and darken the ovals corresponding to the type of tax being remitted (in this case, always "941") and the applicable quarter to which the remittance applies. The information on this form is entered into the IRS database with an optical scanner, so write clearly in order to avoid scanning errors.

Special handling of tax deposits are necessary if an employer is a semi-weekly depositor and has multiple pay days that occur within the same semi-weekly period but apply to different calendar quarters. If this situation arises, the employer must determine which portion of the semi-weekly deposit applies to payroll occurring within each of the two calendar quarters, and make a separate deposit for each portion.

Example: The Red Light Company has a pay date on Saturday, September 28, 2003, as well as another pay date on Tuesday, October 1, 2003. Deposits for the two pay dates are both due on the following Friday, October 4, but must be deposited separately.

Federal Tax Deposit Penalties

The IRS imposes significant penalties if a business does not make its tax deposits on time, makes insufficient deposits, or does not use the EFTPS electronic filing system when it is required to do so. Its penalty structure is as follows:

- 2 percent penalty if deposits are made from one to five days late.
- 5 percent penalty if deposits are made 6 to 15 days late.

- 10 percent penalty if deposits are made 16 or more days late.
- 10 percent penalty if deposits are remitted to the wrong location.
- 10 percent penalty if the EFTPS is not used when it is required.
- 15 percent penalty if funds have not been remitted at least 10 days after the IRS sent a payment warning notification.

Penalties can be avoided for very small payment shortfalls. There is no penalty if a deposit of up to $5,000 is short by no more than $100, or a larger deposit is short by no more than 2 percent of the total. If a shortfall of this size occurs, a semi-weekly depositor must deposit the shortfall by the earlier of the next Form 941 due date or the first Wednesday or Friday following the 15th day of the next month. A monthly depositor must make the deposit with its next Form 941.

If an employer does not file its quarterly Form 941 in a timely manner, it will be penalized 5 percent for the amount of all net unpaid taxes shown on the return for each month during which the form is not filed. This penalty is capped at 25 percent, which essentially means that a business will be penalized for the first five months during which it does not file a Form 941.

Example: The Red Herring Fish Company's controller forgets to file a quarterly Form 941, which would have shown a net tax due of $2,200. Upon discovering the error ten months later and filing the return, the IRS penalizes the firm for 5 percent of the $2,200 due, times fives months, which is a 25 percent penalty, or $550.

It is possible to convince the IRS to mitigate or eliminate these penalties if reasonable cause is proven. However, given the size of the potential penalties, it is best to make the proper remittance of tax deposits a high priority by the payroll staff.

Tax Deposit Problems Related to Acquisitions

A company that acquires another business should closely examine the acquiree's payroll remittances to ensure that all remittances have been made. By doing so, it can determine if there is a potential liability for unpaid withholdings that may not crop up for several years when federal or state auditors file claims that may include stiff penalties and interest charges. This is only an issue if the acquiring entity purchases the other business as a going concern, since it takes on all liabilities of the acquired entity. A purchase of business assets will not present this problem.

A potential flag for remittance problems is if an acquiree does all of its own remittance filings, rather than using the services of a payroll provider. In this case, there is a greater risk that remittances were sporadically made or never made at all.

Anyone conducting a due diligence review of such a company should establish that every remittance was made in sequence, that cashed checks verify the transfer of funds to the government, and that the amounts paid match the amounts calculated as due and payable in the payroll register.

The Employer's Quarterly Federal Tax Return

Form 941 must be filed by employers on a quarterly basis with the federal government. This form identifies the amount of all wages on which taxes were withheld, the amount of taxes withheld, and any adjustments to withheld taxes from previous reporting periods. If there is a shortfall between the amount of withheld taxes on this form and the amount of taxes actually withheld and deposited with the government during the quarter, then the difference must accompany this form when it is submitted. Taxes to be reported on this form include income taxes withheld from wages, including tips, supplementary unemployment compensation benefits, and third-party payments of sick pay, plus Social Security and Medicare taxes. An example of the form is shown in Exhibit 8.6.

Use the following steps to complete the form:

Line 1: Enter the number of employees on the payroll during the pay period that includes March 12. This figure should not include household employees or anyone who received no pay during the period.

Line 2: Enter the total amount of all wages paid, which includes tips, and taxable fringe benefits, but not including supplemental unemployment compensation benefits and contributions to employee pension plans that are not itemized as employee wages.

Line 3: Enter the total amount of income taxes withheld on wages, tips, taxable fringe benefits, and supplemental unemployment compensation benefits.

Line 4: If there were errors in the reported amount of income taxes withheld from previous quarters of the same calendar year, enter the adjustments on this line. Adjustments to reported quarters in previous years are not allowed. The amount of any adjustment must also be included on Line 17, and itemized separately on Form 941c, "Supporting Statement to Correct Information."

Line 5: Net Line 4 against Line 3, and enter the merged amount on this line.

Line 6: Enter the amount of all wages paid on Line 6a, except tips, that are subject to Social Security taxes. For the year 2003, this would be all wages up to $87,000. Multiply this figure by the Social Security tax rate of 12.4 percent, and enter the tax in Line 6b. Enter the same information for tip wages in Line 6c and the tax due in Line 6d.

Line 7: Enter the amount of all wages and tips subject to Medicare taxes; there is no upper wage limitation on the amount subject to this tax.

Exhibit 8.6 *Form 941*

Form **941**
(Rev. January 2003)
Department of the Treasury
Internal Revenue Service (99)

Employer's Quarterly Federal Tax Return

▶ See separate instructions revised January 2003 for information on completing this return.

Please type or print.

Enter state code for state in which deposits were made only if different from state in address to the right ▶ [:] (see page 2 of separate instructions).

Name (as distinguished from trade name)	Date quarter ended
Trade name, if any	Employer identification number
Address (number and street)	City, state, and ZIP code

OMB No. 1545-0029

T
FF
FD
FP
I
T

If address is different from prior return, check here ▶

IRS Use

```
1 1 1 1 1 1 1 1 1        2    3 3 3 3 3 3 3    4 4 4    5 5 5
                                                    
6     7    8 8 8  8 8 8 8   9 9 9 9   10 10 10  10 10 10 10 10 10 10
```

A If you do not have to file returns in the future, check here ▶ ☐ and enter date final wages paid ▶ _____
B If you are a seasonal employer, see Seasonal employers on page 1 of the instructions and check here ▶ ☐

1	Number of employees in the pay period that includes March 12th . ▶ 1	
2	Total wages and tips, plus other compensation	2
3	Total income tax withheld from wages, tips, and sick pay	3
4	Adjustment of withheld income tax for preceding quarters of this calendar year	4
5	Adjusted total of income tax withheld (line 3 as adjusted by line 4)	5
6	Taxable social security wages . . . . . 6a [____] × 12.4% (.124) = 6b	
	Taxable social security tips . . . . . . 6c [____] × 12.4% (.124) = 6d	
7	Taxable Medicare wages and tips . . . 7a [____] × 2.9% (.029) = 7b	
8	Total social security and Medicare taxes (add lines 6b, 6d, and 7b). Check here if wages are not subject to social security and/or Medicare tax . . . . ▶ ☐	8
9	Adjustment of social security and Medicare taxes (see instructions for required explanation) Sick Pay $ _____ ± Fractions of Cents $ _____ ± Other $ _____ =	9
10	Adjusted total of social security and Medicare taxes (line 8 as adjusted by line 9)	10
11	Total taxes (add lines 5 and 10)	11
12	Advance earned income credit (EIC) payments made to employees (see instructions) . . .	12
13	Net taxes (subtract line 12 from line 11). If $2,500 or more, this must equal line 17, column (d) below (or line D of Schedule B (Form 941))	13
14	Total deposits for quarter, including overpayment applied from a prior quarter	14
15	Balance due (subtract line 14 from line 13). See instructions	15
16	Overpayment. If line 14 is more than line 13, enter excess here ▶ $ _____ and check if to be: ☐ Applied to next return or ☐ Refunded.	

- All filers: If line 13 is less than $2,500, do not complete line 17 or Schedule B (Form 941).
- Semiweekly schedule depositors: Complete Schedule B (Form 941) and check here . . . . ▶ ☐
- Monthly schedule depositors: Complete line 17, columns (a) through (d), and check here. . . . . ▶ ☐

17	Monthly Summary of Federal Tax Liability. (Complete Schedule B (Form 941) instead, if you were a semiweekly schedule depositor.)			
	(a) First month liability	(b) Second month liability	(c) Third month liability	(d) Total liability for quarter

Third Party Designee

Do you want to allow another person to discuss this return with the IRS (see separate instructions)? ☐ Yes. Complete the following. ☐ No

Designee's name ▶ _____
Phone no. ▶ (   )
Personal identification number (PIN) ▶ [_ _ _ _ _]

Sign Here

Under penalties of perjury, I declare that I have examined this return, including accompanying schedules and statements, and to the best of my knowledge and belief, it is true, correct, and complete.

Signature ▶ _____
Print Your Name and Title ▶ _____
Date ▶ _____

For Privacy Act and Paperwork Reduction Act Notice, see back of Payment Voucher.   Cat. No. 17001Z   Form **941** (Rev. 1-2003)

Then multiply the result by the Medicare tax rate of 2.9 percent and enter the tax due in Line 7b.

Line 8: Summarize all taxes due from Lines 6 and 7.

Line 9: Enter any adjustments to the reported amounts of Social Security and Medicare taxes previously listed on Lines 6 and 7. These adjustments can include the uncollected employee share of tip taxes, adjustments for the employee share of Social Security and Medicare taxes on group-term life insurance premiums paid to former employees, and adjustments for the employee share of taxes withheld by an independent provider of sick pay. An accompanying statement should itemize these adjustments.

Line 10: Net Lines 8 and 9 to arrive at the adjusted total of Social Security and Medicare taxes.

Line 11: Add Lines 5 and 10 to arrive at the total amount of taxes withheld.

Line 12: Enter the total amount of any earned income credit payments made to employees. If the amount of these credit payments exceeds the total taxes listed on Line 11, you can either claim a refund or let the credit forward into the next quarter.

Line 13: Subtract Line 12 from Line 11 and enter it here.

Line 14: Enter the total deposits made during the quarter, as well as any overpayment remaining from a preceding quarter.

Line 15: Subtract the deposit total on Line 14 from the tax due on Line 13 to arrive at the balance due.

Line 16: If there is a credit balance on Line 15, enter it here and then check off your choice of rolling it forward to the next quarterly return or receiving a refund.

Line 17: Enter the total tax liability for each month of the reporting quarter, as well as the total amount for the quarter.

The form should be signed by a business owner, corporate officer, partner, or fiduciary, depending on the type of business entity filing the report.

If a company only has seasonal operations, one can avoid filling out the report for quarters when there is no activity by checking off the "Seasonal Employers" box above Line 1 on the form. If a company is going out of business, be sure to check off the "Final Return" box above Line 1 of the form.

The form is due one month after each calendar quarter, and is filed at one of three IRS locations, depending on the location of the filing company. Exhibit 8.7 shows the correct filing location for each state of residence.

If an employer is making a payment with Form 941, it must use the Form 941-V Payment Voucher to accompany the payment. This form, which is shown in Exhibit 8.4, is used to identify the taxpayer, as well as the quarter to which the deposit is to be credited, and the amount of the payment. This form is available through the Internal Revenue Service's website in Adobe Acrobat format. An example is shown in Exhibit 8.8.

	Exhibit 8.7 *Filing Address for Form 941*	
Filing Location if No Payment	**Filing Location if Includes a Payment**	**For Employers Located In**
Cincinnati, OH 45999-0005	P.O. 105703 Atlanta, GA 30348-5703	Connecticut, Delaware, District of Columbia, Illinois, Indiana, Kentucky, Maine, Maryland, Massachusetts, Michigan, New Hampshire, New Jersey, New York, North Carolina, Ohio, Pennsylvania, Rhode Island, South Carolina, Vermont, Virginia, West Virginia, Wisconsin
Ogden, UT 84201-0005	P.O. 660264 Dallas, TX 75266-0264	Alabama, Alaska, Arizona, Arkansas, California, Colorado, Florida, Georgia, Hawaii, Idaho, Iowa, Kansas, Louisiana, Minnesota, Mississippi, Missouri, Montana, Nebraska, Nevada, New Mexico, North Dakota, Oklahoma, Oregon, South Dakota, Tennessee, Texas, Utah, Washington, Wyoming
Philadelphia, PA 19255-0005	P.O. 80106 Cincinnati, OH 45280-0006	No legal residence or principal place of business

Summary

Much of the information contained in this chapter is a summarization of the Internal Revenue Service's publications. In particular, you may want to download from the *www.irs.gov* site the following publications. They contain additional information about payroll taxes and remittances:

- *Publication 509, Tax Calendars.* As the name implies, this publication lists the dates on which a variety of taxes are due throughout the year. Of particular use for semi-weekly depositors is a table listing the due dates for deposit of taxes under the semi-weekly rule for all weeks of the current year.

- *Publication 15, Employer's Tax Guide.* This manual itemizes how to obtain an EIN (Employer Identification Number), defines employees, and discusses wages, payroll periods, withholding and depositing taxes, and a variety of other tax-related subjects.

- *Publication 15-A, Employer's Supplemental Tax Guide.* This manual discusses the legal definition of an employee, special types of wage compensation, sick pay reporting, pensions and annuities, and alternative methods for calculating withholding.

- *Publication 15-B, Employer's Tax Guide to Fringe Benefits.* As the name implies, this publication covers a wide range of fringe benefit exclusion rules, ranging from accident and health benefits to working condition benefits. It also address fringe benefit valuation rules as well as rules for withholding, depositing, and reporting taxes.

Exhibit 8.8 *Form 941-V Payment Voucher*

Form 941
Payment Voucher

Purpose of Form

Complete Form 941-V if you are making a payment with Form 941, Employer's Quarterly Federal Tax Return. We will use the completed voucher to credit your payment more promptly and accurately, and to improve our service to you.

If you have your return prepared by a third party and make a payment with that return, please provide this payment voucher to the return preparer.

Making Payments With Form 941

Make your payment with Form 941 only if:

• Your net taxes for the quarter (line 13 on Form 941) are less than $2,500 and you are paying in full with a timely filed return or

• You are a monthly schedule depositor making a payment in accordance with the Accuracy of Deposits Rule. (See section 11 of Circular E (Pub. 15), Employer's Tax Guide, for details.) This amount may be $2,500 or more.

Otherwise, you must deposit the amount at an authorized financial institution or by electronic funds transfer. (See section 11 of Circular E (Pub. 15) for deposit instructions.) Do not use the Form 941-V payment voucher to make Federal tax deposits.

Caution: If you pay amounts with Form 941 that should have been deposited, you may be subject to a penalty. See Deposit Penalties in section 11 of Circular E (Pub. 15).

Specific Instructions

Box 1—Employer identification number (EIN). If you do not have an EIN, apply for one on Form SS-4, Application for Employer Identification Number, and write "Applied For" and the date you applied in this entry space.

Box 2—Amount paid. Enter the amount paid with Form 941.

Box 3—Tax period. Darken the capsule identifying the quarter for which the payment is made. Darken only one capsule.

Box 4—Name and address. Enter your name and address as shown on Form 941.

• Enclose your check or money order made payable to the "United States Treasury." Be sure also to enter your EIN, "Form 941," and the tax period on your check or money order. Do not send cash. Please do not staple this voucher or your payment to the return (or to each other).

• Detach the completed voucher and send it with your payment and Form 941 to the address provided on the back of Form 941.

▼ Detach Here and Mail With Your Payment and Tax Return. ▼ Form 941-V (2003)

Form **941-V** | **Payment Voucher** | OMB No. 1545-0029

Department of the Treasury
Internal Revenue Service (99) ► Do not staple or attach this voucher to your payment. **2003**

| 1 Enter your employer identification number. | 2 Enter the amount of your payment. ► | Dollars | Cents |

3 Tax period		4 Enter your business name (individual name if sole proprietor).
○ 1st Quarter	○ 3rd Quarter	Enter your address.
○ 2nd Quarter	○ 4th Quarter	Enter your city, state, and ZIP code.

9

Benefits

Introduction

Though it may appear that the extension of benefits to employees is more of a paperwork-laden human resources function than a payroll function, there are a number of payroll issues involving the amount and limitation of related payroll deductions, the taxability of benefits received, and the reporting of those benefits to the IRS. This chapter[*] addresses these issues and more in respect to cafeteria plans, various types of medical insurance, leaves of absence, life insurance, pension plans, sick and disability pay, stock options, and workers' compensation insurance.

Cafeteria Plans

A cafeteria plan allows employees to pay for some benefits with pretax dollars, so that the amount of taxable income to them is reduced. In its simplest form, a "Premium-Only Plan" (POP) allows employees to take employer-required medical insurance deductibles from their pretax income. This version of the cafeteria plan requires almost no effort to administer and is essentially invisible to employees. The primary impact to employees is that the amount of taxes taken out of their paychecks will be slightly reduced.

A more comprehensive cafeteria plan includes a Flexible Spending Account (FSA). This option allows employees to have money withheld from their pay on a pretax basis and stored in a fund, which they can draw down by being reimbursed for medical or dependent care expenses.

> **Example:** Allison Schoening has a long-term medical condition that she knows will require a multitude of prescriptions over the plan year. She knows the prescription co-pays will cost her at least $800 during the year. Accord-

---

[*] This chapter is derived with permission from Chapter 6 of Bragg, *Essentials of Payroll* (Hoboken, NJ: John Wiley and Sons, 2003).

ingly, at the beginning of the year, she elects to have a total of $800 deducted from her pay in equal installments over the course of the year. When she pays for a co-pay, she keeps the receipt and forwards it to the payroll department, which reimburses her for it from the funds that she has already had deducted from her pay.

By having funds withdrawn from their pay prior to the calculation of taxes, employees will not pay any taxes (e.g., income taxes, Social Security taxes, or Medicare taxes) on the withdrawn funds.

Example: To continue the previous example, Allison Schoening earns $40,000 per year. The total of all taxes taken out of her pay, including federal and state income taxes, Social Security, and Medicare taxes, is 27 percent. Her net take-home pay, after also taking out $800 for the previously described medical expenses, is $28,400, which is calculated as ([$40,000 × (1 − 27%)] − $800). When she enrolls in the cafeteria plan and has $800 removed from her pay on a pretax basis to pay for the medical expenses, her take-home pay, net of medical costs, increases to $28,616, which is calculated as ([$40,000 − $800] × [1 − 27%]). The increase in her take-home pay of $216 is entirely attributable to the removal of medical costs from her pay before tax calculations and deductions are made.

The cafeteria plan appears to be a surefire way to increase employee take-home pay. However, it has some built-in restrictions that, if not managed carefully, can result in a *reduction* in take-home pay. One issue is that employees are only allowed to choose the total amount of their annual cafeteria plan deductions at the beginning of the plan year and cannot change it again until the plan year has concluded. This lockdown provision can only be altered when there have been changes in an employee's marital status, number of dependents (including adoptions) or the status of those dependents, residential address, or the employment status of the employee or a spouse or dependent. These changes must also result in a change in employee status in the underlying coverage before the amount of the cafeteria plan deduction can be altered.

Example: To continue the previous example, Allison Schoening's long-term medical condition clears up partway through the year, allowing her to stop purchasing prescriptions. Consequently, she wants to reduce the amount of the cafeteria plan deductions being removed from her pay. She claims that there has been a change in her status, because she changed residences midway through the year. This claim is denied by the cafeteria plan administrator, because the change in residence did not alter her eligibility for coverage under the terms of the underlying medical insurance plan.

Example: Allison Schoening decides to adopt a baby after the plan year has begun. This results in a change in her eligibility under the rules of the underlying medical insurance plan, which allows her to add the baby as a dependent. Since this is also an allowable change in status under the cafeteria plan, she is allowed to alter the amount of her cafeteria plan deductions to more closely match her altered medical expenses resulting from the adoption.

The reason why it is so important to closely match the amount of actual expenses incurred to the amount withheld under a cafeteria plan is that if an employee does not submit a sufficient amount of qualified expenses to be reimbursed from the withheld funds, the remaining funds will be lost at the end of the plan year. Only those expenses billed to the employee prior to year-end can be reimbursed through the plan. When a reimbursement request is made, an employee must provide a receipt from the healthcare provider and also make a written statement that he or she has not received reimbursement for this expense from any other source. Consequently, it is best for employees to make a low estimate of the total amount of qualified expenses that they expect to incur by the end of the year, rather than have too much withheld and then lose the unused portion.

Example: Allison Schoening receives a periodic statement from the FSA plan administrator, informing her that she still has $250 of funds left in her cafeteria plan account with one month to go before the plan year-end. Accordingly, she accelerates the purchase of several prescriptions at the local pharmacy on the last day of the plan year, even though she will not need the medication for some time to come. Because this action is acceptable under the cafeteria plan rules, reimbursement of the late purchases from the fund are approved and she does not lose any funds from her FSA account.

Another problem for employees is that contributions into an FSA plan are treated as separate pools of funds if they are intended for medical expense reimbursements or for dependent care reimbursements. Cash from these two types of funds cannot be mixed. For example, if an employee contributes too much money into a dependent care account and cannot use it all by the end of the plan year, these funds cannot be shifted to other uses, such as the reimbursement of medical expenses.

A problem for employers offering an FSA cafeteria plan is that employees may legally make claims against the fund that exceed the amount they have thus far contributed to the plan, and then quit the company—if so, the business cannot seek recompense from the individual for the difference between the amount contributed into the fund and the amount paid out. A company cannot alleviate this potential problem by forcing employees to accelerate the amount of their contributions beyond the preset amount.

Example: Mr. Adolph Armsbrucker contributes $100 per month into the company's FSA fund, which will result in a total contribution of $1,200 at the end of the year. However, he submits expenses to the plan administrator of $550 in February, for which he is reimbursed. He has only contributed $200 into the fund at this point, so the company is essentially supporting the fund for the difference between $550 in expenses and $200 in funding, or $350. Mr. Armsbrucker leaves the company at the end of February, leaving the company with this liability.

The favorable tax treatment accorded to participants in a cafeteria plan is only available if the plan passes several nondiscrimination tests. First, a plan must have the same eligibility requirements for all employees; this involves avoidance of giving plan participation solely to highly compensated employees and having a standard term of employment prior to participation in the plan (not to exceed three years). Second, all plan participants must have equal access to the same nontaxable benefits offered under the plan. Finally, no more than one-quarter of all nontaxable benefits provided under the plan can be given to key employees.

Insurance Benefits

This can include medical, dental, vision, and life insurance. Deductions are usually taken from every paycheck to help defray the cost of the insurance, either in part or in total. A company may contribute to this cost by paying for some portion or all of the insurance itself. Even if employees pay the entire amount of the insurance, it is still usually less expensive than if they had obtained it themselves, since insurance companies generally quote lower prices to businesses employing a number of people. The contribution made by the company to defray the cost of medical insurance is *not* considered income to employees. Furthermore, if the company has a medical expense reimbursement plan under which employees can be reimbursed for any out-of-pocket medical expenses that they incur, these additional payments are also not considered income to employees.

Example: In a sudden burst of generosity, the president of the Humble Pie Company announces at the company business party that all co-payments and deductibles on its medical insurance plan for the upcoming year will be paid by the company. These reimbursements are not taxable income to the employees.

The most common ways to provide medical insurance are through the Health Maintenance organization (HMO), Preferred Provider Organization (PPO), and Point of Service (POS) plan. The HMO arrangement requires employees to go to designated doctors who have signed up to participate in the plan. The PPO option allows employees to consult with doctors outside of the group of designated doctors, but at a higher cost in terms of co-payments and deductibles. The POS plan requires employees to choose a primary care doctor from within the HMO network of doctors, but they can then see doctors outside the HMO's network, as long as the primary care doctor is still the primary point of contact.

Given the high cost of medical insurance provided by third parties, some organizations are turning to self-insurance plans. Under this approach, employee medical claims are submitted directly to the company or a third-party administrator, with the claims in either case being paid by the company. Once total claims reach a certain point, a "stop-loss" insurance policy takes over and pays all remaining claims. This stop-loss coverage prevents the company from incurring inordinate losses by providing umbrella coverage for major insurance claims. This approach eliminates the profit that would otherwise be charged by a third-party medical provider, while also allowing the company to exert more control over employee claims. A key drawback to this arrangement is that, if the plan's benefits are skewed in favor of highly compensated employees, the excess medical payments made on behalf of this group will be considered income to them for tax reporting purposes. Excess payments are considered to be those payments paid that exceed the level of payments made to other employees in the plan. In order not to be considered discriminatory, a self-insured plan should include at least 70 percent of all employees.

Example: The management team of the Humble Pie Company is given free corrective eye surgery, which is not offered to other employees. The CFO is given this surgery, which costs $2,200. The entire cost of this surgery should be added to the CFO's reportable income, since the benefit was not made available to the rest of the company.

Many third-party medical insurance providers do not allow partial-month insurance coverage. This is an important issue in cases where employees are leaving a company near the beginning of a month, since the company will still pay its share of the medical cost for the remainder of the month, even if the employee is no longer working there. The payroll staff should be sure to charge the departing employee his or her full share of the medical insurance for the full month of medical coverage; this deduction is frequently missed in companies where more than one payroll is generated per month, since the employee share of the expense is spread over several paychecks. Despite the additional manual effort involved in altering the medical insurance deduction on an employee's final paycheck, this can result in significant cost savings to the company.

Insurance Continuation Subsequent to Employment

Under the terms of the Consolidated Omnibus Budget Reconciliation Act (COBRA), employees of private sector, state, and local governments who lose their jobs have the right to accept continuing health insurance coverage, as long as the former employer had 20 or more employees in the prior year. If an employee is terminated, then he or she can accept coverage for an additional 18 months. If an employee becomes entitled to Medicare coverage or becomes divorced, then the coverage period becomes 36 months. If a spouse or dependent child of an employee loses coverage due to the death of an employee, then they can obtain coverage for up to 36 months. If a dependent child of an employee loses dependent status, then that person can obtain coverage for up to 36 months.

An employer is required to give notice of potential COBRA coverage to employees when a qualifying event occurs (employees are required to inform the health plan administrator of any divorce, disability, or dependent issues that would bring about qualification for benefits under COBRA). The impacted people then have up to 60 days in which to elect to take COBRA coverage.

If coverage is chosen, an impacted person can be required to pay up to 102 percent of the cost of the insurance. If one does not make timely payments under the terms of the insurance plan (within 30 days of the due date), the COBRA coverage can be terminated. COBRA coverage also will end if the employer stops providing medical coverage to its regular employees, if the covered individual obtains coverage under another health insurance plan subsequent to taking the COBRA coverage, or if the covered individual becomes covered by the Medicare program.

Example: A cook at the Humble Pie Company is laid off at the end of March. She is given paperwork to fill out at the time of termination for COBRA coverage. She submits the documentation accepting coverage after 55 days. The company is required to keep her on COBRA, since she filed in a timely manner. After three months, she obtains work with another company and enrolls in its medical insurance program. Because she is now covered by a different insurance program subsequent to her election to accept COBRA coverage, the Humble Pie Company no longer has to give her COBRA coverage, and so terminates it.

Leaves of Absence

The Family and Medical Leave Act (FMLA) entitles employees at companies with 50 or more employees to take up to 12 weeks of unpaid leave (which may be taken sporadically) each year for a specified list of family and medical reasons. Only those employees who have worked for the employer for a total of at least 12 months, and worked for the employer for at least 1,250 hours in the last 12 months are covered by the Act. A further restriction is that an employee must work at a company location where at least 50 employees are employed within a 75-mile radius of the facility. Valid reasons for taking the leave of absence include the birth of a child, serious illness, or caring for a family member with a serious illness.

During their absence, an employer must continue to provide medical insurance coverage if it had been taken by the employee prior to the leave of absence, though the employee can be charged for that portion of the expense that had been deducted from his or her pay prior to the leave. If the employee does not pay this portion of the expense within 30 days, the insurance can be cancelled for the remainder of the leave (though 15 days written notice must be provided), but it must be restored once the employee returns to work. If the terms of the medical insurance plan are changed by the company during the leave of absence, then the new terms will apply to the person who is on leave. Only medical insurance is subject to these provisions—other types of insurance, such as life and disability insurance, do not have to be maintained during the leave of absence.

Example: Samuel Lamont had a sick parent and took FMLA leave from the Humble Pie Company in order to care for her. Prior to his leave of absence, he paid $120 per month as his share of the cost of a company-provided medical insurance plan. During the leave, the company changed the employee share of the insurance for all employees to $160. Mr. Lamont concluded that he could not afford this additional cost, and stopped paying for his share of the insurance. The company accordingly warned him in writing that coverage would be dropped and then did so after payment became 30 days overdue. When he returned from leave, the company was required to restore his medical coverage.

Because of the large number of provisions of the FMLA and its cost impact on both the employer and employee, it is most useful for the employer to fill out a formal, detailed response to a request for a leave of absence, copies of which should go to the employee's file as well as the employee. The Department of Labor has issued a sample report that covers the key provisions of the FMLA, which is reproduced in Exhibit 9.1. This form, Number WH-381, may be downloaded in Acrobat PDF format from the Department of Labor's website at *www.dol.gov.*

Exhibit 9.1 *Employer Response Form for FMLA Leave Request*

Employer Response to Employee	**U.S. Department of Labor**
Request for Family or Medical Leave	Employment Standards Administration
(Optional Use Form -- See 29 CFR § 825.301)	Wage and Hour Division

(Family and Medical Leave Act of 1993)

Date:

OMB No. : 1215-0181
Expires : 07/31/04

To: _____
(Employee's Name)

From:_____
(Name of Appropriate Employer Representative)

Subject: REQUEST FOR FAMILY/MEDICAL LEAVE

On _____ , you notified us of your need to take family/medical leave due to:
(Date)

☐ The birth of a child, or the placement of a child with you for adoption or foster care; or

☐ A serious health condition that makes you unable to perform the essential functions for your job: or

☐ A serious health condition affecting your ☐ spouse, ☐ child, ☐ parent, for which you are needed to provide care.

You notified us that you need this leave beginning on _____ and that you expect
(Date)
leave to continue until on or about _____ .
(Date)

Except as explained below, you have a right under the FMLA for up to 12 weeks of unpaid leave in a 12-month period for the reasons listed above. Also, your health benefits must be maintained during any period of unpaid leave under the same conditions as if you continued to work, and you must be reinstated to the same or an equivalent job with the same pay, benefits, and terms and conditions of employment on your return from leave. If you do not return to work following FMLA leave for a reason other than: (1) the continuation, recurrence, or onset of a serious health condition which would entitle you to FMLA leave; or (2) other circumstances beyond your control, you may be required to reimburse us for our share of health insurance premiums paid on your behalf during your FMLA leave.

This is to inform you that: *(check appropriate boxes; explain where indicated)*

1. You are ☐ eligible ☐ not eligible for leave under the FMLA.

2. The requested leave ☐ will ☐ will not be counted against your annual FMLA leave entitlement.

3. You ☐ will ☐ will not be required to furnish medical certification of a serious health condition. If required, you must furnish certification by _____*(insert date)* (must be at least 15 days after you are notified of this requirement), or we may delay the commencement of your leave until the certification is submitted.

4. You may elect to substitute accrued paid leave for unpaid FMLA leave. We ☐ will ☐ will not require that you substitute accrued paid leave for unpaid FMLA leave. If paid leave will be used, the following conditions will apply: *(Explain)*

Form WH-381
Rev. June 1997

Exhibit 9.1 *(Continued)*

5. (a) If you normally pay a portion of the premiums for your health insurance, these payments will continue during the period of FMLA leave. Arrangements for payment have been discussed with you, and it is agreed that you will make premium payments as follows: *(Set forth dates, e.g., the 10th of each month, or pay periods, etc. that specifically cover the agreement with the employee.)*

   (b) You have a minimum 30-day *(or, indicate longer period, if applicable)* grace period in which to make premium payments. If payment is not made timely, your group health insurance may be cancelled, *provided* we notify you in writing at least 15 days before the date that your health coverage will lapse, or, at our option, we may pay your share of the premiums during FMLA leave, and recover these payments from you upon your return to work. We ☐ will ☐ will not pay your share of health insurance premiums while you are on leave.

   (c) We ☐ will ☐ will not do the same with other benefits (*e.g.*, life insurance, disability insurance, etc.) while you are on FMLA leave. If we do pay your premiums for other benefits, when you return from leave you ☐ will ☐ will not be expected to reimburse us for the payments made on your behalf.

6. You ☐ will ☐ will not be required to present a fitness-for-duty certificate prior to being restored to employment. If such certification is required but not received, your return to work may be delayed until certification is provided.

7. (a) You ☐ are ☐ are not a "key employee" as described in § 825.217 of the FMLA regulations. If you are a "key employee:" restoration to employment may be denied following **FMLA leave on the grounds that such** restoration will cause substantial and grievous economic injury to us as discussed in § 825.218.

   (b) We ☐ have ☐ have not determined that restoring you to employment at the conclusion of FMLA leave will cause substantial and grievous economic harm to *us. (Explain (a) and/or (b) below. See §825.279 of the FMLA regulations.)*

8. While on leave, you ☐ will ☐ will not be required to furnish us with periodic reports every _____ *(indicate interval of periodic reports, as appropriate for the particular leave situation)* of your status and intent to return to work (see § 825.309 of the FMLA regulations). If the circumstances of your leave change and you are able to return to work earlier than the date indicated on the reverse side of this form, you ☐ will ☐ will not be required to notify us at least two work days prior to the date you intend to report to work.

9. You ☐ will ☐ will not be required to furnish recertification relating to a serious health condition. *(Explain below. if necessary, including the interval between certifications as prescribed in §825.308 of the FMLA regulations.)*

This optional use form may be used to satisfy mandatory employer requirements to provide employees taking FMLA leave with Written notice detailing specific expectations and obligations of the employee and explaining any consequences of a failure to meet these obligations. (29 CFR 825.301(b).)

Note: Persons are not required to respond to this collection of information unless it displays a currently valid OMB control number.

Public Burden Statement

We estimate that it will take an average of 5 minutes to complete this collection of information, including the time for reviewing instructions. searching existing data sources, gathering and maintaining the data needed, and completing and reviewing the collection of information. If you have any comments regarding this burden estimate or any other aspect of this collection of information, including suggestions for reducing this burden. send them to the Administrator, Wage and Hour Division, Department of Labor, Room S-3502. 200 Constitution Avenue, N.W., Washington. D.C. 20210.

DO NOT SEND THE COMPLETED FORM TO THE OFFICE SHOWN ABOVE.

Upon returning from a leave of absence, an employee must be given the same or equivalent job, with the same level of pay and benefits that he or she had before the leave. However, no additional leave or seniority accrues during the term of an employee's leave of absence. In certain cases where job restoration would cause significant economic damage to an employer, key positions will not be restored to returning employees. A key position is defined as a salaried employee whose pay is in the top ten percent of all employees.

Life Insurance

It is common practice for a company to provide group term life insurance to its employees as part of a standard benefit package. This requires some extra reporting from a tax perspective, however. If the amount of the life insurance benefit exceeds $50,000, the company must report the incremental cost of the life insurance over $50,000 (to the extent that the employee is not paying for the additional insurance) on the employee's W-2 form as taxable income. In the less common case where the company provides life insurance that results in some amount of cash surrender value, then the cost of this permanent benefit to the employee must also be included in the employee's W-2 form. The only case in which these costs are not included on an employee's W-2 form is when the company is the beneficiary of the policy, rather than the employee. The opposite situation arises if the company is providing life insurance only to a few key employees, rather than to all employees; in this case, the entire cost of the insurance must be reported on the employee's W-2 form as taxable income.

Pension Plan Benefits

There are an enormous variety of retirement plans available, each of which has a slightly different treatment under the tax laws, resulting in varying levels of investment risk to the employee or different levels of administrative activity. In this section, we will give a brief overview of each type of retirement plan.

A *qualified retirement plan* is one that is designed to observe all of the requirements of the Employee Retirement Income Security Act (ERISA), as well as all related IRS rulings. By observing these requirements, an employer can immediately deduct allowable contributions to the plan on behalf of plan participants. Also, income earned by the plan is not taxable to the plan. In addition, participants can exclude from taxable income any contributions they make to the plan, until such time as they choose to withdraw the funds from the plan. Finally, distributions to participants can, in some cases, be rolled over into an Individual Retirement Account (IRA), thereby prolonging the deferral of taxable income. There are two types of qualified retirement plans:

- *Defined Contribution Plan.* This is a plan in which the employer is liable for a payment into the plan of a specific size, but not for the size of the resulting payments from the plan to participants. Thus, the participant bears the risk of the results of investment of the monies that have been deposited into the plan. The participant can mitigate or increase this risk by having control over a number of different investment options. The annual combined contribution to this type of plan by both the participant and employer is limited to the lesser of $40,000 or all of a participant's annual compensation. Funds received by participants in a steady income stream are taxed at ordinary income tax rates and cannot be rolled over into an IRA, whereas a lump sum payment can be rolled into an IRA. Some of the more common defined contribution plans are:

- *401k Plan.* This is a plan set up by an employer, into which employees can contribute the lesser of $13,000 or 15 percent of their pay, which is excluded from taxation until such time as they remove the funds from the account. All earnings of the funds while held in the plan will also not be taxed until removed from the account. Employers can also match the funds contributed to the plan by employees, and also contribute the results of a profit sharing plan to the employees' 401k accounts. The plan typically allows employees to invest the funds in their accounts in a number of different investment options, ranging from conservative money market funds to more speculative small cap or international stock funds; the employee holds the risk of how well or poorly an investment will perform—the employer has no liability for the performance of investments. Withdrawals from a 401k are intended to be upon retirement or the attainment of age 59 $\frac{1}{2}$, but can also be distributed as a loan (if the specific plan document permits it) or in the event of disability or death.

Example: The Humble Pie Company matches the contributions of its employees for the first three percent of pay they contribute into a 401k plan. Ms. Sally Reed elects to have eight percent of her pay contributed to the 401k plan each month. Her monthly rate of pay is $3,500. Accordingly, the company deducts $280 from her pay (8% × $3,500). The company then adds $105 to her contribution (3% × $3,500). Consequently, the total contribution to her 401k plan is $385, which is comprised of $280 contributed by Ms. Reed and $105 contributed by the company.

- *403b Plan.* This plan is similar to a 401k plan, except that it is designed specifically for charitable, religious, and education organizations that fall under the tax-exempt status of 501(c)(3) regulations. It varies from a 401k plan in that participants can only invest in mutual funds and annuities and also in that contributions can exceed the limit imposed under a 401k plan to the extent that participants can catch up on contributions that were below the maximum threshold in previous years.
- *Employee Stock Ownership Plan (ESOP).* The bulk of the contributions made to this type of plan are in the stock of the employing company. The

employer calculates the amount of its contribution to the plan based on a proportion of total employee compensation and uses the result to buy an equivalent amount of stock and deposit it in the ESOP. When an employee leaves the company, he or she will receive either company stock or the cash equivalent of the stock in payment of his or her vested interest.

- *Money Purchase Plan.* The employer must make a payment into each employee's account in each year that is typically based on a percentage of total compensation paid to each participant. The payments must be made, irrespective of company profits (see next item).

- *Profit Sharing Plan.* Contributions to this type of plan are intended to be funded from company profits, which is an incentive for employees to extend their efforts to ensure that profits will occur. However, many employers will make contributions to the plan even in the absence of profits. This plan is frequently linked to a 401k plan, so that participants can also make contributions to the plan.

■ **Defined Benefit Plan.** This plan itemizes a specific dollar amount that participants will receive, based on a set of rules that typically combine the number of years of employment and wages paid over the time period when each employee worked for the company. An additional factor may be the age of the participant at the time of retirement. Funds received by participants in a steady income stream are taxed at ordinary income tax rates and cannot be rolled over into an IRA, whereas a lump sum payment can be rolled into an IRA. This type of plan is not favorable to the company because it guarantees the fixed payments made to retirees and so bears the risk of unfavorable investment returns that may require additional payments into the plan in order to meet the fixed payment obligations. Some of the more common defined benefit plans are:

- *Cash Balance Plan.* The employer contributes a *pay credit* (usually based on a proportion of that person's annual compensation) and an *interest credit* (usually linked to a publicly available interest rate index or well-known high-grade investment such as a U.S. government security) to each participant's account within the plan. Changes in plan value based on these credits do not impact the fixed benefit amounts to which participants are entitled.

- *Target Benefit Plan.* Under this approach, the employer makes annual contributions into the plan based on the actuarial assumption at that time regarding the amount of funding needed to achieve a targeted benefit level (hence the name of the plan). However, there is no guarantee that the amount of the actual benefit paid will match the estimate upon which the contributions were based, since the return on invested amounts in the plan may vary from the estimated level at the time when the contributions were made.

The preceding plans all fall under the category of qualified retirement plans. However, if a company does not choose to follow ERISA and IRS guidelines, it can create a *nonqualified retirement plan.* By doing so, it can discriminate in favor of paying key personnel more than other participants, or to the exclusion of other employees. All contributions to the plan and any earnings by the deposited funds will remain untaxed as long as they stay within the trust. However, the downside of this approach is that any contribution made to the plan by the company cannot be recorded as a taxable expense until the contribution is eventually paid out of the trust into which it was deposited and to the plan participant (which may be years in the future). Proceeds from the plan are taxable as ordinary income to the recipient, and cannot be rolled over into an IRA.

An example of a nonqualified retirement plan is the 457 plan, which allows participants to defer up to the lesser of $13,000 or their annual compensation per year. It is restricted to the use of government and tax-exempt entities. Distributions from the plan are usually at retirement, but can also be at the point of the employee's departure from the organization or a withdrawal can be requested on an emergency basis. A key difference between the 457 plan and the qualified retirement plans is that the funds deposited in the trust by the employer can be claimed by creditors, unless the employer is a government entity.

A plan that can fall into either the defined contribution or defined benefit plan categories is the Keogh plan. It is available to self-employed people, partnerships, and owners of unincorporated businesses. When created, a Keogh plan can be defined as either a defined contribution or a defined benefit plan. Under a defined benefit plan, contributions are limited to the lesser of $160,000 or 100 percent of a person's average compensation for his or her three highest years. Under a defined contribution plan, contributions are limited to the lesser of $40,000 or 100 percent of a person's annual compensation. It is not allowable to issue loans against a Keogh plan, but distributions from it can be rolled over into an IRA. Premature withdrawal penalties are similar to those for an IRA.

An employer may not want to deal with the complex reporting requirements of a qualified retirement plan, nor set up a nonqualified plan. A very simple alternative is the *personal retirement account* (PRA), of which the most common is the individual retirement arrangement. The primary types of PRAs are as follows:

- *Individual Retirement Account (IRA)*. This is a savings account that is set up for the specific use of one person who is less than $70\frac{1}{2}$ years old. Contributions to an IRA are limited to the lesser of $3,000 per year or a person's total taxable compensation (which can be wages, tips, bonuses, commissions, and taxable alimony). Anyone 50 years old or more can contribute an additional $500 per year. There is no required minimum payment into an IRA. Contributions to an IRA are not tax deductible if the contributor also participates in an employer's qualified retirement plan, and his or her adjusted gross income is greater than $44,000 if a single filer, or $64,000 if filing a joint return. The deductible amount begins to decline at a point $10,000 lower than all of these values. If a working spouse is not covered by an employer's qualified retirement plan, then he or she may make a fully deductible contribution of up to $3,000 per year to the IRA, even if the other spouse has such coverage. However, this deduction is eliminated when a couple's adjusted gross income reaches $160,000, and begins to decline at $150,000. Earnings within the plan are shielded from taxation until distributed from it.

It is mandatory to begin withdrawals from an IRA as of age $70\frac{1}{2}$; if distributions do not occur, then a penalty of 50 percent will be charged against the amount that was not distributed. When funds are withdrawn from an IRA prior to age $59\frac{1}{2}$, they will be taxed at ordinary income tax rates, and will also be subject to a 10 percent excise tax. However, the excise tax will be waived if the participant dies, is disabled, is buying a home for the first time (to a maximum of $10,000), is paying for some types of higher education costs or medical insurance costs that exceed $7\frac{1}{2}$ percent of the participant's adjusted gross income (as well as any medical insurance premiums following at least $\frac{1}{4}$ year of receiving unemployment benefits). The following list reveals the wide range of IRA accounts that can be set up:

- *Coverdell Education IRA*. This type of IRA is established for the express purpose of providing advanced education to the beneficiary. Though contributions to this IRA are not exempt from taxable income, any earnings during the period when funds are stored in the IRA will be tax-free at the time when they are used to pay for the cost of advanced education. The annual contribution limit on this IRA is $2,000, and is limited to the time period prior to the beneficiary reaching the age of 18. The maximum contribution begins to decline at the point when joint household income reaches $190,000, and $95,000 for a single tax filer. The amount in this IRA can be moved to a different family member if the new beneficiary is less than 30 years old. The amount in the IRA must be distributed once the beneficiary reaches the age of 30. If a distribution is not for the express purpose of offsetting education expenses, then the distribution is taxable as ordinary income and will also be charged a 10 percent excise tax.

- *Individual Retirement Annuity*. This is an IRA that is comprised of an annuity that is managed through and paid out by a life insurance company.

- *Inherited IRA*. This is either a Roth or traditional IRA that has been inherited from its deceased owner, with the recipient not being the deceased owner's spouse. After the owner's death, no more than five years can pass before the beneficiary receives a distribution or an annuity can be arranged that empties the IRA no later than the beneficiary's life expectancy. This IRA is not intended to be a vehicle for ongoing contributions from the new beneficiary, so tax deductions are not allowed for any contributions made into it. Also, the funds in this IRA cannot be shifted into a rollover IRA, since this action would circumvent the preceding requirement to distribute the funds within five years.

- *Rollover IRA*. This is an IRA that an individual sets up for the express purpose of receiving funds from a qualified retirement plan. There are no annual contribution limits for this type of IRA, since its purpose is to transfer a preexisting block of funds that could be quite large. Funds deposited in this account, as well as any earnings accumulating in the accounts, are exempt from taxation until removed from it. Rollover funds can also be transferred (tax-free) into another qualified retirement plan. A common use of the rollover account is to "park" funds from the qualified plan of a former employer until the individual qualifies for participation in the plan of a new employer, at which point the funds are transferred into the new employer's plan.

- *Roth IRA.* Under this IRA, there are offsetting costs and benefits. On the one hand, any contribution to the IRA is not deductible; however, withdrawals from the account (including earnings) are not taxable at all, as long as the recipient is either at least 59½ years old, disabled, or made a beneficiary following the death of the IRA participant, or the money is used to buy a first-time home. Contributions are limited to $3,000 per year and can be continued indefinitely, irrespective of the participant's age. Anyone of age 50 or older can contribute an additional $500 to the plan. However, no contribution is allowed once the participant's adjusted gross income reaches $160,000 for a joint filer, or $110,000 for a single filer, and will gradually decline beginning at $150,000 and $95,000, respectively.

    There are special rules for transferring funds into a Roth IRA from any other type of IRA. It is only allowed if the adjusted gross income of the transferring party is $100,000 or less in the year of transfer (the same limitation applies to both single and joint filers). Distributions from the Roth IRA that come from these rolled-over funds will not be taxable, but only if they have been held in the Roth IRA for at least five years following the date of transfer.

- *Savings Incentive Match Plan For Employees (SIMPLE).* Under this IRA format, an employer that has no other retirement plan and employs fewer than 100 employees can set up IRA accounts for its employees, into which each employee can contribute up to $9,000 per year (as of 2004). The employee commits to make a matching contribution of up to 3 percent of his or her employee's pay, depending upon how much the employee has chosen to contribute. Anyone age 50 or older can contribute an additional $500 to the plan. The combined employee/employer contribution to the plan cannot exceed $13,000 per year. The employer also has the option of reducing its contribution percentage in two years out of every five consecutive years, or can commit to a standard 2 percent contribution for all eligible employees, even if the employees choose not to contribute to the plan. Vesting in the plan is immediate. The downside to this plan from an employee's perspective is that the excise tax assessment for a withdrawal within the first two years of participation is 25 percent, rather than the usual 10 percent that is assessed for other types of IRA accounts.

- *Simplified Employee Pension.* This plan is available primarily for self-employed persons and partnerships, but is available to all types of business entities. It can only be established if no qualified retirement plan is already in use. The maximum contribution that an employer can make is the lesser of 25 percent of an employee's compensation for the year or $40,000. The amount paid is up to the discretion of the employer. The contribution is sent at once to an

IRA that has been set up in the name of each employee, and which is owned by the employee. Once the money arrives in the IRA, it falls under all of the previously-noted rules for an IRA.

Sick/Disability Pay

A typical company benefit plan allows for the accrual of a fixed number of sick days per year. When an illness forces an employee to stay home, the sick time accrual is used in place of work hours, so an employee is compensated for a normal number of working hours during his or her time off. Once all the accrued sick time is used up, an employee can use any remaining vacation time in order to continue being paid, and thereafter must take an unpaid leave of absence.

Additional wages may be paid from either short-term or long-term disability insurance plans, which are generally offered through third-party insurance providers. If an employer pays the entire cost of these insurance plans, then any benefits received from them by employees is taxable income to them. However, if the employees pay some portion of the cost of these plans with after-tax dollars, then only the employer-paid portion is recognized as taxable income to them. Alternatively, if employees pay for their share of these plans through a cafeteria plan, then they are doing so with before-tax dollars, which makes the proceeds from the insurance taxable.

Example: Molly Hatcher mistakenly ate a piece of the Humble Pie Company's namesake product and is out sick with a severe case of meekness. She had been paying for 40 percent of the cost of short-term disability insurance, with the company paying for the remainder of this cost. Under the policy, she is entitled to $350 per week. Of this amount, 60 percent will be recognized as taxable income to her, which is $210 per week.

Example: Molly Hatcher has elected to pay for half of her 40 percent share of the short-term disability insurance through the corporate cafeteria plan, which means that 20 percent of the total payments are made with pretax funds, 20 percent with after-tax funds, and 60 percent by the company. Under this scenario, 80 percent of the weekly short-term disability payments are subject to income taxes, thereby increasing her proportion of taxable income to $280.

Under a third-party liability insurance plan, the insurance carrier is responsible for all withholding, if the recipient asks it to do so by filing a Form W-4S. If the insurance carrier transfers this responsibility to the company, then the company must report the amount of taxable liability income received by an employee on its W-2 form at year-end.

Stock Options

A stock option gives an employee the right to buy stock at a specific price within a specific time period. Stock options come in two varieties: the *incentive stock option* (ISO) and the *nonqualified stock option* (NSO).

Incentive stock options are not taxable to the employee at the time they are granted nor at the time when the employee eventually exercises the option to buy stock. If the employee does not dispose of the stock within two years of the date of the option grant or within one year of the date when the option is exercised, then any resulting gain will be taxed as a long-term capital gain. However, if the employee sells the stock within one year of the exercise date, then any gain is taxed as ordinary income. An ISO plan typically requires an employee to exercise any vested stock options within 90 days of that person's voluntary or involuntary termination of employment.

The reduced tax impact associated with waiting until two years have passed from the date of option grant presents a risk to the employee that the value of the related stock will decline in the interim, thereby offsetting the reduced long-term capital gain tax rate achieved at the end of this period. To mitigate the potential loss in stock value, one can make a Section 83(b) election to recognize taxable income on the purchase price of the stock within thirty days following the date when an option is exercised and withhold taxes at the ordinary income tax rate at that time. The employee will not recognize any additional income with respect to the purchased shares until they are sold or otherwise transferred in a taxable transaction, and the additional gain recognized at that time will be taxed at the long-term capital gains rate. It is reasonable to make the Section 83(b) election if the amount of income reported at the time of the election is small and the potential price growth of the stock is significant. On the other hand, it is not reasonable to take the election if there is a combination of high reportable income at the time of election (resulting in a large tax payment) and a minimal chance of growth in the stock price, or that the company can forfeit the options. The Section 83(b) election is not available to holders of options under an NSO plan.

The alternative minimum tax (AMT) must also be considered when dealing with an ISO plan. In essence, the AMT requires that an employee pay tax on the difference between the exercise price and the stock price at the time when an option is exercised, even if the stock is not sold at that time. This can result in a severe cash shortfall for the employee, who may only be able to pay the related taxes by selling the stock. This is a particular problem if the value of the shares subsequently drops, since there is now no source of high-priced stock that can be converted into cash in order to pay the required taxes. This problem arises frequently in cases where a company has just gone public, but employees are restricted from selling their shares for some time after the IPO date, and run the risk of losing stock value during that interval. Establishing the amount of the gain reportable under AMT rules is especially difficult if a company's stock is not publicly held, since there is no clear consensus on the value of the stock. In this case, the IRS will use the value of the per-share price at which the last round of funding was concluded. When the stock is eventually sold, an AMT credit can be charged against the reported gain, but there can be a significant cash shortfall in the meantime. In order to avoid this situation, an employee could choose to exercise options at the point when the estimated value of company shares is quite low, thereby reducing the AMT payment; however, the employee must now find the cash to pay for the stock that he or she has just purchased, and also runs the risk that the shares will not increase in value and may become worthless.

An ISO plan is only valid if it follows these rules:

- Incentive stock options can only be issued to employees. A person must have been working for the employer at all times during the period that begins on the date of grant and ends on the day three months before the date when the option is exercised.
- The option term cannot exceed 10 years from the date of grant. The option term is only five years in the case of an option granted to an employee who, at the time the option is granted, owns stock that has more than 10 percent of the total combined voting power of all classes of stock of the employer.
- The option price at the time it is granted is not less than the fair market value of the stock. However, it must be 110 percent of the fair market value in the case of an option granted to an employee who, at the time the option is granted, owns stock that has more than 10 percent of the total combined voting power of all classes of stock of the employer.
- The total value of all options that can be exercised by any one employee in one year is limited to $100,000. Any amounts exercised that exceed $100,000 will be treated as a nonqualified stock option (to be covered shortly).
- The option cannot be transferred by the employee and can only be exercised during the employee's lifetime.

If the options granted do not include these provisions or are granted to individuals who are not employees under the preceding definition, then the options must be characterized as nonqualified stock options.

A *nonqualified stock option* is not given any favorable tax treatment under the Internal Revenue Code (hence the name). It is also referred to as a *nonstatutory stock option*. The recipient of an NSO does not owe any tax on the date when options are granted unless the options are traded on a public exchange. In that case, the options can be traded at once for value and tax will be recognized on the fair market value of the options on the public exchange as of the grant date. An NSO option will be taxed when it is exercised, based on the difference between the option price and the fair market value of the stock on that day. The resulting gain will be taxed as ordinary income. If the stock appreciates in value after the exercise date, then the incremental gain is taxable at the capital gains rate.

There are no rules governing an NSO, so the option price can be lower than the fair market value of the stock on the grant date. The option price can also be set substantially higher than the current fair market value at the grant date, which is called a *Premium Grant*. It is also possible to issue *Escalating Price Options*, which use a sliding scale for the option price that changes in concert with a peer group index, thereby stripping away the impact of broad changes in the stock market and forcing the company to outperform the stock market in order to achieve any profit from granted stock options. Also, a *Heavenly Parachute* stock option can be created that allows a deceased option holder's estate up to three years in which to exercise his or her options.

Company management should be aware of the impact of both ISO and NSO plans on the company, not just employees. A company receives no tax deduction on a stock option transaction if it uses an ISO plan. However, if it uses an NSO plan, the company will receive a tax deduction equal to the amount of the income that the employee must recognize. If a company does not expect to have any taxable income during the stock option period, then it will receive no immediate value from having a tax deduction (though the deduction can be carried forward to offset income in future years) and so would be more inclined to use an ISO plan. This is a particularly common approach for companies that have not yet gone public. On the other hand, publicly held companies, which are generally more profitable and so must search for tax deductions, will be more inclined to sponsor an NSO plan. Research has shown that most employees who are granted either type of option will exercise it as soon as possible, which essentially converts the tax impact of the ISO plan into an NSO plan. For this reason also, many companies prefer to use NSO plans.

Stock Purchase Plans

Some companies offer stock purchase plans that allow employees to buy company stock at a reduced price. The purchases are typically made through ongoing deductions from employee paychecks and are usually capped at specified percentage of employee pay, such as 15 percent.

Example: The Humble Pie Company offers its stock to employees at a 20 percent discount from the market price. Deductions are made from employee paychecks to cover the cost of shares. Ms. Sally Reed has chosen to have $10 deducted from her pay on an ongoing basis in order to buy this stock. During the first pay period, company stock is publicly traded at $17.50, so the price at which Ms. Reed can buy it from the company is $14.00 ($17.50 market price times [1 − 20%]). However, the deduction is not sufficient to purchase a share, so the company places the funds in a holding account until the next pay period, when another $10 brings the total available funds to $20. The company then deposits one share of stock in the account of Ms. Reed and transfers $14 to its equity account, leaving $6 on hand for the next stock purchase.

Workers' Compensation Benefits

Businesses are required by law to obtain workers' compensation insurance, which provides their employees with wage compensation if they are injured on the job. This insurance may be provided by a state-sponsored fund or by a private insurance entity. The key issue from the payroll perspective is in calculating the cost of the workers' compensation insurance. This calculation occurs once a year, when the insurer sends a form to the company, asking it to list the general category of work performed by the various groups of employees (such as clerical, sales, or manufacturing), as well as the amount of payroll attributable to each category. It behooves the person filling out the form to *legitimately* shift as many employees as possible out of high-risk manufacturing positions, since the insurance cost of these positions is much higher than for clerical positions. Also, be sure to reduce the amount of payroll attributable to each group by any expense reimbursements or nonwage benefits that may be listed as wages, as well as the overtime premium on hours worked. By reducing the total amount of reported payroll expense, the total cost of the workers' compensation insurance will also be reduced.

Example: The payroll manager of the Humble Pie Company was responsible for managing the cost of workers' compensation. In the previous year, she was aware that the 58 manufacturing positions reported to the insurance company were subject to a 4x multiplier for insurance pricing purposes because they worked in risky jobs, while the clerical staff only had a 1x multiplier. Thus, by *legitimately* shifting employees from the manufacturing category to the clerical category, she could reduce the cost of workers' compensation insurance for those positions by 75 percent. In reviewing the payroll records, she found that three production supervisors and one security guard were classified as manufacturing positions. She shifted the classification of these positions to clerical ones.

Benefit Deduction Tracking

A company could be laying itself open to a lawsuit if it makes some types of deductions from employee paychecks without their authorization. The best way to avoid this problem is to have employees sign an authorization notice that clearly specifies the amount and type of any deductions, as well as the start and stop dates for the deductions. An example of such a form is noted in Exhibit 9.2.

These forms should be kept in employee payroll files for immediate access in case an employee later challenges the amount of a deduction. To keep these challenges from occurring, it is useful to have all deductions separately identified on the remittance advice that accompanies each paycheck. For example, if there are deductions for short-term disability and long-term disability insurance, the amount of these deductions should be separately listed.

Exhibit 9.2 *Deduction Authorization Form*

Deduction Authorization Form

I hereby authorize that the following deductions be made from my pay:

Deduction Type	Deduction Amount	Start Date	Stop Date
☐ Cafeteria Plan—Dependent Care			
☐ Cafeteria Plan—Medical			
☐ Dental Insurance			
☐ Dependent Life Insurance			
☐ Long-Term Disability Insurance			
☐ Medical Insurance			
☐ Short-Term Disability Insurance			
☐ Supplemental Life Insurance			

Signature	Date

Summary

The payroll manager is required to have an increasingly in-depth knowledge of the rules associated with a wide range of benefits, partially because they impact record-keeping, withholding, and tax reporting issues, and partially because the payroll department is generally perceived to be similar to the human resources department and may be asked detailed questions about many of these topics by employees. Consequently, it behooves the payroll staff to obtain a high degree of knowledge over benefits-related issues.

10

Payments to Employees

Introduction

This chapter[*] covers the ostensibly simple topic of physically paying employees for their work. Just cut a check? Not exactly. There are a multitude of considerations, such as the allowable and practical frequency of payment, the type of payment to be made (such as in cash, by check or direct deposit, or even directly into an employee's credit card account). There are also a number of state laws governing the allowable time period that can elapse before a terminated employee must be paid—and which varies based on a voluntary or involuntary termination. Finally, there are state-specific laws concerning what to do with unclaimed payments to employees. All of these topics are covered in this chapter.

Frequency of Payment

The frequency of payment to employees covers two areas—the number of days over which pay is accumulated before being paid out and the number of days subsequent to this period before payment is physically made.

Organizations with a large proportion of employees who are relatively transient or who are at very low pay levels usually pay once a week, since their staffs do not have sufficient funds to make it until the next pay period. If these businesses attempt to lengthen the pay period, they usually find that they become a bank to their employees, constantly issuing advances. Consequently, the effort required to issue and track advances offsets the labor savings from calculating and issuing fewer payrolls per month.

The most common pay periods are either biweekly (once every two weeks) or semi-monthly (twice a month). The semi-monthly approach requires 24 payrolls per year, as opposed to the 26 that must be calculated for biweekly payrolls, so there is not much labor difference between the two time periods. However, it is much easier from an accounting perspective to use the semi-monthly approach,

---

[*] This chapter is derived with permission from Chapter 9 of Bragg, *Essentials of Payroll* (Hoboken, NJ: John Wiley and Sons, 2003).

because the information recorded over two payrolls exactly corresponds to the monthly reporting period, so there are fewer accruals to calculate. Offsetting this advantage is the slight difference between the number of days covered by a semi-monthly reporting period and the standard one-week time sheet reporting system. For example, a semi-monthly payroll period covers 15 days, whereas the standard seven-day timecards used by employees mean that only 14 days of timecard information is available to include in the payroll. The usual result is that employees are paid for two weeks of work in each semi-monthly payroll, except for one payroll every three months, in which a third week is also paid that catches up the timing difference between the timecard system and the payroll system.

A monthly pay period is the least common, since it is difficult for low-pay workers to wait so long to be paid. However, it can be useful in cases where employees are highly compensated and can tolerate the long wait. Because there are only 12 payrolls per year, this is highly efficient from the accounting perspective. One downside is that any error in a payroll must usually be rectified with a manual payment, since it is so long before the adjustment can be made to the next regular payroll.

The general provision for payroll periods under state law is that hourly employees be paid no less frequently than biweekly or semi-monthly, while exempt employees can generally be paid once a month. Those states having no special provisions at all or generally requiring pay periods of one month or more are Alabama, Colorado, Florida, Idaho, Iowa, Kansas, Minnesota, Montana, Nebraska, North Dakota, Oregon, Pennsylvania, South Carolina, South Dakota, Washington, and Wisconsin. These rules vary considerably by state, so it is best to consult with the local state government to be certain of the rules.

The other pay frequency issue is how long a company can wait after a pay period is completed before it can issue pay to its employees. A delay of several days is usually necessary in order to provide sufficient time to compile timecards, verify totals, correct errors, calculate withholdings, and create checks. If a company outsources its payroll, there may be additional delays built into the process, due to the payroll input dates mandated by the supplier. A typical range of days over which a pay delay occurs is typically three days to a week. The duration of this interval is frequently mandated by state law and is summarized in Exhibit 10.1.

The days of delay noted in the preceding table are subject to slight changes under certain situations, so one should check applicable state laws to be certain of their exact provisions. Also, any states not shown in the table have no legal provisions for the maximum time period before which payroll payments must be made.

Cash Payments

Cash payments are still used, though this practice tends to be limited to day laborers who work for short periods. It is not a recommended payment approach, since it requires a considerable amount of labor to calculate and distribute cash, and also presents a high risk that the large quantities of cash involved may be stolen. In order to make cash payments, follow these steps:

Exhibit 10.1 *Allowable Days of Payment Delay by State*

Allowable Days of Delay	State
5	Arizona
6	Massachusetts, Vermont
7	Delaware, Hawaii, New York, Washington
8	Connecticut, Maine, New Hampshire
9	Rhode Island
10	California, Colorado, District of Columbia, Indiana, Louisiana, Mississippi, Montana, New Jersey, New Mexico, Utah
11	Oklahoma
12	Iowa
15	Idaho, Kansas, Michigan, Minnesota, Nevada, Ohio, Pennsylvania, Wyoming
16	Missouri
18	Kentucky
20	Tennessee
31	Wisconsin
Special Provisions	Illinois (varies by length of pay period)

1. Calculate the amount of gross pay, deductions, and net pay due to each employee. This can be calculated manually or through the use of payroll software.
2. Write a check to the local bank for the total amount of the payroll that will be paid in cash. This check will be converted into cash.
3. Determine the exact amount of bills and coins required to pay each employee; the form used in Exhibit 10.2 can assist in this process. To use the form, list the net pay due to each person in the second column, and then work across the form from left to right, listing the number of the largest denominations allowable that

Exhibit 10.2 *Payroll Bill and Coin Requirements Form*

Payroll Bill & Coin Requirements Form								Payroll Period Ended _____ May 15 _____	
Employee Name	Net Pay	$20	$10	$5	$1	$0.25	$0.10	$0.05	$0.01
Anderson, John	$129.12	6		1	4		1		2
Brickmeyer, Charles	207.03	10		1	2				3
Caldwell, Dorian	119.82	5	1	1	4	3		1	2
Devon, Ernest	173.14	8	1		3		1		4
Franklin, Gregory	215.19	10	1	1			1	1	4
Hartwell, Alan	198.37	9	1	1	3	1	1		2
Inglenook, Mary	248.43	12		1	3	1	1	1	3
	$1,291.10	60	4	6	19	5	5	3	20

will pay off each person. For example, to determine the exact number of bills and coins required to pay the first person in the form, John Anderson, we determine the maximum number of $20 bills that can be used, which is six. His net pay is $129.12, so six $20 bills will reduce the remainder to $9.12. The next largest useable denomination is the $5 bill, of which one can be used, followed by four $1 bills. This leaves coinage, of which one dime and two pennies are required to complete the payment. After completing the calculation for each employee, cross-foot the form to ensure that the bills and coinage for all employees add up to the total amount of the check that will be cashed at the bank.

4. Highlight the totals row on the form. Take the completed form to the bank along with the check and requisition the correct amount of each type of currency.

5. Obtain a set of pay envelopes, which can be a simple mailing envelope with a stamped fill-in-the-blanks form on the outside. An example of this stamp is shown in Exhibit 10.3. This stamp separately lists the regular and overtime hours worked and then combines this information into a single total earnings amount from which standard deductions are made, with the net pay figure noted at the bottom. If there are other deductions, such as for employee purchases, 401k deductions, and so on, the stamp can be altered to include these items. Write the total earnings, deductions, and net pay in the spaces provided, and as shown in the exhibit. This gives each employee a complete breakdown of how his or her pay was calculated.

Exhibit 10.3 Stamp for Pay Envelope

Employee Name	Wilbur Smythe		
Pay Period Beginning Date	May 8		
Pay Period Ending Date	May 15		
Hours Worked	**Regular:** 40	**Overtime:**	5
Earnings	**Regular:** $ 400	**Overtime:** $	75
Total Earnings	$ 475		
Pay Deductions			
Social Security Tax	$ 29		
Federal Income Tax	$ 100		
Medicare Tax	$ 12		
State Income Tax	$ 47		
Total Deductions	$ 188		
Net Pay	$ 287		

6. When an employee takes receipt of his or her pay envelope, there must be some evidence that the money has shifted into that person's possession, so there are no later claims of not having been paid. This issue is readily solved by creating a pay receipt, an example of which is shown in Exhibit 10.4. This receipt manually lists the name of each employee and the amount of money paid. Each employee must sign this document at the time of cash receipt. It is also useful to have them enter the date when they received the cash, in case there are later claims that moneys were paid out later than the state-mandated date.

The main problem with the form shown in Exhibit 10.4 is that each employee signing the receipt can see the net amount paid to every other employee on the list, which does nothing to preserve the confidentiality of employee pay rates. If this is a problem, use a separate pay receipt page for each employee.

Exhibit 10.4 *Pay Receipt*

For Pay Period Ended May 15, 2003

Employee Name	Cash Paid	Date Received	Employee Signature
Barclay, David	$231.14	May 19, 2003	*David Barclay*
Fairchild, Enoch	$402.19	May 19, 2003	*Enoch Fairchild*
Harley, Jeff	$300.78	May 19, 2003	*Jeff Harley*
Jimenez, Sandra	$220.82	May 19, 2003	*Sandra Jimenez*
Nindle, Allison	$275.03	May 19, 2003	*Allison Nindle*

Check Payments

A far more common method for paying employees is to create a check payment for each one. It is increasingly rare to see a company manually calculate and create payroll checks, since very inexpensive software can be obtained to tackle these chores, as well as the services of any of the dozens of payroll suppliers.

Nonetheless, if checks are prepared manually, one should carefully copy down the information from the payroll register onto the check, using ink so the results cannot be altered. Also, to prevent fraudulent modifications to the check, be sure to write a line through all blank spots on the check, and begin writing as far to the left in each space provided as possible. Once all checks are complete, conduct a final comparison of each one to the payroll register again, possibly including an independent recalculation of the payment to each person.

The much more common method for issuing checks is to integrate their completion into the workings of a standard payroll software package. Under this approach, the software creates a payroll register report, which the payroll manager reviews and approves. If it is acceptable, blank checks are loaded into the local printer and the software quickly churns out completed checks. Checks are then taken to an authorized signer for a final review and signature, though even this step can be avoided by adding a signature image to the checks when they are printed. If the cashed checks are not returned by the bank, then one can either contact it to have a check image mailed to the company or the image can be accessed online and printed out.

If a payroll supplier is used, it will print checks and send them to the company for distribution to employees. Additional services include the incorporation of a signature image to the stamps, stuffing the checks into envelopes, and sending them directly to multiple company locations.

When a company has a sufficient number of employees to warrant issuing a large number of payroll checks, it usually opens a separate bank account from which to issue them. This makes it much easier to reconcile the account at month-end. However, if payroll is outsourced, the checks are run through the supplier's bank account, with only two deductions being made from the company's account—a total deduction for all payroll taxes and a total deduction for all net pay amounts. With only two entries being made per payroll, there is no longer a need for a separate payroll account at the bank.

Direct Deposit Payments

Direct deposit is the most prevalent method for paying employees. It involves the direct transfer of funds from the company payroll account to the personal savings or checking accounts of its employees. By arranging for direct deposit, employees avoid taking paychecks anywhere for cashing, which avoids wasted time and possibly a check-cashing fee. They also avoid the risk of losing a paycheck. It is particularly useful for people who are either on the road or on vacation on payday, since the deposit will be made without their presence.

Direct deposit works most simply if a company uses a payroll supplier, since this third party will have an automated direct deposit linkage. If payroll is processed in-house, then a company must send an electronic file containing information about where money is to be transferred, as well as the accounts into which they will be deposited, to a financial institution that is equipped to process direct deposit transactions. This file is processed through the Automated Clearing House (ACH) network, which transfers the funds. The employer then issues a payment advice to employees, either on paper or electronically, that details their gross pay, taxes and other deductions, and net pay.

Employers can require employees to accept direct deposit, though this requirement is frequently overridden by state laws that require employee concurrence. Consequently, it is best to obtain written permission from employees prior to setting them up for direct deposit payments. This permission should include the routing number of the bank to which payments are to be sent, as well as the account number within that bank, plus the amount of funds to be deposited in each account. Typically, funds may be deposited in multiple accounts, such as $100 in a savings account and the remainder in a checking account. When asking for written permission from employees, it is best to also obtain a voided check for the account to which the funds are to be sent, in order to verify the routing and account numbers. Using a deposit slip to verify this information is not recommended, since the identification numbers on the slip may not match those of the bank.

When an employee signs up for direct deposit, one should inform him that the next paycheck will still be issued as a check, since the direct deposit transaction must first be verified with a prenotification transaction to make sure that a regular paycheck will properly arrive in the employee's account. A prenotification transaction, in which a zero-dollar payment is sent to the employee, is quite useful for verifying that a standard direct deposit transaction will process properly. Consequently, though it is not required, a company should always insist on a prenotification transaction when first setting up an employee on direct deposit.

If a company has locations in multiple states and processes its payroll from a single central location, then the checks sent to outlying locations will take longer to clear (since they are drawn on an out-of-state bank). This issue should be brought to the attention of employees in the outlying locations, which may convince them to switch over to direct deposit payments, which require no timing delay in making payments.

Payments to Employee Credit Cards

Some companies employ people who, for whatever reason, either are unable to set up personal bank accounts or do not choose to. In these cases, they must take their paychecks to a check-cashing service, which charges them a high fee to convert the check into cash. Not only is it expensive, but the check-cashing service can have a long approval process. Also, employees will be carrying large amounts of cash just after cashing their checks, which increases their risk of theft. They also run the risk of losing their paychecks prior to cashing them. Thus, the lack of a bank account poses serious problems for a company's employees.

A good solution to this problem is to set up a Visa debit card, called the Visa Paycard, for any employees requesting one, and then shift payroll funds directly into the card. This allows employees to pull any amount of cash they need from an ATM, rather than the entire amount at one time from a check-cashing service. The card can also be used like a credit card, so that there is little need to make purchases with cash. Further, the fee to convert to cash at an ATM is much lower than the fee charged by a check-cashing service. There is also less risk of theft through the card, since it is protected by a personal identification number (PIN). Employees will also receive a monthly statement showing their account activity, which they can use to get a better idea of their spending habits.

Using this card can be difficult for anyone who speaks English as a second language, or who cannot understand ATM instructions. However, Visa offers multilingual customer service personnel, which reduces the severity of this problem.

The Paycard has only recently been rolled out by Visa and is only available through a few banks. One must contact the company's bank to see if it has this option available. If not, an alternative is to switch the payroll function to the Pay-maxx Internet site (found at *www.paymaxx.com*), which offers the Paycard option.

Termination Payments

There are a variety of state laws that govern how soon employees are to be paid after their employment is terminated. The key factor in these laws is whether or not an employee leaves a company under his or her own volition or if the termination was forced by the company. Exhibit 10.5 lists the time periods by state by which termination pay must be given to those employees who have voluntarily left employment. In all cases, the intervals listed are for the *earlier* of the next regularly scheduled pay date or the number of days listed in the first column. If a state is not listed in the table, then assume that the termination payment is required at the time of the next regularly scheduled pay date.

Exhibit 10.5 *Required Pay Interval for Voluntary Terminations*	
Maximum Payment Delay	**Applicable States**
4 Days	California
5 Days	Oregon, Wyoming
7 Days	District of Columbia, Nevada
10 Days	Idaho
14 Days	Kentucky, Maine, Nebraska
15 Days	Louisiana, Montana
20 Days	Minnesota
21 Days	Tennessee

Exhibit 10.6 lists the time periods by state by which termination pay must be given to those employees who have involuntarily left employment. In all cases, the intervals listed are for the *earlier* of the next regularly scheduled pay date or the number of days listed in the first column. If a state is not listed in the table, it does not regulate the required pay interval. Also, note that many more states have adopted early-payment laws for involuntary terminations, indicating a much greater degree of interest in paying off employees who fall into this category.

If the human resources department is coordinating an employee layoff, it is best to notify the payroll supervisor at least a day in advance, so this person can coordinate the proper calculation, printing, and signing of termination payments before the layoffs are begun. By doing so, an employer can hand out final paychecks at the time of termination and not have to worry about state laws that sometimes mandate immediate payments to employees. Also, by calculating these payments in advance, there is less chance of incorporating a calculation error, which is likelier to occur when under the pressure of having a terminated employee waiting for the final payment.

Exhibit 10.6 *Required Pay Interval for Involuntary Terminations*

Maximum Payment Delay	Applicable States
Immediately	California, Colorado, Hawaii, Illinois, Massachusetts, Michigan, Minnesota, Missouri, Montana, Nevada
Next Regular Payday	Delaware, Idaho, Indiana, Iowa, Kansas, Louisiana, Maine, Maryland, New Jersey, New York, North Carolina, North Dakota, Oklahoma, Pennsylvania, Puerto Rico, Rhode Island, South Dakota, Tennessee, Virginia, Washington, Wisconsin
1 Day	Connecticut, District of Columbia, Oregon, Utah
2 Days	South Carolina
3 Days	Alaska, Arizona
4 Days	New Hampshire, Vermont, West Virginia
5 Days	New Mexico, Wyoming
6 Days	Texas
7 Days	Arkansas
14 Days	Kentucky, Nebraska

Unclaimed Pay

Sometimes when an employee is terminated or becomes aware of a garnishment order that is about to be implemented against him, an employee will disappear without taking receipt of a final paycheck. These paychecks should not be cancelled and the funds retained by the company. Instead, individual state laws typically mandate some effort to contact an employee, followed by the state taking ownership of the pay after a designated waiting period. The amount of the waiting period by state is shown in Exhibit 10.7.:

Exhibit 10.7 *Years Required to Hold Unclaimed Pay, by State*

Number of Years to Hold	Applicable States
1	Alabama, Alaska, Arizona, Arkansas, Colorado, District of Columbia, Florida, Georgia, Hawaii, Idaho, Indiana, Kansas, Louisiana, Maine, Michigan, Minnesota, Montana, Nebraska, Nevada, New Hampshire, New Jersey, New Mexico, Ohio, Oklahoma, Rhode Island, South Carolina, South Dakota, Tennessee, Utah, Virginia, Washington, West Virginia, Wisconsin, Wyoming
2	North Carolina, North Dakota, Vermont
3	California, Connecticut, Iowa, Maryland, Massachusetts, New York, Oregon, Pennsylvania, Texas
5	Delaware, Illinois, Mississippi, Missouri
7	Kentucky

Most states also require that these unclaimed pay amounts be listed on an annual report that is filed with the state.

Summary

The state-imposed limitations noted in the "Frequency of Payment" section are generally not a problem, since all states allow at least a one-week delay between the termination of a reporting period and required payments to employees. It is much easier to run afoul of state laws in the area of termination payments, since many states require payments either immediately or within one day to employees who are involuntarily terminated. Making sure that these payments are made in a timely manner requires tight coordination between the payroll and human resources departments. State laws regarding the remittance of unclaimed wages are usually easy to follow, since this is a rare circumstance. Of the options presented for paying employees, cash payments are the least recommended, since this option requires additional controls over increased levels of cash on hand, and is more labor intensive to process than other payment methods.

11

Unemployment Insurance

Introduction

Federal and state unemployment taxes were initiated in order to create unemployment funds, which give former employees some money to tide them over until they can find work again. The laws supporting these actions were the Social Security Act and the Federal Unemployment Tax Act (see Chapter 14 for descriptions).

Benefits are paid by the state-sponsored programs, which require a short waiting period (usually a week, plus the vacation, holiday, and severance pay portion of any final payment) before payments can be made to unemployed persons. The amount paid is a percentage of a person's former pay, up to a low maximum level. If an employee looks for work and proves it by reporting back to the state agency, then payments can continue for up to half a year. The amount of benefits, their calculation, and the terms of payment vary by state program.

In this chapter,[*] we review several components of the unemployment tax program, including the calculation of both federal and state unemployment taxes, the calculation of the contribution rate, the reason for filing voluntary unemployment tax contributions, and how to fill out the 940 and 940-EZ forms.

The Federal Unemployment Tax

The Federal Unemployment Tax (FUTA) is paid by employers only. It is currently set at 6.2 percent of the first $7,000 of a person's wages earned in a year. However, the actual amount paid to the federal government is substantially lower, since employers take a credit based on the amount of funds paid into their state unemployment programs (not including any FUTA payments deducted from employee pay, additional penalties paid as part of the state-assigned percentage, and any voluntary contributions to the state unemployment fund). Employers with a history of minimal layoffs can receive an extra credit above amounts paid into their state funds that brings their total credit against the federal tax to 5.4 percent. When the maximum credit amount is applied to the federal tax rate, the effective

---

[*]This chapter is derived with permission from Chapter 10 of Bragg, *Essentials of Payroll* (Hoboken, NJ: John Wiley and Sons, 2003).

rate paid drops to 0.8 percent. This maximum credit is based on 90 percent of the total federal rate.

If a state experiences a large amount of unemployment claims and uses up its funds, it can borrow money from the federal fund, which must be paid back by the end of the next calendar year. If not, then the amount of the FUTA credit is reduced for employers within that state, which brings in enough additional funds to eventually pay back the loan.

According to government instructions accompanying the Form 940 (see the later section describing it), FUTA taxes are *not* payable in the following situations:

- When a household employer pays cash wages of less than $1,000 for all household employees in any calendar quarter for household work in a private home, local college club, or local chapter of a college fraternity or sorority.

- When an agricultural employer pays cash wages of less than $20,000 to farm workers in any calendar quarter, or employs fewer than 10 farm workers during at least some part of a day during any 20 or more different weeks during the year.

- When wages are paid to an H-2(A) visa worker.

- When services are rendered to a federally-recognized Indian tribal government.

- When the employer is a religious, educational, or charitable organization that qualifies as a 501(c)(3) entity under the federal tax laws.

- The employer is a state or local government.

Also, wages are not subject to the tax if they are noncash payments, expense reimbursements, or various disability payments. Also, there is no FUTA requirement for full-commission insurance agents, working inmates, work within a family, work by nonemployees (such as consultants), and several other limited situations.

An employer must calculate the amount of FUTA tax owed at the end of each calendar quarter, after which it must be deposited (see next section). If there are no new hires during the year, this usually results in nearly all FUTA taxes being paid in the first quarter, with the remainder falling into the second quarter.

If payroll is outsourced, the supplier makes money by withholding the FUTA tax in every pay period and retaining the funds in an interest-bearing account until they are due for payment to the government at the end of the quarter.

Depositing FUTA Taxes

When a company applies for an Employer Identification Number (EIN), the IRS will send a Federal Tax Deposit Coupon book containing a number of Form 8109s, which are used as an attachment that identifies each type of deposit made to the IRS. When making a deposit, black out the "940" box on the form. Deposits should be made at a local bank that is authorized to accept federal tax deposits; deposits should not be mailed to the IRS. It is also useful to list the business's EIN, form number, and period for which the payment is being made on the accompanying check, in case the IRS loses the Tax Deposit Coupon. The check should be made out to the "United States Treasury."

FUTA deposits are made once a quarter, and must be completed within 30 days of the end of the preceding calendar quarter. However, if the 30th day of the filing period falls on a weekend or federal holiday, then it may be filed on the following business day. The deposit schedule for a typical year is shown in Exhibit 11.1.

Exhibit 11.1 *FUTA Deposit Schedule*

For the first quarter	January thru March	Must pay by	April 30
For the second quarter	April thru June	Must pay by	July 31
For the third quarter	July thru September	Must pay by	October 31
For the fourth quarter	October thru December	Must pay by	January 31

If the total amount of FUTA due in any quarter is less than $100, then the deposit can be skipped for that quarter. Instead, roll the outstanding amount into the next quarter. If the sub-$100 amount continues for multiple quarters, it must still be paid following the year-end quarter, when the Form 940 is filed.

If FUTA deposits are filed late, a penalty will be assessed by the IRS. The amount is 2 percent of the amount of the late deposit if it is no more than 5 days late; 5 percent if between 6 and 15 days late; 10 percent if more than 15 days late; or 15 percent if not paid within 10 days from the date of the company's receipt of a delinquency notice from the IRS. This penalty may be waived for small businesses or those who have just started filing payments.

Filing the 940 and 940-EZ Forms

The FUTA tax return is used to calculate how much was paid out in wages during the preceding year, how much of this amount was subject to the FUTA tax, the amount of the tax, and any prior quarterly deposits made to reduce the payable tax, resulting in a net payment due to the government. The form must be filed no later than January 31 of the year following the reporting year, or by February 10 if all quarterly deposits for the calendar year were made in a timely manner. The form can be filed at an even later date if the company requests an extension from the IRS, but this is only for submission of the form—all quarterly payments must still be filed by the required dates.

A company can file the Form 940-EZ instead of the Form 940 if it paid unemployment contributions to only one state, paid all state unemployment taxes by January 31, and all wages that were taxable for the FUTA tax were also taxable for its state unemployment tax. An IRS chart showing the logic steps for this decision is shown in Exhibit 11.2.

Exhibit 11.2 *Decision Steps for Use of the 940-EZ Form*

Form 940-EZ (2002)   Page **2**

Who May Use Form 940-EZ

The following chart will lead you to the right form to use—

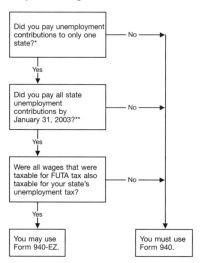

***Do not file Form 940-EZ if—**
- **You owe FUTA tax only for household work in a private home. See Schedule H (Form 1040).**
- **You are a successor employer claiming a credit for state unemployment contributions paid by a prior employer. File Form 940.**

****If you deposited all FUTA tax when due,you may answer "YES" if you paid all state unemployment contributions by February 10, 2003.**

The Form 940 is shown in Exhibit 11.3. To fill out the form, follow these steps:

1. *Identification section.* If the form is not preaddressed, fill in the business's address and employer identification number (EIN). If there is no EIN, apply for one with the Form SS-4. If no EIN has been received from the government by the time the form is due to be filed, print "Applied For" and the date of application in this area.

2. *Questions A-C.* If the answers to all three questions posed in this section are "Yes," then one may file the simpler Form 940-EZ instead. Any "No" answers require completion of the Form 940. The questions match the logic steps noted earlier in Exhibit 11.2.

3. *Amended or final return.* There are two check-off boxes immediately above the "Part I" section. Check off the first box if there will be no future FUTA

Exhibit 11.3 *The Form 940*

Form **940**	Employer's Annual Federal	OMB No. 1545-0028
Department of the Treasury Internal Revenue Service (99)	Unemployment (FUTA) Tax Return ▶ See separate Instructions for Form 940 for information on completing this form.	2002

You must complete this section. ▶	⌐ Name (as distinguished from trade name) Calendar year ⌐ Trade name, if any Address and ZIP code Employer identification number	T
		FF
		FD
		FP
		I
	L ⌐	T

A   Are you required to pay unemployment contributions to only one state? (If "No," skip questions B and C) .   ☐ Yes   ☐ No

B   Did you pay all state unemployment contributions by January 31, 2003? ((1) If you deposited your total FUTA tax when due, check "Yes" if you paid all state unemployment contributions by February 10, 2003. (2) If a 0% experience rate is granted, check "Yes." (3) If "No," skip question C.) . . . .   ☐ Yes   ☐ No

C   Were all wages that were taxable for FUTA tax also taxable for your state's unemployment tax? . . . . .   ☐ Yes   ☐ No

If you answered "No" to any of these questions, you must file Form 940. If you answered "Yes" to all the questions, you may file Form 940-EZ, which is a simplified version of Form 940. (Successor employers, see Special credit for successor employers   on page 2 of the instructions.) You can get Form 940-EZ by calling 1-800-TAX-FORM (1-800-829-3676) or from the IRS Web Site at www.irs.gov.

If you will not have to file returns in the future, check here   (see Who Must File   in separate instructions) and complete and sign the return   . . . . ▶ ☐

If this is an Amended Return, check here   (see Amended Returns   on page 2 of the separate instructions) . . . . ▶ ☐

Part I   Computation of Taxable Wages

1   Total payments (including payments shown on lines 2 and 3) during the calendar year for services of employees . . . . | 1 |

2   Exempt payments. (Explain all exempt payments, attaching additional sheets if necessary.) ▶ --------------------------------------
-- | 2 |

3   Payments of more than $7,000 for services. Enter only amounts over the first $7,000 paid to each employee. (see separate instructions) Do not include any exempt payments from line 2. The $7,000 amount is the Federal wage base. Your state wage base may be different. Do not use your state wage limitation . . . . | 3 |

4   Add lines 2 and 3 . . . . | 4 |

5   Total taxable wages   (subtract line 4 from line 1) . . . . ▶ | 5 |

Be sure to complete both sides of this form, and sign in the space provided on the back.

For Privacy Act and Paperwork Reduction Act Notice, see separate instructions.   ▼ DETACH HERE ▼   Cat. No. 11234O   Form 940 (2002)

Form **940-V**	Form 940 Payment Voucher	OMB No. 1545-0028
Department of the Treasury Internal Revenue Service	Use this voucher only when making a payment with your return.	2002

Complete boxes 1, 2, and 3. Do not send cash, and do not staple your payment to this voucher. Make your check or money order pa yable to the "United States Treasury." Be sure to enter your employer identification number, "Form 940," and "2002" on your payment.

1 Enter your employer identification number.	2		Dollars	Cents
	Enter the amount of your payment. ▶			
	3 Enter your business name (individual name for sole proprietors).			
	Enter your address.			
	Enter your city, state, and ZIP code.			

Exhibit 11.3 *(Continued)*

Form 940 (2002)   Page 2

Part II	Tax Due or Refund		
1	Gross FUTA tax. (Multiply the wages from Part I, line 5, by .062)	1	
2	Maximum credit. (Multiply the wages from Part I, line 5, by .054) .	2	
3	Computation of tentative credit (Note: All taxpayers must complete the applicable columns.)		

(a) Name of state	(b) State reporting number(s) as shown on employer's state contribution returns	(c) Taxable payroll (as defined in state act)	(d) State experience rate period		(e) State experience rate	(f) Contributions if rate had been 5.4% (col. (c) x .054)	(g) Contributions payable at experience rate (col. (c) x col. (e))	(h) Additional credit (col. (f) minus col.(g)) If 0 or less, enter -0-	(i) Contributions paid to state by 940 due date
			From	To					

3a	Totals . . . ▶			
3b	Total tentative credit (add line 3a, columns (h) and (i) only—for late payments, also see the instructions for Part II, line 6) . . . . ▶	3b	
4			
5			
6	Credit: Enter the smaller of the amount from Part II, line 2 or line 3b; or the amount from the worksheet on page 5 of the separate instructions	6	
7	Total FUTA tax (subtract line 6 from line 1). If the result is over $100, also complete Part III . .	7	
8	Total FUTA tax deposited for the year, including any overpayment applied from a prior year . .	8	
9	Balance due (subtract line 8 from line 7). Pay to the "United States Treasury." If you owe more than $100, see Depositing FUTA Tax on page 3 of the separate instructions . . . . . . ▶	9	
10	Overpayment (subtract line 7 from line 8). Check if it is to be: ☐ Applied to next return or ☐ Refunded . . . . ▶	10	

Part III	Record of Quarterly Federal Unemployment Tax Liability (Do not include state liability.) Complete only if line 7 is over $100. See page 6 of the separate instructions.				
	Quarter	First (Jan. 1–Mar. 31)	Second (Apr. 1–June 30)	Third (July 1–Sept. 30)	Fourth (Oct. 1–Dec. 31)	Total for year
Liability for quarter					

Third Party Designee	Do you want to allow another person to discuss this return with the IRS (see instructions page 6)? ☐ Yes. Complete the following. ☐ No
	Designee's name ▶ Phone no. ▶ ( ) Personal identification number (PIN) ▶ ☐☐☐☐☐

Under penalties of perjury, I declare that I have examined this return, including accompanying schedules and statements, and, t o the best of my knowledge and belief, it is true, correct, and complete, and that no part of any payment made to a state unemployment fund claimed as a credit was, or is t o be, deducted from the payments to employees.

Signature ▶   Title (Owner, etc.) ▶   Date ▶

✹   Form **940** (2002)

filings, or the second one if this is an amended return. Otherwise, continue to "Part I."

4. *Total payments (Part I, Line 1).* Enter the total gross wages paid during the calendar year to employees, including wages not eligible for the FUTA tax. Total gross wages should include commissions, bonuses, 401k plan contributions, the fair value of goods paid, and vacation and sick pay.

5. *Exempt payments (Part 1, Line 2).* Include all wages that are exempt from the FUTA tax. Many of these exemptions were noted earlier under the "Federal Unemployment Tax" section. Do not include in this line any wages exceeding the statutory $7,000 annual wage limitation on the FUTA tax, since this is addressed by the next line item.

6. *Wages exceeding $7,000 (Part I, Line 3).* Enter the total amount of wages paid that exceed the $7,000 annual wage limitation on the FUTA tax.

7. *Total taxable wages (Part I, Line 5).* Subtract the total exempt payments and total payments exceeding $7,000 from the total payments to arrive at this figure.

8. *Gross FUTA tax (Part I, Line 2).* Multiply the total taxable wages noted in the last line by 6.2 percent to arrive at the maximum possible FUTA tax liability.

9. *Maximum credit (Part II, Line 2).* Multiply the total taxable wages calculated two lines ago by 5.4 percent to arrive at the maximum possible FUTA tax credit.

10. *Computation of credit (Part II, Line 3).* This is a table requiring entries in a number of columns. The information to be entered in these columns is:

   - *Name of state.* Enter the two-letter abbreviation representing the state in which wages were paid.

   - *State reporting number.* Enter the State Identification Number assigned to the company by the state referenced in the first column.

   - *Taxable payroll.* Enter the total wages paid within the identified state that each state has defined as being subject to unemployment taxes.

   - *State experience rate period.* Enter the beginning and ending dates covered by the state experience rate that is listed in the following column. If an experience rate is granted partway through a year, then enter one line for the period of the calendar year covered by the first experience rate, and a second line for the period covered by the succeeding experience rate.

   - *State experience rate.* Enter the experience rate percentage. This is the percentage assigned to a company by each state in which it does business. It is based on the amount of unemployment tax paid, as well as the amount of unemployment compensation paid to former employees. The latest experience rate is usually mailed to an employer once a year, but one may also call the state unemployment office to obtain it.

   - *Contributions if rate had been 5.4 percent.* Multiply the taxable payroll from the third column by 5.4 percent.

   - *Contributions payable at experience rate.* Multiply the taxable payroll from the third column by the state experience rate.

   - *Additional credit.* Subtract the total contributions payable at the experience rate from the total contributions if the rate had been 5.4 percent. If the result is zero or less, enter a zero in this field. Otherwise, enter the difference.

   - *Contributions paid to state by 940 due date.* Enter the total amount of all payments actually paid to the state by the due date for this tax. Any amounts not paid are excluded from this calculation, which essentially imposes a significant penalty on any FUTA late payers.

11. *Total tentative credit (Part II, Line 3b).* Combine the totals from the additional credit and state contributions columns. The result is the minimum total amount of the credit that can potentially be applied against the FUTA tax.

12. *Credit (Part II, Line 6).* This is the actual amount of credit used to offset the FUTA tax. It is the *lesser* of the total tentative credit (which is based on ac-

tual payments to state governments) or the theoretical maximum credit of 5.4 percent of applicable wages.

13. *Total FUTA tax (Part II, Line 7).* Subtract the preceding credit from the total amount of the gross FUTA tax listed in Line 2 of Part II. If the amount of this tax exceeds $100, be sure to complete Part III of the form as well.

14. *Total FUTA tax deposited (Part II, Line 8).* Summarize all FUTA payments already made, as well as any overpayment carry forward from the previous year.

15. *Balance due (Part II, Line 9).* Subtract the total amount of FUTA taxes already deposited from the total amount of the tax to arrive at the net liability. If the amount due is less than $1, do not pay it.

16. *Record of quarterly FUTA liability (Part III).* This section should only be completed if a company's total annual FUTA tax exceeds $100. If so, enter the amount of the liability for each quarter of the year, as well as the grand total.

The Form 940-EZ is significantly easier to complete, though it only applies to a restricted number of situations, as outlined earlier in Exhibit 11.2. The Form 940-EZ is shown in Exhibit 11.4. To fill out the form, follow these steps:

1. *Identification section.* If the form is not preaddressed, fill in the business's address and employer identification number (EIN). If there is no EIN, apply for one with the Form SS-4. If no EIN has been received by the government by the time the form is due to be filed, print "Applied For" and the date of application in this area.

2. *Amount of contributions paid.* List the total amount of contributions made to the unemployment fund of the state in which the company does business.

3. *State and identification number.* Enter the name of the state where the company does business, as well as the identification number assigned to the company by the state.

4. *Total payments (Part I, Line 1).* Enter the total gross wages paid during the calendar year to employees, including wages not eligible for the FUTA tax. Total gross wages should include commissions, bonuses, 401k plan contributions, the fair value of goods paid, and vacation and sick pay.

5. *Exempt payments (Part I, Line 2).* Include all wages that are exempt from the FUTA tax. Many of these exemptions were noted earlier under the "Federal Unemployment Tax" section. Do not include in this line any wages exceeding the statutory $7,000 annual wage limitation on the FUTA tax, since this is addressed by the next line item.

6. *Wages exceeding $7,000 (Part I, Line 3).* Enter the total amount of wages paid that exceed the $7,000 annual wage limitation on the FUTA tax.

Exhibit 11.4 *The Form 940-EZ*

Form **940-EZ**	Employer's Annual Federal	OMB No. 1545-1110

Department of the Treasury
Internal Revenue Service   (99)

Employer's Annual Federal
Unemployment (FUTA) Tax Return

▶ See separate Instructions for Form 940-EZ for information on completing this form.

2002

			T	

You must complete this section. ▶

Name (as distinguished from trade name)   Calendar year

Trade name, if any

Address and ZIP code   Employer identification number

FF
FD
FP
I
T

Answer the questions under Who May Use Form 940-EZ on page 2. If you cannot use Form 940-EZ, you must use Form 940.

A   Enter the amount of contributions paid to your state unemployment fund. (see separate instructions)   .   .   ▶ $ ....

B   (1) Enter the name of the state where you have to pay contributions   .   .   .   .   ▶ ----------------------------------

      (2) Enter your state reporting number as shown on your state unemployment tax return ▶

If you will not have to file returns in the future, check here   (see Who Must File in separate instructions) and complete and sign the return.   ▶ ☐

If this is an Amended Return, check here   (see Amended Returns on page 2 of the separate instructions)   .   .   .   .   ▶ ☐

Part I   Taxable Wages and FUTA Tax

1	Total payments (including payments shown on lines 2 and 3) during the calendar year for services of employees	1	
2	Exempt payments. (Explain all exempt payments, attaching additional sheets if necessary.) ▶	2	
3	Payments of more than $7,000 for services. Enter only amounts over the first $7,000 paid to each employee. (see separate instructions)	3	
4	Add lines 2 and 3	4	
5	Total taxable wages (subtract line 4 from line 1) . . . . ▶	5	
6	FUTA tax. Multiply the wages on line 5 by .008 and enter here. (If the result is over $100, also complete Part II.)	6	
7	Total FUTA tax deposited for the year, including any overpayment applied from a prior year	7	
8	Balance due (subtract line 7 from line 6). Pay to the "United States Treasury." . . . . ▶	8	
	If you owe more than $100, see Depositing FUTA tax in separate instructions.		
9	Overpayment (subtract line 6 from line 7). Check if it is to be: ☐ Applied to next return or ☐ Refunded ▶	9	

Part II   Record of Quarterly Federal Unemployment Tax Liability   (Do not include state liability.) Complete only if line 6 is over $100.

Quarter	First (Jan. 1 – Mar. 31)	Second (Apr. 1 – June 30)	Third (July 1 – Sept. 30)	Fourth (Oct. 1 – Dec. 31)	Total for year
Liability for quarter					

Third Party Designee

Do you want to allow another person to discuss this return with the IRS (see instructions page 5)? ☐ Yes. Complete the following.   ☐ No

Designee's name ▶		Phone no. ▶ ( )		Personal identification number (PIN) ▶	

Under penalties of perjury, I declare that I have examined this return, including accompanying schedules and statements, and, t o the best of my knowledge and belief, it is true, correct, and complete, and that no part of any payment made to a state unemployment fund claimed as a credit was, or is t o be, deducted from the payments to employees.

Signature ▶   Title (Owner, etc.) ▶   Date ▶

For Privacy Act and Paperwork Reduction Act Notice, see separate instructions.   ▼ **DETACH HERE** ▼   Cat. No. 10983G   Form **940-EZ** (2002)

Form **940-EZ(V)**	Form 940-EZ Payment Voucher	OMB No. 1545-1110

Department of the Treasury
Internal Revenue Service

Use this voucher only when making a payment with your return.

2002

Complete boxes 1, 2, and 3. Do not send cash, and do not staple your payment to this voucher. Make your check or money order pa yable to the "United States Treasury." Be sure to enter your employer identification number, "Form 940-EZ," and "2002" on your payment.

1 Enter your employer identification number.

2		Dollars	Cents
	Enter the amount of your payment. ▶		

3 Enter your business name (individual name for sole proprietors).

Enter your address.

Enter your city, state, and ZIP code.

7. *Total taxable wages (Part I, Line 5)*. Subtract the total exempt payments and total payments exceeding $7,000 from the total payments to arrive at this figure.

8. *Gross FUTA tax (Part I, Line 6)*. Multiply the total taxable wages noted in the last line by 6.2 percent to arrive at the maximum possible FUTA tax liability.

9. *Total FUTA tax deposited (Part I, Line 7)*. Summarize all FUTA payments already made, as well as any overpayment carry forward from the previous year.

10. *Balance due (Part I, Line 8)*. Subtract the total amount of FUTA taxes already deposited from the total amount of the tax to arrive at the net liability. If the amount due is less than $1, do not pay it.

11. *Record of quarterly FUTA liability (Part II)*. This section should only be completed if a company's total annual FUTA tax exceeds $100. If so, enter the amount of the liability for each quarter of the year, as well as the grand total.

For both the Form 940 and Form 940-EZ, if a fourth quarter payment of less than $100 is due, fill out the Payment Voucher located at the bottom of either form, listing the amount of the payment, the business name and address, and its EIN number. It is also useful to list the EIN, form number, and payment period covered on the accompanying check, in case the IRS loses the accompanying voucher.

The State Unemployment Tax

Tax rates imposed by states can be quite low, but can range up to 5.4 percent (the amount of the credit allowed against the federal unemployment tax), and some states even exceed this amount. The rate charged is based on a company's history of avoiding layoffs, which is called an experience rating. If it lays off a large proportion of its employees, then this action will likely drain a significant amount from the state's unemployment funds through the payment of unemployment benefits. Thus, a layoff in one year will likely be followed by a notice increasing the state unemployment tax (or "contribution") rate. Keeping this in mind, if a possible layoff is coming up, it may be worthwhile to verify the exact time period over which the next contribution rate calculation will be made (usually the calendar year), and then time the layoff for a period immediately thereafter, so that the contribution rate for the next year will not be affected. By taking this action, the contribution rate in the *following* year will increase as a result of the layoff, thereby pushing the added expense further into the future.

A business that is buying another company may have the opportunity to do so because the acquiree has fallen on hard times, and so can be purchased for a minimal price. However, if the acquiree has been laying off staff in the year leading up to the acquisition (quite likely, if there have been cash shortfalls), the acquirer may find itself saddled with a very high state unemployment contribution rate in the upcoming year. The acquirer can avoid this problem by purchasing the assets of the acquiree, rather than the entire business entity, thereby eliminating the acquiree's poor experience rating as tracked by the state unemployment agency.

The taxable wage base used by states is required by federal law to be at least as much as the federal level, which is currently set at $7,000. Exhibit 11.5 shows the employer tax rates, employee tax rates (where rarely applicable), taxable wage limits, and coverages for all 50 states, plus the District of Columbia and Puerto Rico. There is also a column covering the *new* employer tax rate, which lists the default tax rate given to any company that does not yet have an experience rating. This default rate can change in some cases (see Note 1 to the exhibit), depending upon the industry in which a new organization is based; industries with historically high employee turnover rates deplete the state unemployment funds more rapidly, so companies operating in those industries are assigned a higher contribution rate.

When a person's employment is terminated, he or she goes to the local state unemployment office and applies for unemployment benefits. The state agency then sends a form to the company, asking it to verify basic information about the former employee, such as the amount of hourly pay at the time of termination and the amount and composition of the severance payment. After verification, the state sends the employer another form, notifying it of the maximum amount of unemployment benefits that can be paid to the employee (which can be greatly reduced if the employee finds work soon). A key issue in this process is whether an employee was terminated for cause (such as theft), was laid off, or voluntarily resigned. Unemployment benefits are not paid when a person quits or is terminated for cause, so be sure to contest employee benefit claims if either case was the cause for termination. Proper documentation of the termination is crucial to this determination, which is made by an employee of the state division of employment. If determination is made in favor of the former employee, then any benefits paid will be charged against the company, which will impact its experience rating and therefore increase the amount of its contribution rate in the following year.

States have a preference for defining contractors as employees, since an employer can then be required to pay unemployment taxes based on the pay of these individuals. To determine the status of an employee under a state unemployment insurance program, one can use some portion or all of the ABC Test, which means that a person is a contractor only if:

- There is an **A**bsence of control by the company,
- **B**usiness conducted by the employee is substantially different from that of the company, or is conducted away from its premises, and
- The person **C**ustomarily works independently from the company as a separate business.

Twenty-six states use all three of these tests in determining the status of an employee or contractor, while eight use just the first and third tests.

Exhibit 11.5 State Wage Bases Used for State Unemployment Tax Calculations

State	Employer Tax Rate	New Employer Tax Rate	Employee Withholding Rate	Taxable Wage Limit	Coverage
Alabama	2.7%–6.8%	2.7%	None	$8,000	Same as federal
Alaska	5.4%	(1)	0.5%–1.0%	$26,700	Any company paying 1+ employees for at least a day in the year
Arizona	5.4% Std	2.7%	None	$7,000	Same as federal
Arkansas	0.5%–10.4%	3.3%	None	$9,500	Any company paying 1+ employees for at least 10 days in the current or preceding year
California	0.7%–5.4%	3.4%	None	$7,000	Any company paying 1+ employees in the current or preceding year
Colorado	1.7% Std	1.7%	None	$10,000	Any company paying 1+ employees for at least a day in the year
Connecticut	0.5%–5.4%	2.1%	None	$15,000	Same as federal
Delaware	5.4% Std	1.8%	None	$8,500	Same as federal
District of Columbia	2.7% Std	2.7%	None	$9,000	Any company paying 1+ employees in the current year
Florida	0.1%–5.4%	2.7%	None	$7,000	Same as federal
Georgia	5.4% Std	2.7%	None	$8,500	Same as federal
Hawaii	0%–5.4%	3.0%	None	$30,200	Any company paying 1+ employees in the current year
Idaho	1.5% Std	—	None	$27,600	Any company with 1+ employees in 20 weeks of the current or preceding year
Illinois	0.6%–7.2%	3.3%	None	$9,000	Same as federal
Indiana	5.4% Std	2.7%	None	$7,000	Same as federal
Iowa	0%–7.5%	—	None	$19,200	Same as federal
Kansas	0.6%–5.4%	2%	None	$8,000	Same as federal
Kentucky	0%–10%	2.7%	None	$8,000	Same as federal
Louisiana	0.14%–6.2%	(1)	None	$7,000	Same as federal
Maine	5.4% Std	0.14%–1.3%	None	$12,000	Same as federal
Maryland	0.3%–7.5%	1.8%	None	$8,500	Same as federal
Massachusetts	1.4%–7.3%	2.2%	None	$10,800	Any company with 1+ employees in 13 weeks of the current or preceding year

192

State	Employer Tax Rate	New Employer Tax Rate	Employee Withholding Rate	Taxable Wage Limit	Coverage
Michigan	0.1%–9%	2.7%	None	$9,000	Any company with 1+ emloyees in 20 weeks of the current or preceding year or is subject to FUTA
Minnesota	0.47%–8.63%	1.51%	None	$22,000	Same as federal
Mississippi	5.4% Std	2.7%	None	$7,000	Same as federal
Missouri	0%–9%	3.51%	None	$7,500	Same as federal
Montana	6.5% Max	(1)	None	$19,700	Any company with payroll of $1,000+ in current or preceding year
Nebraska	.05%–5.4%	3.5%	None	$7,000	Same as federal
Nevada	0.25%–5.4%	2.95%	None	$21,500	Any company paying 1+ employees in the current year
New Hampshire	0.05%–6.5%	2.7%	None	$8,000	Same as federal
New Jersey	0.3%–5.4%	(2)	None	$23,900	Any company paying wages of $1,000+ in current or preceding year
New Mexico	0.05%–5.4%	2.7%	None	$16,000	Any company with 1+ employees in 20 weeks of the current or preceding year
New York	1.1%–9.5%	4.1%	None	$8,500	Any company paying $300+ in wages in any calendar quarter
North Carolina	0%–5.7%	1.2%	None	$15,900	Same as federal
North Dakota	0.49%–10.09%	2.08%	None	$18,000	Same as federal
Ohio	0.1%–6.5%	2.7%	None	$9,000	Same as federal
Oklahoma	0.1%–5.5%	1.0%	None	$11,700	Same as federal
Oregon	1.2%–5.4%	3.1%	None	$26,000	Any company with 1+ employees in 18 weeks of the year
Pennsylvania	5.4%–9.2%	3.5%	None	$8,000	Any company with 1+ employees in the calendar year
Puerto Rico	1.0%–5.4%	2.9%	None	$7,000	Any company with 1+ employees in the current or preceding calendar year
Rhode Island	0.06%–10%	1.79%	None	$12,000	Any company with 1+ employees in the year
South Carolina	0.74%–6.1%	2.7%	None	$7,000	Same as federal
South Dakota	0%–7.0%	1.9%	None	$7,000	Same as federal
Tennessee	0%–10%	2.7%	None	$7,000	Same as federal

Exhibit 11.3 *(Continued)*

State	Employer Tax Rate	New Employer Tax Rate	Employee Withholding Rate	Taxable Wage Limit	Coverage
Texas	0%–6.24%	2.7%	None	$9,000	Same as federal
Utah	0.1%–8%	(1)	None	$22,500	Any company paying $140+ in wages during any quarter of current or preceding year, or that is subject to FUTA
Vermont	0.4%–8.4%	(1)	None	$8,000	Same as federal
Virginia	0%–6.2%	2.5%	None	$8,000	Same as federal
Washington	0.47%–5.4%	(1)	Optional	$29,700	Any company with 1+ employees during the year
West Virginia	0%–8.5%	2.7%	None	$8,000	Same as federal
Wisconsin	5%–8.9%	3.05%	None	$10,500	Same as federal
Wyoming	0.15%–10%	(1)	None	$14,700	Any company with 1+ employees during the year

[1] Industry-based rate is applied for a new employer.

[2] Depends on fund reserve ratio

An important issue is to retain the notice of contribution rate change that the state unemployment division will mail to every company at least once a year. The new rate listed in the notice must be used in the calculation of the state unemployment tax payable, as of the date listed on the notice. If a company outsources its payroll, this notice should be forwarded to the supplier, who incorporates it into its payroll tax calculations.

Calculating the Unemployment Tax Contribution Rate

The contribution rate is the percentage tax charged by a state to an employer to cover its share of the state unemployment insurance fund. The contribution rate is based on the "experience rating," which is essentially the proportion of unemployment claims made against a company by former employees it has laid off, divided by its total payroll. In essence, those organizations with lower levels of employee turnover will have a better experience rating, which results in a smaller contribution rate.

States can choose the method by which they calculate the contribution rate charged to employers. The four methods currently in use are as follows:

1. *Benefit ratio method.* This is the proportion of unemployment benefits paid to a company's former employees during the measurement period, divided by the total payroll during the period. A high ratio implies that a large proportion of employees are being laid off and are therefore using up unemployment funds, so the contribution rate assessed will be high. This calculation method is used by Alabama, Connecticut, Florida, Illinois, Iowa, Maryland, Michigan, Minnesota, Mississippi, Oregon, Texas, Utah, Vermont, Virginia, Washington, and Wyoming.

2. *Benefit wage ratio method.* This is similar to the benefit ratio method but uses in the numerator the total taxable wages for laid-off employees, rather than the benefits actually paid. A high ratio has the same implications as for the benefit ratio method—the contribution rate assessed will be high. This method is used by Delaware and Oklahoma.

3. *Payroll stabilization.* This method links the contribution rate to fluctuations in a company's total payroll over time, with higher rates being assessed to those with shrinking payrolls, on the grounds that these entities are terminating an inordinate proportion of their employees. This method is only used by Alaska.

4. *Reserve ratio.* This is the most common method, being used by 32 states (all those not listed for the preceding three methods). Under this approach, the ongoing balance of a firm's unclaimed contributions from previous years is reduced by unemployment claims for the past year and then divided by the average annual payroll, resulting in a "reserve ratio." Each state then applies a tax rate to this ratio in inverse proportion to the amount (i.e., a low reserve ratio indicates that nearly all contributed funds are being used, so a high tax will be assessed).

Making Voluntary Unemployment Tax Contributions

If a state uses the "Reserve Ratio" method described in the last section to arrive at the contribution rate charged to a business, then the business may have the option to contribute additional funds into its account. By doing so, it can improve its experience rating and thereby reduce the contribution rate charged by the state. In most cases, a company must make the decision to contribute additional funds within 30 days of the date when a state mails its notice of contribution rates to the company. The decision to pay additional funds to the state should be based on a cost-benefit analysis of the amount of funding required to reduce the contribution rate versus the reduced amount of required contributions that will be gained in the next calendar year by doing so.

The State Disability Tax

A few states maintain disability insurance funds, from which payments are made to employees who are unable to work due to illness or injury. This tax is sometimes a joint payment by both employees and employers, and in other cases is borne only by employees. Exhibit 11.6 shows the range of employer tax rates, employee withholding rates, taxable wage limits, and employee coverages for each state where a disability fund is used.

Exhibit 11.6 *Specifics of State Disability Funds*

State	Employer Tax Rate	Employee Withholding Rate	Taxable Wage Limit
California	None	0.9%	$56,916
Hawaii	Half of plan costs	0.5%	$36,524
New Jersey	0.1%–0.75%	0.5%	$23,900
New York	(1)	0.5% (2)	$6,240
Puerto Rico	0.3%	0.3%	$9,000
Rhode Island	None	1.7%	$45,300

1 Employers pay for excess benefit costs exceeding amount of employee contributions.
2 Not to exceed $0.60 per week for each employee.

Summary

Unemployment insurance may appear to be a nuisance tax that a company is forced by federal and state laws to pay out at regular intervals. However, as noted in this chapter, there are ways to manage the calculation of these taxes so they can be reduced to some extent. A knowledge of the authorizing laws and underlying calculations used to create federal and state employment taxes is key to these potential reductions.

12

Payroll Recordkeeping

Introduction

The payroll function requires a significant amount of recordkeeping, primarily under the regulations of the Internal Revenue Service and the Fair Labor Standards Act; other federal and state laws require some additional record storage. The core recordkeeping area involves basic employee contact information, wages paid, and tax withholdings. Layered on top of this information are storage requirements pertaining to the verification of employee eligibility to work, unemployment pay, garnishments, leaves of absence, and unclaimed wages. Details about each of these areas are discussed in this chapter. We also address the time periods over which documents should be retained and the proper procedures to use for planned document destruction.

Keeping Records about Wage Information

A variety of wage-related information must be stored for examination by the federal government. The following information should be retained about employees for at least four years, which is the maximum retention period required by the Internal Revenue:

- Service
- Name
- Address
- Social Security Number
- Sex
- Employee W-4 certificate
- Job title
- Dates of employment
- Fringe benefits
- Regular pay rate
- Hours worked each day
- Regular and overtime pay

- Additions to and subtractions from regular pay
- Tax withholdings and adjustments to withholdings
- Total wage payments, noting the payment period covered
- W-2 form issued to the employee

Of the above information, there is no need to retain information about hours worked, regular and overtime pay, or wage deductions for any exempt employees.

In addition to the above employee-specific information, a business should also retain information about the dates and amounts of total tax deposits and pension payments made.

If an employer is paying tipped employees less than the minimum wage, then the above pay information must also include the following information:

- The amount of employee-reported tip income.
- The amount of pay reduction taken as a tip credit by the employer.
- The hours worked and related pay for time worked as both a tipped and non-tipped employee.

There is no requirement that the above information be stored in any particular format or order. However, it must be made available for examination within 72 hours of a request being made by the government, so it must be sufficiently well indexed to be easily located in the storage area, whether it be on-site or off-site. If these records are intentionally destroyed or lost, the government can impose fines of up to $10,000 and even add imprisonment penalties if the violations continue.

Keeping Records about New Employees

Employee identification and eligibility to work records are key to the implementation of several federal laws. Accordingly, one must retain the I-9 form for a new employee for the later of one year following the termination of employment or three years from the date of hire. If copies were made of supporting documents to the I-9 form, they should be stored alongside the completed form.

A W-4 form should be filled out at the time of hire. This document, and all subsequent updates of it by the employee, should be stored for four years. Also, if the business requires new hires to fill out a form stating their veteran status for later itemization in the annual VETS-100 report, then this form should be retained until one year following employee termination.

Keeping Records about Unemployment Information

A company must retain sufficient information for four years after the filing date of its Annual Federal Unemployment Tax Return to back up the information itemized in the return. This should include at least the following information:

- Total wage payments made to employees during the year.
- The subset of wages paid that is subject to FUTA taxes.
- Minus payments made to state unemployment funds.

Keeping Records about Garnishments

There is no legal requirement for retaining payroll deduction information related to any types of garnishments. However, a company should have a standard retention policy that retains this information for the same time period listed for wage information retention, since this information is a deduction from wages. Also, if a lawsuit arises in which the records may be called into question, they should be retained for the duration of the lawsuit, even if this time period extends beyond that of the wage information retention policy.

Base-level information to retain should include the court order that garnishes the wages, a record of the periodic deductions from employee pay that met the requirements of the court order, any administrative fees charged, and a record of when garnishments were stopped. Most of this information is probably contained within a company's standard wage records or can be reconstructed from them, so much of it is already addressed by recordkeeping policies for wage information. Thus, the primary additional record to retain is the court order document.

Keeping Records about Leaves of Absence

When employees take leaves of absence, the Family and Medical Leave Act (FMLA) requires that the following records be kept, in addition to the basic wage information items noted earlier:

- The hours when leave was taken, if the leave was less than a day.
- The days when leave was taken, if whole days were used.
- The written leave notification signed by the employee.
- Notes regarding any disputes with the employee over the leave designation.
- Premium payments made for the benefits of employees who are on leave.

Please note that these recordkeeping requirements only apply to those businesses that fall under the jurisdiction of the FMLA, which is described in Chapter 14.

Keeping Records about Unclaimed Wages

Many states have laws requiring a business to pay them the amount of any wages that have not been claimed by employees after a certain period of time. Under these laws, one must usually retain a record of an employee's name and last known address for whatever time period is specified by the relevant state. The typical retention period is between five and ten years.

The Document Destruction Policy*

A company that is in business for any length of time will find itself spending an increasing amount to maintain an ever-increasing storage facility for its payroll records. To avoid this issue, there should be a document destruction policy that requires the accounting staff or records administrator to remove and destroy certain types of records after they have exceeded a preset age. The number of years used before document destruction is authorized will vary by company, since they may be located in states that require extra time periods before certain types of records can be eliminated.

By using a retention schedule and document destruction policy, a company can more or less automatically destroy records after a document's retention period has expired. However, some companies prepare and execute a form similar to that shown in Exhibit 12.1, which requires specific authorization to destroy records. This permits a recheck of the decision to destroy, even if a document is on a retention schedule. This might be necessary if the retention periods are changed by law, litigation is in process that may require use of the documents, or other circumstances arise. However, records should generally be destroyed in accordance with a document destruction policy so that a company can use its consistent application as a defense in the event of a lawsuit where the litigant attempts to obtain access to the records.

Each record scheduled for destruction should be checked, because it is far too easy to destroy vital records through erroneous filing. In no event should a box of records be destroyed on the basis of the label; the contents must be reviewed.

There are many ways to destroy records. For paper, the cleanest and most efficient method is shredding. An alternative is to pulverize and recycle, although this may be unacceptable for confidential material. Finally, there is incineration, which is not good for the environment and also often leaves pieces of unburned paper. Whatever method is used, strict accountability as to what was done, when, and how successful it was is needed to ensure adequate control of the process.

Record Storage Issues

When storing records, be sure to separate those items requiring permanent storage, such as board minutes and articles of incorporation, from other documents created during the same year, and shift them into a more secure location where they can be more clearly identified. This added storage step avoids throwing out important corporate documents along with other payroll documents when the document destruction policy specifies that the other items be eliminated.

In situations where a large number of storage boxes are required for each year's documents, it is common to simply put an identifying index number on each box

---

* This section was adapted with permission from Willison et al., pages 1283–1284 of the Sixth Edition of *Controllership* (Hoboken, NJ: John Wiley and Sons, 1999).

Exhibit 12.1 *Authorization for Destruction of Records Form*

Authorization for Destruction of Records
and Destruction Certificate

No. _____

Date _____

To: (Controller)
Authority is requested for destruction of the following records:

Form Number	Description of Records	Date of Records		Recommended Retention Period
		From	To	

Destruction Recommended by _____

Destruction Approved by _____

I hereby certify that I have this day destroyed the accounts, records, and memoranda listed above, and further that no accounts, records, or memoranda other than those named were destroyed herewith.

(Witness) _____   (Signed) _____

(Location) _____   (Position) _____

and then list each box's contents on a separate index document. However, it is possible that the index number will be improperly transcribed onto the master index document, so anyone referring to it will not know where some documents are stored. To avoid this problem, it is useful to list the general contents of each box on the outside of the box, using a marker pen. This way, there is no risk of losing track of documents and someone without access to the master index to still find stored documents with minimal search time.

Summary

This chapter summarized the basic document storage requirements for all types of payroll-related documents. Most of these requirements are based on a small number of federal laws and regulations. However, there are cases where more stringent state laws will require that additional information be retained or kept for longer periods than what is mandated by the federal government. To be sure, contact your local state government to see if any of these overriding state laws apply to your specific situation.

13

Payroll Journal Entries

Introduction

Once a payroll has been completed, one must figure out how to transfer the information on the payroll reports into the general ledger, so that company management can determine the total amount of payroll expense for each department, as well as any payroll-related liabilities. In addition, accruals must be consistently generated for period-end financial reporting that accurately shows the amount of various unpaid expenses, such as vacation time. Of particular concern is how to keep errors from creeping into journal entries, so that payroll information is consistently and accurately reported in the financial statements. This chapter shows how to create journal entries for each of a wide range of payroll-related transactions, as well as where to find the underlying information, and how to ensure that the entries are made in a reliable and consistent manner.

Benefits Accrual Journal Entry

Create a benefits accrual journal entry[1] whenever there are employee benefit expenses that have been incurred during the reporting period but for which an associated supplier billing has not yet been received. For example, a company's provider of disability insurance may only bill the company on a quarterly basis, so the payroll staff should create an entry for the first two months of the quarter that accrues the cost of the insurance and then reverses the accumulated liability when the bill arrives. A sample of this transaction is shown below:

	Debit	*Credit*
Medical insurance expense	xxx	
Dental insurance expense	xxx	
Disability insurance expense	xxx	
Life insurance expense	xxx	
Accrued benefits liability		xxx

This entry should be *reversed* in the following accounting period or in the period in which the offsetting supplier invoice is received. The information needed for this entry can be derived from the last supplier invoice. It usually itemizes specific individuals and the amount of the benefit expense for each one, so it is a simple matter to estimate the accrual based on these expenses for each person, adjusted for any changes in headcount since the last invoice was received, as well as any notification of changes in the cost of benefits. If benefit costs are quite small, one should consider avoiding this entry, since the increased accuracy of the resulting financial statements will be minimal, while the payroll staff must spend valuable time creating the journal entry.

Bonus Accrual and Payment Journal Entries

Create a bonus accrual journal entry whenever the expected financial or operational performance of the company matches or exceeds the levels required in the bonus plans for various employees. For example, the management team may be given a year-end bonus if profits exceed 10 percent of sales, or the sales staff may receive an override commission if the entire group's sales exceed $10 million. A sample of this transaction is:

	Debit	*Credit*
Bonus expense (by department)	xxx	
Accrued bonus liability		xxx

When the bonus is eventually paid, the resulting journal entry will clear out the accrued bonus liability, while also recording any payroll tax liabilities associated with the bonus payment:

	Debit	*Credit*
Accrued bonus liability	xxx	
Cash		xxx
Federal withholding taxes payable		xxx
Social Security withholding taxes payable		xxx
Medicare withholding taxes payable		xxx
Federal unemployment taxes payable		xxx
State withholding taxes payable		xxx
State unemployment taxes payable		xxx

The decision to make the bonus expense entry is extremely judgmental, since the eventual awarding of the bonus may be subject to results in future months that one can only guess at early in the bonus measurement period. Consequently, it is common to either only make the entry after several months of performance have been completed, or to enter smaller amounts early in the measurement period and larger ones later on, after the likelihood of success has become more clear.

The source information for the bonus calculation should be stored in the human resources department, which should have control over the underlying bonus plans for all employees. The payroll staff should convert these sometimes complex documents into a brief summary document that clearly outlines the potential amounts of any bonuses, as well as the goals that must be achieved in order to be awarded them.

Cafeteria Plan Journal Entry

Create a cafeteria plan journal entry whenever there is a cafeteria plan in existence for which employees have authorized the deduction of preset amounts from their pay. These funds are then stored for the use of employees, who can withdraw funds for dependent care or medical expenses. For example, an employee may authorize a deduction of $200 per month, which is stored in a separate bank account by the company. The employee submits receipts for child care once a month, which are used as authorization to reimburse her for the requested amounts from the bank account. A sample of the transaction for the initial deduction of funds is:

	Debit	*Credit*
Cash (transfer to cafeteria plan bank account)	xxx	
Cash (transfer from payroll bank account)		xxx
Salaries and wages expense	xxx	
Cafeteria plan liability		xxx

When a request for reimbursement is received from an employee, the following transaction shifts the funds from the cafeteria plan and reduces the liability account:

	Debit	*Credit*
Cafeteria plan liability	xxx	
Cash (cafeteria plan bank account)		xxx

The information for this entry should come from a deduction authorization form that is completed by participating employees at the beginning of each year, and which is usually retained by the human resources department.

Manual Check Journal Entry

Create a manual check journal entry when an employee must be paid with a manual check, rather than through the standard computerized payroll system. For example, the management team decides to lay off several employees midway through the payroll reporting period, so the payroll staff creates a manual check, which is handed to the employees when they are informed of the layoff. Each manual check is then entered into the computerized payroll system. A journal entry is required to record the cash payment, while the manual check will be entered into the company's computerized payroll system, which will record the amount of all other payroll taxes and other deductions due. A sample of the transaction is:

	Debit	*Credit*
Salaries and wages expense	xxx	
Cash		xxx

Once the manual check has been recorded in the payroll system, the computer should seamlessly include in its periodic payroll summary a transaction that accounts for all payroll taxes and other deductions, *net of the entry already made.* The computer-generated transaction should look something like this:

	Debit	*Credit*
Salaries and wages expense (net of entry already made)	xxx	
Cash		xxx
Federal withholding taxes payable		xxx
Social Security withholding taxes payable		xxx
Medicare withholding taxes payable		xxx
Federal unemployment taxes payable		xxx
State withholding taxes payable		xxx
State unemployment taxes payable		xxx
Garnishments payable		xxx
Union dues payable		xxx

The information required for the initial journal entry comes from the remittance advice attached to the manual check. The proper amount of payroll tax deductions used for the manual check may have been derived from an Internet-based wage calculation site, a phone-in automated calculation site maintained by a payroll supplier, from tax tables, or from a wage calculator in a computerized in-house payroll system.

Outsourced Payroll Journal Entry

Create an outsourced payroll journal entry when the payroll processing function is being handled by an outside entity that returns to the company a listing of all funds expended and an itemization of all expense accounts. This is a simpler entry than is required for in-house payroll systems, since the supplier generally undertakes to pay all government entities on behalf of the company, thereby eliminating all payroll-related liability accounts that the company would otherwise use. A sample of the transaction is:

	Debit	*Credit*
Salaries and wages expense	xxx	
Payroll taxes expense	xxx	
Cash		xxx
Garnishments payable		xxx
Union dues payable		xxx

Note that all payroll taxes are compressed into a single expense account. One can split these expenses into a larger number of expense accounts, but the increase in reporting information is usually not worth the effort of maintaining additional expense accounts. Also note that some nontax deductions are still paid out by the company, such as garnishments and union dues, so they are still listed as credits.

The information required for this entry is obtained from payroll reports issued by the payroll supplier. Since the exact format of these reports varies by supplier, it is impossible to specify exactly where the information will be derived from. However, if a supplier's reports are unclear, one can generally pay the supplier to construct a custom report that itemizes exactly what expenses and liabilities have been generated as a result of a payroll transaction.

Salaries and Wages Accrual Journal Entry[2]

Create a salaries and wages accrual entry when employees have worked some hours at the end of the reporting period for which they have not yet been paid. If a company pays on a weekly or biweekly basis, then this entry will probably be required for both the salaried and hourly employees. If it pays bimonthly or monthly, then the entry is probably only needed for hourly employees, since salaried personnel will have been paid through the last day of the reporting period. For example, if a company pays its employees once a month, based on time sheets completed through the preceding weekend, then it must accrue for unpaid wages for any hourly personnel who worked any days between the end of the last time reporting period and the end of the month. A possible calculation under this assumption is shown in Exhibit 13.1, where the pay rates of all hourly personnel are listed as well as the number of unpaid working days in the month. The spreadsheet automatically uses this initial information to calculate the wage and payroll tax accrual, even listing the account numbers to which the expenses should be charged.

Exhibit 13.1 *Wage Accrual Calculation Spreadsheet*

Wage Accrual Spreadsheet
Note: Hourly personnel are paid through the Sunday prior to the payroll date.

Hourly Full Time Personnel:	Pay Rate per Hour	Unpaid Business Days in Month	Pay Accrual
Barlow, Cindy	$ 15.50	5	$ 620.00
Davis, Humphrey	$ 15.00	5	$ 600.00
Dunning, Mortimer	$ 16.00	5	$ 640.00
Guthrie, James	$ 18.15	5	$ 726.00
Hortense, Alice	$ 15.50	5	$ 620.00
Innsbruck, Ingmar	$ 15.00	5	$ 600.00

Journal Entry	Acct. No.	Amount
Wage Accrual	50100	$ 3,806.00
FICA Accrual	62250	$ 235.97
Total Accrual	22800	$ 4,041.97

A sample of the transaction is:

	Debit	Credit
Direct labor expense	xxx	
[Salaries—itemize by department]	xxx	
Accrued salaries		xxx
Accrued payroll taxes		xxx

This entry should be *reversed* in the following accounting period, when the unpaid time will be included in the next payroll.

Companies with predominantly salaried staffs frequently avoid making this entry, on the grounds that the wages due to a small number of hourly personnel at the end of the reporting period will have a minimal impact on reported financial results.

The information for this entry is most easily derived from an electronic spreadsheet that itemizes all employees to whom the calculation applies, the number of unpaid days, and the standard rate of pay for each person. It is generally not necessary to also compile actual or estimated overtime costs for the unpaid days, partially because the timekeeping system may not readily accumulate this information for the last few days of the reporting period, and partially because it may require an excessive amount of effort to calculate this additional cost.

Transfer to General Ledger from Payroll Journal Entry[3]

Create an entry to transfer information to the general ledger for an entire payroll when the accounting system does not automatically perform this chore itself, or if the payroll information is derived from a separate payroll system. This entry should not be for individual employees, but rather in sum total for the entire set of employees paid through a payroll transaction. For example, a company has purchased a separate payroll processing software package and must transfer the payroll expense and liability information from this package to the general ledger module of its accounting software. A sample of the transaction is as follows:

	Debit	*Credit*
Direct labor expense	xxx	
(Salaries—itemize by department)	xxx	
Cash		xxx
Federal withholding taxes payable	xxx	
Social Security withholding taxes payable		xxx
Medicare withholding taxes payable		xxx
Federal unemployment taxes payable		xxx
State withholding taxes payable		xxx
State unemployment taxes payable		xxx
Garnishments payable		xxx
Union dues payable		xxx

The information needed for this entry will be acquired from different fields on different reports, depending on the system used to process the payroll. If the source of this information is unclear, try to create a custom report within the payroll processing system, or perhaps with a third-party report-writing package, such as Crystal Reports, that will clearly lay out the information that must be included in the journal entry.

Vacation Accrual Journal Entry[4]

Create an entry to accrue vacation pay earned by employees but not yet used by them, subject to any year-end maximum vacation carry-forward limitation. The same entry can be used to record accrued sick time. For example, one can itemize the vacation time earned for each employee, subtract out all vacation time already used, and multiply the remaining amount by the hourly pay of each person. An example of this calculation is shown in Exhibit 13.2. The exhibit shows a list of employees, their annualized pay rates, and the maximum amounts of vacation that each one is allowed to carry forward into the next year. The spreadsheet solves for a vacation accrual that matches the maximum allowable vacation time at year-end,

---

Exhibit 13.2 *Vacation Accrual Calculation*

Vacation Accrual   **6** ← Months to Date in Year

Name	Annualized Salary	Maximum Hours	Maximum Accrual	YTD Accrual
Barlowe, Cindy	$32,240	80	$1,240	$620
Bosley, Sandra	$51,039	80	$1,963	$982
Caraway, Lisa	$200,000	80	$7,692	$3,846
Chantilly, Edward	$46,200	80	$1,777	$888
Davis, Humphrey	$31,200	80	$1,200	$600
Dunning, Mortimer	$33,280	80	$1,280	$640
Dunwiddy, Alexandra	$42,400	80	$1,631	$815
Greenstreet, James	$53,000	80	$2,038	$1,019
Guthrie, James	$37,752	80	$1,452	$726
Halverston, Eric	$80,250	80	$3,087	$1,543
Johnson, Noyes	$76,000	40	$1,462	$731
Montrose, Wesley	$57,500	40	$1,106	$553
Mortimer, Victoria	$100,000	40	$1,923	$962
Penway, Alice	$46,824	40	$900	$450
Quarterstaff, Molly	$80,000	40	$1,538	$769
Rosencrantz, Albert	$50,000	40	$962	$481
Saunders, Ricardo	$49,920	40	$960	$480
Von Gundle, Gerta	$60,000	40	$1,154	$577
Zeta, Xavier	$47,700	40	$917	$459
			$34,282	$17,141

YTD accrual through last month:	$16,025
Required entry for this month:	**$1,116**

Journal Entry	Acct. No.	Amount
Accrued vacation expense	62150	$1,116
Vacations payable	22700	$1,116

---

which is the annual pay rate divided by 2,080 working hours per year and multiplied by the maximum number of carry-forward hours. The accrual is then reduced by the proportion of months that have thus far occurred in the year (six months in the example), resulting in a required vacation accrual in the example of $17,141 through the first six months of the year. The spreadsheet then subtracts the accrual that was already made earlier in the year to arrive at a required entry for the month of $1,116, which is then listed in a suggested journal entry format at the bottom of the page.

The vacation accrual calculation used in Exhibit 13.2 assumes that one is gradually building the vacation accrual to be at the correct level at the end of the year, presumably for external reporting purposes. If the vacation accrual going into the year is already fully recognized, then for future calculations, one simply solves for the maximum number of carry-forward hours without regard to the proportional calculation in the final column and makes smaller incremental adjustments to match the vacation accrual to the total assumed year-end vacation accrual.

An example of the resulting journal entry is:

	Debit	Credit
Payroll taxes	xxx	
(Salaries—itemize by department)	xxx	
Accrued salaries		xxx
Accrued payroll taxes		xxx

This entry *should not be reversed* in the following accounting period, since the vacation time may not be used in the following period. Instead, recalculate the vacation accrual in Exhibit 14.2 for the next period, and incrementally adjust the total amount of vacation accrued in the next period to match the calculated total vacation accrual. For example, if the accrued vacation expense at the end of January is $10,000 and the calculation in Exhibit 14.2 results in a total vacation accrual of $12,000 as of the end of February, then the February entry should be for the difference between the two months, or $2,000.

Ensuring Journal Entry Accuracy

Payroll-related journal entries tend to be long and complex, and so are easy to enter incorrectly, leading to excessively high or low payroll expense or liability totals, which can be difficult to spot and correct. One way to resolve this problem is to create and save a set of standard journal entries in the accounting computer system. By doing so, one can call up the template every time an entry must be made, and simply plug the correct amounts into the prepositioned journal entry fields.

However, the use of a journal entry template does not prevent one from entering an incorrect dollar amount, or a debit instead of a credit (or vice versa), even when the account number into which the information is going is accurate. To avoid these two additional problems, it is useful to create a monthly comparison of all income statement and balance sheet accounts and compare the trend line of accounts from month to month to see if there are any anomalies. If so, one can go to the supporting general ledger accounts and check the underlying entries to see where problems may have occurred. This error-correction routine usually occurs during the financial statement creation process, when there are lots of tasks to complete and available accounting labor is in short supply. To reduce the number of review hours used during this time period, try reviewing the information near the end of the reporting period, so that any errors have already been corrected by the end of the period.

Another review option is to create separate income statements for each department, as well as a month-to-month comparison of the information. This is useful on a more detailed level for finding unusual changes in journal entry amounts, where the total payroll expense as shown on the summarized income statement is correct, but the allocation of payroll costs among departments is wrong.

Most payroll accruals require a reversal of the entry in the following reporting period, when the actual incurrence of an expense replaces the accrual. For example, the wage accrual should be reversed. If this reversal does not occur, then payroll costs will be permanently too high. To correct this problem, be sure to set the permanent journal entry template to be a reversing entry. Also, one should always check the contents of all accrued liability accounts at the end of each month as part of the standard closing procedures to see if any excess payroll accruals have been mistakenly left in an account.

The payroll reports created by a company's accounting system form the basis for any additional journal entries that must be entered into the general ledger. If payroll is generated in-house, then the software may automatically shift some payroll transactions into the general ledger with no operator intervention. However, some companies may use a separate payroll package or the services of a supplier, either of which requires a manual journal entry transaction to shift the payroll information into the general ledger. If either of the later two situations are the case, create a highly detailed procedure that describes exactly how the source payroll information is summarized and how it is then coded into a journal entry. Otherwise, problems may arise when a new person is charged with entering this information and has no idea how to do so or there are consistency problems when an old-timer summarizes the payroll information in a different manner from payroll to payroll. Reporting consistency is the key to making accurate journal entries every time and good procedures lead to reporting consistency.

The bulk of these recommendations require that errors <u>be caught *after*</u> they have occurred, which leads to little efficiency in the correction of payroll journal entries. Accordingly, be sure to create standard journal entry templates since this is the best way to keep journal entry errors from occurring.

Account Reduction Possibilities

One can create many accounts in which to store a wide array of payroll information, such as payables for garnishments, Medicare, Social Security, and state income tax reimbursements. However, having a large number of accounts requires additional effort to keep track of outstanding balances. There are cases where the number of payroll-related accounts can be drastically reduced. For example, if payroll is being outsourced, there is no need for any payroll payable or payroll tax payable account since the supplier is taking care of these payments. If there is a choice between keeping the responsibility for a payment in-house or giving the responsibility to a supplier, then give the chore to the supplier, thereby eliminating the related payroll account.

Also, if the amount of funds itemized in a separate payroll account is quite small, it may not be worth the effort to store it separately. Instead, cancel the account and shift the funds to a related account. However, there may be cases where significant legal liability is associated with funds payable, as is the case for garnishments withheld, where one may be justified in separately identifying the funds in a different payroll account.

Summary

This chapter showed how to create journal entries for any payroll situation that is likely to arise, and noted the differences between journal entries derived from in-house versus outsourced payroll systems. A key issue noted several times is the prevention of inconsistencies in the reporting of information through journal entries—this can be a major problem, especially since payroll costs can comprise the bulk of all company expenses. Consequently, pay close attention to the prevention of payroll transactional errors.

Notes

1. This journal entry was derived with permission from Appendix B of Bragg, *Accounting Reference Desktop* (Hoboken, NJ: John Wiley and Sons, 2002).
2. Ibid.
3. Ibid.
4. Ibid.

14

Payroll-Related Laws

Introduction

A large number of federal regulations apply to the payroll function. This chapter provides an overview of all the major laws that have some impact on it. Many of these laws commonly include provisions relating to discrimination, workplace safety, and other human resources issues; though these elements of the laws are important, they fall outside the boundaries of this book. Given the extremely lengthy nature of some laws, only those portions of their texts that impact the payroll function are summarized here.

For a more complete presentation of these comprehensive laws, go to the Department of Labor's website at *www.dol.gov* or look up the complete text of the laws through an Internet search engine, such as Google (at *www.google.com*).

The law summaries noted here *generally* describe the original laws, which may have been heavily amended since that time. Consequently, the intent is to give a general idea of the source of various types of legislation, rather than a precise rendering of the subsequent laws that have been derived from these foundation regulations.

Employment Eligibility

Employers are required to verify the identity and employment eligibility of any newly hired employees. The Immigration Reform and Control Act required the use of the Form I-9 to control the documentation of this process, while the Illegal Immigration Reform and Immigrant Responsibility Act filled some loopholes in the earlier law. Summaries of the Acts are:

■ *Illegal Immigration Reform and Immigrant Responsibility Act of 1996 (IIRIRA).* This Act shields employers from liability if they have made a good-faith effort to verify a new employee's identity and employment eligibility and were subsequently found to have committed a technical or procedural error in the identification. If a violation is found, an employer will have ten business days in which to correct the violation. Noncompliance penalties were greatly increased over those of earlier legislation; in particular, employers can now incur a penalty for each paperwork violation, rather than in total, so the potential fines are much higher.

■ *Immigration Reform and Control Act of 1986.* This Act requires all employers having at least four employees to verify the identity and employment eligibility of all regular, temporary, casual, and student employees. This is done through a form I-9, which must be completed within three days of an employee's hire date, and retained for the longer of three days from the date of hire or one year following the date of termination.

The I-9 form includes a complete list of documents that are considered allowable to prove identity and employment eligibility. In brief, those documents proving both identity and employment eligibility include a U.S. passport, a certificate of U.S. citizenship or naturalization, and an Alien Registration Receipt Card or green card. Those documents proving identity *only* include a driver's license, government ID card, and voter's registration card. Those documents proving work eligibility *only* include a U.S. Social Security card, Certificate of Birth Abroad, and certified birth certificate. One should consult the I-9 form for a complete list.

If an employer does not comply with this Act, penalties can range from $100 to $1,000 per employee hired, plus possible imprisonment if a continuing pattern of noncompliance can be proven. Also, any employee whose identity and employment eligibility has not been proven through the I-9 form must be terminated from employment.

Garnishments

Employers are responsible for garnishing the wages of their employees and remitting the resulting funds to various entities in order to reduce the personal debts of the employees. The focus of legislation in this area has been the amount of deductions that may be made, which jurisdiction shall have precedence in issuing garnishment orders, and how to track the location of employees who switch jobs in order to avoid garnishment orders. The Consumer Credit Protection Act specifies the proportion of total pay that may be garnished, while the Personal Responsibility and Work Opportunity Reconciliation Act addresses the reporting of new hires into a national database. Finally, the Uniform Interstate Family Support Act specifies which jurisdiction shall issue family support-related garnishment orders. Summaries of the Acts are:

■ *Consumer Credit Protection Act.* This Act limits the maximum payroll deduction from an employee's wages for spouse or child support to 60 percent of his or her disposable earnings, or 50 percent if the employee is also supporting another spouse or children. Disposable earnings are calculated by subtracting all government-mandated deductions from an employee's gross pay, such as Social Security, Medicare, income taxes of all kinds, and any unemployment or disability insurance. Deductions that are chosen by the employee, such as medical insurance deductions, are *not* included in the disposable earnings calculation.

■ *Personal Responsibility and Work Opportunity Reconciliation Act of 1996.* This Act requires individual states to provide time-limited assistance to welfare recipients in exchange for work, essentially forcing many people off the welfare roles. The key issue impacting the payroll manager is that each state must now maintain an employer new hire tracking system that rolls up into a Federal Case Registry and National Directory of New Hires. This information is then used to track parents who are delinquent in making child support payments across state lines.

Employers must report new hires (e.g., any person who is paid wages and is hired to work more than 30 days, including part-time employees) to their state of residence within 20 days of each hire, or at the time of the first regular payroll after the date of hire, whichever is later. The report must be made with a W-4 or equivalent form, which must include the name, address, and Social Security number of the employee, as well as the name, address, and federal tax identification number of the employer.

States can assess penalties for noncompliance at their option, charging $25 for failing to submit new hire information and up to $500 if it can be proven that there is a conspiracy between the employer and an employee to avoid reporting this information to the government.

■ *Uniform Interstate Family Support Act of 1996 (UIFSA).* This Act limits the modification of family support orders to a single state if one party to the dispute resides in that state, thereby eliminating interstate jurisdictional disputes. However, jurisdiction can be shifted to a different state if none of the parents or children continue to reside in the state, or if there is mutual agreement to move the case to another state. This Act has been adopted by every state.

The key results of this Act from a payroll perspective are that only one support order can be in effect at one time and that an income withholding order can be sent to an employer directly from another state. When a withholding order arrives, an employer must follow the rules stated on the order, which will probably specify the address to which payments must be sent, the amount and duration of payments, and possibly the amount of administrative fees that may be withheld.

Health Insurance

Employers can offer health insurance to their employees. If they do so, regulations require them to continue to offer insurance subsequent to employment under certain circumstances, and to offer insurance during employee leaves of absence. The Consolidated Omnibus Budget Reconciliation Act contains the requirements for offering insurance to departed employees, which is expanded upon in the Health Insurance Portability and Accountability Act. The Family and Medical Leave Act contains the rules for offering health insurance to employees who are on leave. Summaries of the Acts are:

- *Consolidated Omnibus Budget Reconciliation Act of 1986 (COBRA).* This Act allows employees of private sector, state, and local governments who lose their jobs the right to accept continuing health insurance coverage, as long as the former employer had 20 or more employees in the prior year. If an employee is terminated, then he or she can accept coverage for an additional 18 months. If an employee becomes entitled to Medicare coverage or becomes divorced, then the coverage period becomes 36 months. If a spouse or dependent child of an employee loses coverage due to the death of an employee, then they can obtain coverage for up to 36 months. If a dependent child of an employee loses dependent status, then that person can obtain coverage for up to 36 months.

  An employer is required to give notice of potential COBRA coverage to employees when a qualifying event occurs (employees are required to inform the health plan administrator of any divorce, disability, or dependent issues that would bring about qualification for benefits under COBRA). The impacted people then have up to 60 days in which to elect to take COBRA coverage.

  If coverage is chosen, an impacted person can be required to pay up to 102 percent of the cost of the insurance. If the person does not make timely payments under the terms of the insurance plan (within 30 days of the due date), the COBRA coverage can be terminated. COBRA coverage also will end if the employer stops providing medical coverage to its regular employees.

  The penalty to an employer for not complying with the provisions of COBRA is $100 per day for each impacted individual, though the penalty will not be imposed if the employer can prove reasonable cause for the failure and also corrects the situation within 30 days from the point when noncompliance was uncovered.

- *Family and Medical Leave Act of 1993 (FMLA).* This Act entitles employees at companies with 50 or more employees to take up to 12 weeks of unpaid leave (which may be taken sporadically) each year for a specified list of family and medical reasons. Only those employees who have worked for the employer for a total of at least 12 months, and worked for the employer for at least 1,250 hours in the last 12 months are covered by the Act. A further restriction is that an employee must work at a company location where at least 50 employees are employed within a 75-mile radius of the facility. Valid reasons for taking the leave of absence include the birth of a child, serious illness, or caring for a family member with a serious illness.

  During their absence, an employer must continue to provide medical insurance coverage if it had been taken by the employee prior to the leave of absence, though the employee can be charged for that portion of the expense that had been deducted from his or her pay prior to the leave. If the employee does not pay this portion of the expense within 30 days, the insurance can be cancelled for the remainder of the leave, but must be restored once the employee returns to work.

Upon returning from a leave of absence, an employee must be given the same or equivalent job with the same level of pay and benefits that he or she had before the leave. In certain cases where job restoration would cause significant economic damage to an employer, key positions will not be restored to returning employees.

This Act is enforced by the U.S. Labor Department's Employment Standards Administration, Wage and Hour Division. If violations are not resolved by this entity, the department can sue employers to compel compliance.

- **Health Insurance Portability and Accountability Act of 1996 (HIPAA).** This Act ensures that small (50 or fewer employees) businesses will have access to health insurance, despite the special health status of any employees. Also, insurance carriers must offer coverage renewals in subsequent periods once they have sold coverage to an employer. The key payroll-related aspect of this Act is its changes to COBRA regulations. The Act entitles anyone who is disabled during the first 60 days of COBRA coverage to receive up to 29 months of COBRA coverage, as well as that person's family members. Also, COBRA coverage cannot be terminated in cases where a former employee is denied coverage in a new plan due to a preexisting condition, thereby ensuring that the individual will continue to receive medical insurance coverage.

Pensions

Employers may offer participation in pension plans to their employees. If so, government regulations control the documentation and administration of the plans and also allow ex-military employees to make extra contributions into them. The Employee Retirement Income Security Act covers the documentation and administration of plans, while the Uniformed Services Employment and Reemployment Rights Act governs the additional contribution of funds by ex-military employees into contribution retirement plans. Summaries of the Acts are:

- **Employee Retirement Income Security Act of 1974 (ERISA).** This Act sets minimum operational and funding standards for employee benefit plans. It covers most private sector employee benefit plans, but does not cover government plans.

The Act requires plan administrators to provide a plan description to any plan participants and to file an annual report about the plan's performance. Plan fiduciaries are required to operate the plan only to the benefit of plan participants and to act prudently in doing so.

The Pension and Welfare Benefits Administration of the Department of Labor enforces this Act, with the assistance of the Internal Revenue Service for some provisions. The department can bring a civil action to correct law violations and can bring criminal actions for willful violations. Annual reporting violations can result in a penalty of $1,000 per day.

- **Uniformed Services Employment and Reemployment Rights Act of 1994.** This Act encourages people to serve in the armed forces by minimizing the impact on their careers when they return to civilian employment by avoiding discrimination and increasing their opportunities for employment. The primary payroll impact is that an employee returning to a civilian job from the armed forces is allowed to make contributions to his or her 401k pension plan up to the amount that would have been allowed if the person had continued employment through the period of service in the armed forces. If the person elects to make these contributions, he or she must do so within a period of three times the service period in the armed forces, up to a maximum of five years.

Taxes

A number of Acts govern the types and amounts of payroll taxes to be withheld from employee paychecks. The Current Tax Payment Act authorizes employer withholding of income taxes from employee pay, while the Social Security Act and Federal Insurance Contributions Acts set up Social Security and authorized deductions from pay in order to fund it. The Federal Unemployment Tax Act set up a federal unemployment fund and authorized deductions to pay for it, while the Self-Employment Contributions Act required self-employed parties to pay these taxes themselves. Summaries of the Acts are:

- **Current Tax Payment Act of 1943.** This Act requires employers to withhold income taxes from employee pay and to remit these deductions to the government on a quarterly basis. This "pay as you go" approach to tax collection surmounts the problem of individuals not having the funds available at year-end to pay their income taxes by enforcing incremental payments as wages are initially earned. This Act puts the onus of tax collection squarely on employers.
- **Federal Insurance Contributions Act of 1935 (FICA).** This Act authorizes the government to collect Social Security and Medicare payroll taxes. These taxes are sometimes referred to as contributions to the social security system, since they are eventually returned to tax payers. Currently, an employer must pay 6.2 percent of an employee's first $87,000 (which varies each year) in annual earnings, which are matched by the employee. Consequently, the total contribution to Social Security by both parties is 12.4 percent. The same calculation applies to a 1.45 percent Medicare tax rate that is based on all taxable pay, with no upper limit. If an employee has multiple employers in a single year, then each one must withhold this tax up to the wage cap of $84,900, even if the grand total employee earnings for the year exceeds that amount.

  The Act allows no deductions from the base wage when calculating the total tax due for Social Security or Medicare taxes. Also, a company must retain payroll records for four years from the later of the due date or payment date of these taxes.

- *Federal Unemployment Tax Act (FUTA)*. This Act requires employers to pay a tax on the wages paid to their employees, which is then used to create a pool of funds that can be used for unemployment benefits. The tax is based on only the first $7,000 of wages paid to each employee in a calendar year. If an employee has multiple employers in a single year, then each one must withhold this tax up to the wage cap of $7,000, even if the grand total employee earnings for the year exceeds that amount.

  The FUTA tax rate is currently 6.2 percent, which can then be reduced by the amount of state unemployment taxes paid, usually resulting in a net tax of 0.8 percent (even though the amount of state unemployment taxes paid may be quite small).

  The FUTA tax applies to an employer if it either employs at least one person during each of any 20 weeks in a calendar year, or pays at least $1,500 in wages during any calendar quarter during the current or preceding year. As soon as liability under FUTA is proven, a business is liable for the tax for the full calendar year (even if the test is first applied later in the year), as well as the next calendar year (even if it fails the test in the next calendar year).

- *Self-Employment Contributions Act (SECA)*. This Act requires self-employed business owners to pay the same total tax rates for Social Security and Medicare taxes that are split between employees and employers under the Federal Insurance Contributions Act. One is never forced to pay under both FICA and SECA—only one applies in any given situation.

  The taxes only apply if an individual's total annual self-employed income is greater than $400, in which case the tax must be applied to *all* income up to a maximum annual limit of $87,000. Also, some deductions are allowed from business income before the tax is calculated. These deductions include income from interest and dividends, the sale of business property or other assets, and rental income from real estate or personal property (though these deductions do not apply if the generation of these types of income comprises one's core business activity).

- *Social Security Act of 1935*. This groundbreaking Act established Old Age and Survivor's Insurance, which was funded by compulsory savings by wage earners. The savings were to be paid back to the wage earners upon their retirement at age 65. The initial payments were 1 percent of gross wages by both the employee and employer, gradually ramping up to 3 percent by 1948. Employers were held responsible for withholding this tax from employee pay. The Act also created the Federal Unemployment Trust Fund through additional withholding, which could be reduced by up to 90 percent if an employee also contributed to a state unemployment fund.

  Originally, only employees engaged in commercial or industrial occupations were covered by this Act, though numerous later changes to the Act have greatly expanded its coverage.

Wages and Overtime

Employers are required to pay their employees at least a minimum wage and over-time rates for work performed in excess of 40 hours per week. These basic issues were originally addressed in the Fair Labor Standards Act (FLSA). The FLSA's provisions were expanded to include contractors working on federal service and construction projects with the Contract Work Hours and Safety Standards Act, and to contractors working on federal construction and repair projects with the Davis-Bacon Act. The McNamara-O'Hara Service Contract Act expanded this coverage to the employees of contractors engaged in federal services contracts, while the Walsh-Healey Public Contracts Act extended coverage to the employees of contractors who sell supplies to the federal government. In addition, the Equal Pay Act required employers to pay both sexes an equal amount for performing the same types of work. Summaries of these Acts are:

■ *Contract Work Hours and Safety Standards Act.* This Act requires federal contractors to pay their blue-collar workers one and one-half times their basic pay rates for all hours worked over 40 hours during a work week.

The Act applies to all contractors working on federal service and construction projects exceeding $100,000, as well as any federally assisted construction contracts where the government is not the direct contracting agency. Exemptions from the Act include contracts for intelligence agencies, transportation, or open market materials purchases. It also does not apply to projects where the government is only guaranteeing a loan or providing insurance.

The compensation aspects of this Act are enforced by the Wage and Hour Division of the Employment Standards Administration. An intentional violation of this Act can be punished by a fine of up to $1,000 or six months imprisonment. In addition, a violation of the overtime provisions of the Act can result in a $10 penalty per employee for each day that overtime is not paid. The government can assure that these penalties will be paid by withholding them from the contract payments being made to a contractor. Employees can also sue their employers for any unpaid overtime amounts. In addition, intentional violation of this Act can result in the termination of all federal contracts and a contractor's exclusion from receiving future federal contracts for up to three years.

■ *Davis-Bacon Act of 1931.* This act provides wage protection to nongovernment workers by requiring businesses engaged in federal construction projects to pay their employees prevailing wages and fringe benefits. Applicable types of federal construction projects include airports, dams, highways, and sewer treatment plants involving either construction or repair work, and exceeding $2,000 in funding.

The Act covers blue-collar employees, such as mechanics and laborers. Managerial, clerical, and administrative positions are not covered by the Act. If an employee is within the correct labor category but is a trainee or apprentice, then that person can receive less than prevailing pay rates if registered as such with the Department of Labor or with a state's apprenticeship agency.

The *prevailing* wage rates and fringe benefits referred to in the Act are the wages and fringe benefits paid to a majority of workers in each labor classification in the geographic region. Alternatively, if there is no majority rate, then the average rate must be paid. These prevailing rates are based on labor information from similar private construction projects in the region, exclusive of other Davis-Bacon federal projects (unless there are no comparable private projects). If a federal project is based in a rural area, then the prevailing wage data must also be derived from rural regions, while wage data for projects in urban areas must similarly be derived from urban data.

If a contractor violates this Act, the agency funding the project can withhold enough funds to pay any underpaid employees of the contractor who fall within the labor categories of the Act, while the contractor can be prevented from bidding on federal contracts for three years.

- **Equal Pay Act of 1963.** This Act is an extension of the Fair Labor Standards Act, requiring that both sexes receive equal pay in situations where work requires equivalent effort, responsibility, and skills, performed under similar working conditions. Under this Act, it is irrelevant if specific individuals of either sex who perform the work have extra skills beyond those needed for designated work. The key issue is whether one can perform those specific skills required for the work. However, wage differentials can exist if they are based on some other factor than sex, such as a piece-rate payment system or seniority in a position.

  The Equal Employment Opportunity Commission enforces this Act, including the receipt of employee complaints and the conduct of subsequent investigations.

- **Fair Labor Standards Act of 1938.** This important Act created standards of overtime pay, minimum wages, and payroll recordkeeping. It applies to any business entity that does at least $500,000 in annual business across interstate lines, as well as all schools and governments. It also covers any domestic service workers who work at least eight hours per week and receive a minimum amount in annual wages. Individual positions that are exempt from its provisions include white-collar salaried employees, fishermen, newspaper deliverers, farmers, and casual babysitters. Individual positions that are exempt only from its overtime pay provisions include railroad employees, certain broadcasting positions, seamen on American vessels, and news editors (the list is quite detailed, and longer than presented here).

  The Act (as amended) requires that covered employees be paid at least the minimum wage of $5.15 per hour, or at least $2.13 to employees who also receive tips. Piece-rate pay is also legal, but the resulting pay must at least match the minimum wage. If an applicable state law requires a higher hourly rate, then the state law will prevail. Overtime pay of one and one-half times the regular rate of pay is also required for all hours worked in excess of 40 in a work week.

The Act prohibits the shipment of goods in interstate commerce that were produced in violation of these provisions. Employees may file a complaint with the Wage and Hour Division of the Department of Labor, or can file suit individually to obtain up to three years of unpaid back pay. The Wage and Hour Division can bring criminal proceedings against a willful violator and issue fines of up to $1,000 per violation.

■ *McNamara-O'Hara Service Contract Act of 1965.* This Act covers contractors who work on federal government contracts involving services by "service employees." These are nonexempt employees who are not categorized as administrative, professional, or executive. The covered federal contracts do not include services performed outside the geographical boundaries of the United States, for public utilities, for transport contracts involving published tariff rates, construction or building repairs, employment contracts directly to a government agency, or for services to the communications industry.

Under this Act, contractors performing services in excess of $2,500 must pay those employees working on a federal contract at least as much as the wage and benefit levels prevailing locally. If a contract is less than $2,500, then the federal minimum wage rate must be paid. Also, employers must pay overtime at a rate of one and one-half times the regular pay rate for work hours exceeding 40 in a work week. Furthermore, employers must inform those employees working on federal contracts of their pay rates and benefits under this Act.

The Wage and Hour Division of the Employment Standards Administration handles complaints related to the wage and benefits provisions of this Act. If a violation occurs, the government can withhold sufficient amounts from its contractual payments to a contractor to cover any underpayments to employees, pursue legal action to recover underpayments, and prevent a contractor from bidding for future federal contracts for up to three years.

■ *Walsh-Healey Public Contracts Act of 1936.* This Act forces government contractors to comply with the government's minimum wage and hour rules. It applies to those contractors who sell equipment and supplies to the government, as long as the value of contracts is at least $10,000. Under the Act, employers must pay their employees one-and-a-half times their regular rate of pay for overtime hours worked within a work week. Employees must be paid at least the prevailing minimum wage for the same or similar type of work in the region when production is occurring.

Suppliers in areas that have statutory or regulatory exemptions, such as periodical deliveries, public utilities, and common carriers, are exempted from this Act.

The Wage and Hour Division of the Employment Standards Administration handles complaints related to the wage and benefits provisions of this Act. A contractor who does not comply with this Act can be liable for damages for the amount of unpaid wages, and can be prevented from receiving government contracts for a three-year period.

Tax Law Research

An excellent source of information for payroll-related regulations is the Department of Labor's website. Go to *www.dol.gov* and click on the "Compliance Assistance" option. This takes you to the following series of options:

- *Major laws and regulations.* Summarizes the key labor-related laws and regulations.
- *Compliance tools.* Lists a number of sources for gathering additional information about labor-related laws and regulations, principally call centers.
- *Employment law guide.* Resummarizes labor laws by category, such as wages and hours of work, safety and health standards, health benefits and retirement standards, and regulations for specific industries. This is the most comprehensive source of information on the site.
- *Rulemaking.* Describes how labor-related regulations are promulgated by the department and how they are enforced.

Another excellent source of information, though more tightly restricted to the reporting of labor-related taxes, is the website of the Internal Revenue Service. Go to the main IRS Web page at *www.irs.gov*, and click on the "Corporations" option and then the "Topics" option under the "Contents" heading. This brings you to a lengthy list of topics that can be clicked to access further detailed information, such as employment taxes, taxes for persons living abroad, and the complete Internal Revenue Code. Of particular interest is the "Operating a Business" option, which brings up another set of topics, including federal unemployment insurance taxes and wage reporting.

Summary

This chapter presented the most important pieces of legislation that have formed the basis of the current set of payroll regulations, including the calculation of overtime pay, use of the minimum wage, garnishments, pension plan contributions, employee identification and right to work, social security taxes, and unemployment insurance. Though one will not learn about the precise nature of existing regulations by reviewing these legal summaries, they do give a good historical overview of how today's payroll environment was shaped by yesterday's legislation.

15

Outsourcing Payroll

Introduction

Outsourcing the payroll function means that the collection of payroll-related data is still kept in-house, but that the processing of that data is now the responsibility of a payroll supplier. The supplier's facility contains a set of payroll processing programs and a related database that contains the payroll records submitted by its many customers. The facility does routine payroll tax calculations on the submitted data and creates payroll checks or issues direct deposit payments back to the employees of its customers. In addition to these basic tasks, the facility calculates all taxes due to various government entities and submits the tax payments along with any required tax forms. Other services include the issuance of annual W-2 forms, quarterly wage reports, and the federal unemployment tax return.

Shifting the payroll function to such a supplier is nearly automatic for smaller firms, which can thereby avoid an array of in-house payroll costs, as well as avoiding the risk of incurring tax penalties for making late or incorrect tax payments to various government entities. The decision to shift to a supplier is more difficult for large firms, who may find that the supplier's fees do not adequately offset the services rendered.

In this chapter,[*] we will explore the advantages and disadvantages of outsourcing the payroll function, cover the contractual, transition, and control issues associated with the change, and also note how the supplier's performance may be measured and managed.

Advantages and Disadvantages of Outsourcing Payroll

There are a variety of good reasons for outsourcing payroll, which has led thousands of companies to pursue this option. Here are some of the reasons:

- *Avoid filing tax payments.* One of the primary reasons for outsourcing payroll is to avoid having to file payroll tax payments in a timely manner. The gov-

---

[*] This chapter is largely adapted with permission from Chapter 4, "Outsourcing the Accounting Function," in *Outsourcing* by Bragg (Hoboken, NJ: John Wiley and Sons, 1998).

ernment requires quite rapid tax filings and has imposed stiff penalties if taxes are not filed on time. For those companies with a chronic tax-filing problem, handing over this task to a supplier may save them more money in tax penalties avoided than the total cost of having the supplier handle the payroll.

- *Avoid paying for software updates.* Companies do not want to pay their software providers for new tax tables every year so they can correctly calculate payroll taxes through their in-house software packages. Since there are some incremental tax rate changes somewhere every year, a company that runs its payroll on an in-house software package must incur this expense every year in order to stay current. By outsourcing payroll, there is no need for this software or related updates.

- *Avoid fixed costs.* By using a payroll supplier, there is no need to maintain any in-house software and its attendant annual maintenance fees. It is also possible, though unlikely in smaller firms, that some in-house payroll personnel would no longer be needed.

- *Avoid nonstrategic activities.* If a company's management team wants to focus on only the most mission-critical activities, then payroll should be one of the first activities to go. Paying employees is certainly an important function, but generally has little to do with a corporation's strategic direction.

- *Avoid creating W-2 forms.* A payroll supplier will accumulate all annual payroll information into W-2 tax reports for the company. Otherwise, the in-house system would produce these documents and send them to employees.

- *Avoid printing paychecks.* A payroll printing can tie up a printer for a long time if a company has a large number of employees and this printing must be monitored by an employee to ensure that there is no jamming. When the function is outsourced, the company can use both the printer and the employee for other purposes.

- *Use direct deposit.* Many in-house payroll systems do not allow direct deposit, since this requires a software interface that can be read by the local bank. All major payroll suppliers, however, offer direct deposit. This is a major advantage for those companies whose employees are constantly traveling and who are frequently not on-site to pick up and deposit their paychecks. There is always a fee associated with direct deposit, so this is not a cost-saving feature, but it is very good for employee relations.

- *Use check stuffing.* A further convenience is for the supplier to automatically stuff all checks into envelopes for delivery to employees, which eliminates a clerical task for the accounting staff.

- *Use check delivery to multiple locations.* Though most payroll services will not mail checks to individual employees, they will send batches of checks to multiple company locations for distribution to employees. This eliminates the risk that the company will forget to distribute checks, which can easily happen if the person responsible for this distribution is on vacation or sick.

- *Stamp signatures on checks.* Some company officers are burdened with the task of signing a multitude of checks every payday. Ostensibly, this is necessary so that someone reviews all checks prior to delivery to employees. However, since checks can easily be reviewed subsequent to distribution by perusing the accompanying payroll reports provided by the supplier, it is easy to correct payroll errors in the next payroll. Taking this view allows a company to deliver signature samples to the payroll supplier, which automatically affixes a signature to each check and saves an officer the trouble of doing so.

- *Use custom and standard reports.* Most payroll suppliers provide a plethora of reports that cover the needs of most companies. For special reporting needs, there is usually a custom report-writing tool available that allows the company to create any additional reports it needs, without special programming.

- *Link to 401k plan.* Some suppliers now link their payroll systems to an array of 401k investment options so that deductions can be made automatically from employee paychecks and deposited into employee retirement accounts, which eliminates a great deal of paperwork.

Despite the formidable array of advantages just noted, some organizations persist in not outsourcing their payroll activities. There are a variety of reasons for this, ranging from inertia to company politics. The two most legitimate complaints are excessive costs and the difficulty of converting the more complex payroll systems to a supplier's system. Some of the more realistic disadvantages are:

- *Cost.* Payroll suppliers can be quite expensive if all possible payroll services are used. The most typical supplier ploy is to initially charge very low rates for the basic service of printing paychecks. This is done to keep a company from shifting to the services of a competitor. However, once the company has signed on with the supplier, it will find that additional services may easily exceed the cost of the basic service. For example, additional fees will be charged for automatic signature printing, check stuffing, delivery to multiple locations, access to custom reporting software, and direct deposits. A very large company that represents a major portion of a supplier's business has more sway in negotiating prices than will a small company.

- *Conversion problems.* There are a number of data items that must be properly converted over to the supplier's software to ensure that employees will continue to receive paychecks in the correct amounts and with accurate deductions. If the conversion does not go well, the company may become so disenchanted with the supplier that it will revert to the in-house processing solution. Conversions can be a problem because many companies want to convert to a supplier at the beginning of each year, which creates a considerable work overload for system-conversion employees of suppliers. This problem can be avoided by conducting a gradual conversion of data to the supplier, so that only the most basic features are shifted to the supplier and debugged before more advanced features are added. However, some highly complex payroll systems must be converted at once, so employees see no difference in the payroll services provided to them; in these cases, the risk of excessive error rates and company dissatisfaction is high.

- *Create manual paychecks.* Some companies complain that they cannot easily determine the correct tax amounts to charge when cutting a manual paycheck for an employee. This is usually needed when an employee is being released, and government regulations require that final payment be made to the employee at once, rather than when the next payroll processing period arrives. However, several payroll suppliers now allow companies to dial up the database of information on each employee, plug in the special payment amount, and have the system automatically tell the company the appropriate amount of taxes to deduct from the paycheck.

- *Last minute changes.* Suppliers prefer to obtain all payroll information three or four days prior to the actual payroll date, so they have sufficient time to process the payroll. However, this means that any last-minute changes to payroll information cannot be processed through the supplier's payroll system. The result is usually the creation of manual checks by the company to reflect these last-minute changes, which must then be entered into the next payroll transmission to the supplier.

- *Must collect payroll data.* The payroll supplier does not collect payroll information. The company must still collect it from a variety of sources, organize it, and input it into the supplier's system. As this may be the primary source of clerical time in computing payroll, some companies may not see how they are saving money by outsourcing their payroll.

- *No control over supplier disaster recovery planning.* It is possible that a disaster may occur at the supplier's processing facility that will destroy a company's payroll database. This is not much of a problem for large national suppliers, which have clearly defined disaster recovery plans, but may be an issue for smaller regional providers that have fewer resources available to set up such systems.

In short, outsourcing is an attractive option for smaller organizations, though the economics of doing so are less obvious to very large entities that can internally process payroll for thousands of employees at less cost than the rates charged by suppliers.

Contract-Specific Issues

A contract for payroll services will only be negotiable on prices. This is because a payroll supplier has thousands of clients and prefers to use a standard contract for all of them—it cannot hope to track slight contract changes for all of those companies and so it does not allow them. However, suppliers have modified their computer systems to allow for different prices for each customer, so this one area is subject to negotiation. Pricing is typically on a per-person basis, plus a fixed baseline fee for various services. Each of these fees can be changed. A company has the most negotiating power if it has a large number of employees to put on the supplier's payroll system; the prospect of losing all of that revenue will normally elicit price cuts by the supplier. A small company will likely have no luck in negotiating reduced prices, for it has no basis for demanding a price reduction. The one exception to this rule is that a payroll supplier will sometimes grant a price cut if the company employee who is sponsoring the supplier has brought the supplier into other companies as well—this loyalty to the supplier can be worth a small discount. Thus, payroll suppliers allow no contract changes, but price alterations are possible if the company has a large payroll.

Transition Issues

When transitioning the payroll function to a supplier, the first step is to meet with the supplier about one month in advance of the conversion date (or earlier if the payroll system to be converted is especially large or complex). This meeting should cover all key conversion dates and who is to perform which tasks by those dates. Since the payroll function must usually be brought online with the supplier as of the first day of the year, this is a very time-sensitive process, so the initial meeting with the supplier is especially important. If various extra payroll features, such as automated check signing, are to be added to the payroll later on, these dates should also be agreed upon by both parties during the meeting.

The next transition step will be to transfer all payroll information for all employees to the supplier at the end of the year or slightly prior to that date. This may require either the conversion of existing computer data to a format that is readable by the supplier's computer system or a large rekeying effort by the company's payroll staff. It is particularly important during this step to provide time and personnel resources to review all rekeyed information to ensure that it is correct. There must also be enough time to adequately train the staff members who will be inputting information into the payroll system on an ongoing basis. Supplier representatives should be on hand during the first few data-entry sessions to ensure that all problem areas are adequately addressed.

If company management is interested in purchasing a number of extra features offered by the supplier, such as vacation time tracking or the addition of 401k services to the payroll, it is best to gradually add these features only after all baseline functionality has been converted and proven to be functioning correctly. It can be quite difficult to add many features to a newly outsourced system and expect them all to work properly, so a little delay in adding some features will ensure that the entire system works better in the long run.

Creating Control Points

The primary control point is the internal audit. The internal audit team should follow an audit program that takes it through a review of the payroll supplier's activities regularly enough for the supplier to know that it will be undergoing an audit about once a year.

There are many audit objectives related to the payroll function, some of which apply to the supplier and some to the data entry and inputting functions that are retained by the company. Possible control objectives relating to the supplier are:

- Verify that payroll taxes are being deposited.
- Verify that 401k deductions are terminated once they reach annual maximums.
- Verify that garnishments are being sent to the appropriate legal authorities.
- Verify that only authorized services and reports are being billed to the company.
- Verify that prices charged match those listed in the original contract or its addendums.
- Verify that payroll tax deduction percentages used by the supplier are up-to-date.

Once the audit team has completed its audit program for the payroll supplier, it should go over its findings with the supplier's representative to verify that all audit findings are accurate and then meet with company management to present its findings and recommendations.

Another control is to create a separate line item in the corporate budget that shows the estimated cost of the payroll supplier. When this information is listed in the monthly financial statements alongside actual costs, company management gains a clear understanding of the cost of the supplier and how that cost is changing in comparison to the budget. If there are significant cost overruns appearing in the financial statements, management can take action to reduce them, either through negotiations, less use of the supplier's services, or by switching to a new supplier.

A final control area is the scheduled review meeting. This is useful for going over the results of internal audits, reviewing progress toward predetermined goals, and discussing any problems that have arisen since the last meeting. An agenda should be distributed in advance and strictly followed to ensure that all major areas are addressed. The company should have a secretary record the minutes of each meeting, distribute them to all participants, and require that the chief representatives from each side sign off on the minutes as being accurate (or modify them as necessary and then sign off). These minutes should be kept on file in case there are questions later on about what was agreed upon during meetings. Once a payroll system has been fully converted to that of a supplier, it should not be necessary to have more than one such formal meeting per year.

The combination of internal audits, financial comparisons to budgeted costs, and formal review meetings provides an effective mix of controls over a payroll supplier.

Measuring the Outsourced Payroll Function

A payroll supplier can be measured in terms of its cost, timeliness in providing information, and ability to provide services. Here are some of the more common measurements that can be used to judge performance:

- *Timeliness in paying payroll taxes.* One of the primary tasks of the supplier is to pay all payroll taxes on behalf of the company. This greatly reduces the labor and risk of penalties for nonpayment by the company. It is a very easy measurement to track, for the government will notify the company of any late payments. If there are no notifications, then the supplier has filed tax payments at the appropriate times. The measurement is to divide the total number of missed tax payments by the number of payrolls per year to determine the average timeliness in paying payroll taxes.

- *Transaction fees per person.* A payroll supplier's services are billed as a mix of per-person costs and fixed costs that are not linked to headcount. The bulk of these fees is based on per-person costs, however, and is therefore an excellent way to determine the per-unit cost of this service. Most payroll providers send out highly detailed billing statements after each payroll, so the information used to derive this measurement is easily obtained. To calculate it, summarize all costs per payroll for each person for whom a paycheck was created. This may include fees for check preparation, check stuffing, extra calculations for vacations or 401k deductions, and direct deposits. All of these per-person fees should be compiled when deriving the transaction fee per person. The total fees are then divided by the total number of employees paid in the period to come up with the per-person amount. If a company has different payrolls of different lengths (e.g., once a week or twice a month), the costs should be annualized to properly account for the costs of *all* payrolls.

- *Proportion of fees for extra services.* A payroll supplier likes to gain business by charging low fees for basic payroll processing services, since companies make the decision to use suppliers based on these initial fees. The suppliers then charge exceedingly high rates for all additional services, which companies ask for after they have enrolled with the supplier and are "locked in." One should separate these extra costs from the baseline fees to gain an understanding of incremental costs. The calculation should be the total additional fees per reporting period, divided by the total fees during that period.

- *Proportion of payrolls delivered to correct locations.* One service provided by payroll suppliers is guaranteed delivery of payrolls to the company's various locations by payday, usually using overnight mail delivery. If a payroll is sent to the wrong location or lost, this causes major personnel problems (since employees are not being paid), and therefore should be measured. The measurement is to summarize all instances when payroll was incorrectly delivered and to divide this by the total number of payroll deliveries in the reporting period. There is never a problem with collecting the information for the missing payrolls—company employees will bring this information to your attention very quickly.

Managing the Outsourced Payroll Function

Outsourcing the payroll function usually means that the payroll processing has been shifted to an outside entity, while the payroll data collection and inputting chores are still conducted internally. This means that at least some portion of a company's payroll staff, and its management, will be retained after the shift to an outsourcing arrangement has occurred. The manager will probably be a payroll supervisor or assistant controller, though the controller may be directly responsible for this area in smaller organizations.

Though the manager of the payroll function will probably still be on staff, his or her job description will change to some extent. Responsibility for data collection and inputting, as well as distribution of paychecks, will remain unchanged. Responsibility for payroll processing will shift from a hands-on role to an examination of the payroll documents returned by the payroll supplier to ensure that processing has been completed and is accurate. The supervisor must also ensure that the supplier is billing the company for services rendered at price levels that were agreed upon in the original contract, and should be the lead person in later negotiations if the supplier wishes to increase its prices.

The company's account will be assigned to a salesperson or technical consultant within the payroll supplier. The company's payroll supervisor should meet with this person from time to time to discuss ongoing issues, training needs for the company's staff, and any prospective changes in the supplier's staff that have been assigned to the company's account.

In short, there is still a strong need for supervision of the payroll function within a company, though the responsibilities assigned to this position will shift away from payroll processing and towards monitoring of supplier activities and performance.

Potential Employee Service Issues

Payroll problems can result in extremely dissatisfied employees. Potential problems can include incorrect pay rates, inaccurate vacation accruals, late issuance of paychecks, or issuances to the wrong company locations. If the problems involve data inaccuracies, the fault may lie with the company employees that input this information into the supplier's payroll system. However, if the data entry is communicated by phone to the supplier and then keyed into the system by an employee of the supplier, then the fault can also lie with the supplier. If the problems relate to the late or inaccurate processing of payroll information, then the fault is almost certainly the supplier's. Continuing problems in the later area should result in the eventual replacement of the supplier, while the former problems require additional investigation to see where the underlying problem is originating. In either case, problems must be dealt with quickly, since employees will not tolerate problems with their paychecks.

Getting Out of the Outsourcing Arrangement

Canceling an outsourcing contract with a payroll supplier is easy to do, but a company should think through the ramifications before going forward with this step.

The main problem involves tax and pay accumulators. If a single payroll supplier accumulates all of this information for a full calendar year, then it will agree to issue W-2 forms to the company for its employees at the end of the year. However, if the supplier is taking over for only part of a year, it will not guarantee the accuracy of the W-2 forms, only issue a W-2 for the period during which it provided services, or not agree to issue the forms at all. This means that the company must manually produce all W-2 forms at the end of the year (which can be a considerable chore if there are thousands of employees) or else allow the supplier to issue a W-2 for just that portion of the year during which it provided services to the company and then issue a second W-2 either internally or with the services of yet another supplier. The best way to avoid this problem is to only switch payroll suppliers at the end of the calendar year, when payroll and tax accumulators are complete and can be reported as such on employee W-2 forms.

Summary

Outsourcing the payroll function makes a great deal of sense to many smaller companies, and is even practiced by some quite large ones that do not want to deal with the tax reporting issues surrounding the payroll function. Given the large number of companies interested in using this service, it is no surprise that there are a number of good payroll suppliers. Some have been in business for several decades and service thousands of companies each. Others are local suppliers that cater to smaller geographic regions. There is also a new crop of suppliers that offer their services through Internet sites. A representative sample of the larger national and Internet payroll providers is listed in Appendix A.

16

International Payroll Issues

Introduction

This chapter addresses the primary area of concern for U.S. citizens that a company sends to work in a foreign country—what taxes must an employee pay? It discusses the situations in which income tax withholding may be avoided, as well as the tax exclusions available to employees working outside the United States, payroll taxes and related Totalization Agreements, state income taxes, and the recognition of business expense reimbursements as taxable income.

Withholding of Federal Income Taxes

The general rule is that a U.S. employer must deduct federal income taxes from the wages of all U.S. citizens working outside the country. Though there are essentially no exemptions to this rule for resident aliens, U.S. citizens are subject to the following exemptions:

- *Work in U.S. possessions.* The wages of an employee working in Puerto Rico for a full year are exempt from withholding. If at least 80 percent of an employee's annual wages are earned in any other U.S. possession, their wages are also exempt from withholding.
- *Legally mandated foreign income tax withholding.* If a foreign country requires the company to withhold income taxes from an employee's wages on its behalf, then the company does not have to withhold U.S. income taxes as well. The employer should request a signed statement from the affected employee, attesting to the requirement by the foreign country to withhold income taxes and keep this statement on file.
- *A credit against U.S. taxes paid, matching foreign income taxes paid.* An employee can claim a foreign tax credit against U.S. income taxes owed to the extent that foreign income taxes have been paid, thereby avoiding double taxation. An employer can reduce the amount of an employee's income tax withholding up to the expected amount of the foreign tax credit. An employee

can claim this credit using Form 1116, "Computation of Foreign Tax Credit," as shown in Exhibit 16.1.

■ *Foreign earned income exclusion.* If an employee feels that he or she will qualify for the foreign earned income exclusion (see next section), they should complete Form 673 and give it to the employer, who uses it as evidence for a reduction in income tax withholding from the employee's pay. An employee can also give the employer a signed statement instead of a completed Form 673. The form is shown in Exhibit 16.2. In addition, the employee must file either Form 2555 or Form 2555-EZ as an attachment to the standard 1040 tax form.

Receipt of a Form 673 or signed statement from an employee does not, however, provide a company with a rock-solid reason to stop withholding federal income taxes. If the employer has reason to believe that the employee will not qualify for the exclusion, the employer should continue to withhold income taxes.

The Foreign Earned Income Exclusion

An employee qualifies for the federal foreign earned income exclusion by meeting the tax home test *and* either the bona fide residence test *or* the physical presence test, as noted in the attached Form 2555 in Exhibit 16.3, which a taxpayer must attach to his or her annual 1040 tax return. The tests are as follows:

■ *Tax home test.* An employee must physically *reside or be present in*[1] a foreign country for a full year. This test is covered in Part I of Form 2555.

■ *Bona fide residence test.* An employee must be a bona fide resident of a foreign country for a full tax year and must intend to reside in the foreign country for an extended, indefinite period of time, not to reside there for a temporary purpose. He or she should demonstrate proof of long-term residency, such as having signed a long-term housing lease in the foreign country. The employee can still qualify under the terms of this test even if there are moves between several foreign countries during the year or if he or she makes brief temporary visits to the United States. This test is covered in Part II of Form 2555.

■ *Physical presence test.* An employee must be *present* in one or more foreign countries for at least 330 full days during a twelve-month period that does not have to match the calendar year. This test is covered in Part III of Form 2555.

The IRS can waive these requirements in cases where a person is forced to leave a country due to war or similar conditions. However, even if a waiver is granted, only the number of days during which the employee resided in the country can be used to calculate the foreign earned income exclusion.

Under no circumstances can a person use the foreign earned income exclusion if the foreign country in which the person is residing is one to which the United States government has banned travel by its citizens.

Exhibit 16.1   *Computation of Foreign Tax Credit Form*

Form **1116**	**Foreign Tax Credit**	OMB No. 1545-0121
	(Individual, Estate, or Trust)	**2002**
Department of the Treasury Internal Revenue Service (99)	► Attach to Form 1040, 1040NR, 1041, or 990-T. ► See separate instructions.	Attachment Sequence No. 19

Name	Identifying number as shown on page 1 of your tax return

Use a separate Form 1116 for each category of income listed below. See Categories of Income   on page 3 of the instructions. Check only one box on each Form 1116. Report all amounts in U.S. dollars except where specified in Part II below.

a ☐ Passive income

b ☐ High withholding tax interest

c ☐ Financial services income

d ☐ Shipping income

e ☐ Dividends from a DISC or former DISC

f ☐ Certain distributions from a foreign sales corporation (FSC) or former FSC

g ☐ Lump-sum distributions

h ☐ Section 901(j) income

i ☐ Certain income re-sourced by treaty

j ☐ General limitation income

k Resident of (name of country) ►

Note: If you paid taxes to only one foreign country or U.S. possession, use column A in Part I and line A in Part II. If you paid taxes to more than one   foreign country or U.S. possession, use a separate column and line for each country or possession.

Part I   Taxable Income or Loss From Sources Outside the United States (for Category Checked Above)

		Foreign Country or U.S. Possession			Total
		A	B	C	(Add cols. A, B, and C.)
l	Enter the name of the foreign country or U.S. possession . . . . ►				
1	Gross income from sources within country shown above and of the type checked above (see page 7 of the instructions):				
	....				**1**
	Deductions and losses (Caution: See pages 9, 12, and 13 of the instructions):				
2	Expenses definitely related to the income on line 1 (attach statement)				
3	Pro rata share of other deductions not definitely related:				
a	Certain itemized deductions or standard deduction (see instructions)				
b	Other deductions (attach statement)				
c	Add lines 3a and 3b				
d	Gross foreign source income (see instructions)				
e	Gross income from all sources (see instructions)				
f	Divide line 3d by line 3e (see instructions) . .				
g	Multiply line 3c by line 3f				
4	Pro rata share of interest expense (see instructions):				
a	Home mortgage interest (use worksheet on page 12 of the instructions)				
b	Other interest expense				
5	Losses from foreign sources				
6	Add lines 2, 3g, 4a, 4b, and 5				**6**
7	Subtract line 6 from line 1. Enter the result here and on line 14, page 2 . . . . ►				**7**

Part II   Foreign Taxes Paid or Accrued   (see page 13 of the instructions)

Country	Credit is claimed for taxes (you must check one)			Foreign taxes paid or accrued								
			In foreign currency				In U.S. dollars					
	(m) ☐ Paid (n) ☐ Accrued		Taxes withheld at source on:			(s) Other foreign taxes paid or accrued	Taxes withheld at source on:			(w) Other foreign taxes paid or accrued	(x) Total foreign taxes paid or accrued (add cols. (t) through (w))	
	(o) Date paid or accrued	(p) Dividends	(q) Rents and royalties	(r) Interest		(t) Dividends	(u) Rents and royalties	(v) Interest				
A												
B												
C												

8 Add lines A through C, column (x). Enter the total here and on line 9, page 2 . . . . ►	**8**

For Paperwork Reduction Act Notice, see page 16 of the instructions.	Cat. No. 11440U	Form 1116 (2002)

Exhibit 16.1 *(Continued)*

Part III   Figuring the Credit

9   Enter the amount from line 8. These are your total foreign taxes paid
    or accrued for the category of income checked above Part I . . .   **9**

10 Carryback or carryover (attach detailed computation) **10**

11 Add lines 9 and 10 . . . .   **11**

12 Reduction in foreign taxes (see page 13 of the instructions) . . .   **12**

13 Subtract line 12 from line 11. This is the total amount of foreign taxes available for credit **13**

14 Enter the amount from line 7. This is your taxable income or (loss) from
    sources outside the United States (before adjustments) for the category
    of income checked above Part I (see page 14 of the instructions) . .   **14**

15 Adjustments to line 14 (see page 14 of the instructions) **15**

16 Combine the amounts on lines 14 and 15. This is your net foreign
    source taxable income. (If the result is zero or less, you have no foreign
    tax credit for the category of income you checked above Part I. Skip
    lines 17 through 21. However, if you are filing more than one Form
    1116, you must complete line 19.) **16**

17 Individuals: Enter the amount from Form 1040, line 39. If you are a
    nonresident alien, enter the amount from Form 1040NR, line 37.
    Estates and trusts: Enter your taxable income without the deduction
    for your exemption **17**

    Caution: If you figured your tax using the special rates on capital gains, see page 15 of the instructions.

18 Divide line 16 by line 17. If line 16 is more than line 17, enter "1" **18**

19 Individuals: Enter the amount from Form 1040, line 42. If you are a nonresident alien, enter the
    amount from Form 1040NR, line 40.

    Estates and trusts: Enter the amount from Form 1041, Schedule G, line 1a, or the total of Form 990-T,
    lines 36 and 37 . . . .   **19**

    Caution: If you are completing line 19 for separate category g (lump-sum distributions), see page 15 of the instructions.

20 Multiply line 19 by line 18 (maximum amount of credit) **20**

21 Enter the smaller of line 13 or line 20. If this is the only Form 1116 you are filing, skip lines 22 through
    30 and enter this amount on line 31. Otherwise, complete the appropriate line in Part IV (see
    page 16 of the instructions) . . . . ▶   **21**

Part IV   Summary of Credits From Separate Parts III   (see page 16 of the instructions)

22 Credit for taxes on passive income **22**

23 Credit for taxes on high withholding tax interest **23**

24 Credit for taxes on financial services income **24**

25 Credit for taxes on shipping income **25**

26 Credit for taxes on dividends from a DISC or former DISC and certain
    distributions from a FSC or former FSC **26**

27 Credit for taxes on lump-sum distributions **27**

28 Credit for taxes on certain income re-sourced by treaty **28**

29 Credit for taxes on general limitation income **29**

30 Add lines 22 through 29 . . . .   **30**

31 Enter the smaller of line 19 or line 30 . . . .   **31**

32 Reduction of credit for international boycott operations. See instructions for line 12 on page 13 . .   **32**

33 Subtract line 32 from line 31. This is your foreign tax credit. Enter here and on Form 1040, line 45;
    Form 1040NR, line 43; Form 1041, Schedule G, line 2a; or Form 990-T, line 40a . . . . . ▶   **33**

⊕

Form **1116** (2002)

Exhibit 16.2   *Withholding Exemption Statement*

Form **673** (Rev. June 2003) Department of the Treasury Internal Revenue Service	Statement For Claiming Exemption From Withholding on Foreign Earned Income Eligible for the Exclusion(s) Provided by Section 911	OMB No. 1545-0666

The following statement, when completed and furnished by a citizen of the United States to his or her employer, permits the employer to exclude from income tax withholding all or a part of the wages paid for services performed outside the United States.

Name (please print or type)   Social security number

Part I   Qualification Information for Foreign Earned Income Exclusion

I expect to qualify for the foreign earned income exclusion under either the bona fide residence or physical presence test for calendar year _____ or other tax year beginning _____ and ending _____ .

Please check applicable box:

☐ Bona Fide Residence Test

     I am a citizen of the United States. I have been a bona fide resident of and my tax home has been located in _____ (foreign country or countries) for an uninterrupted period which includes an entire tax year that began on _____ , 20 _____ .
                                                                     (date)

     I expect to remain a bona fide resident and retain my tax home in a foreign country (or countries) until the end of the tax year for which this statement is made. Or, if not that period, from the date of this statement until _____ , 20 _____ .
              (date within tax year)

     I have not submitted a statement to the authorities of any foreign country named above that I am not a resident of that country. Or, if I made such a statement, the authorities of that country thereafter made a determination to the effect that I am a resident of that country.

     Based on the facts in my case, I have good reason to believe that for this period of foreign residence I will satisfy the tax home and the bona fide foreign resident requirements prescribed by section 911(d)(1)(A) of the Internal Revenue Code and qualify for the exclusion Code section 911(a) allows.

☐ Physical Presence Test

     I am a citizen of the United States. Except for occasional absences that will not disqualify me for the benefit of section 911(a) of the Internal Revenue Code, I expect to be present in and maintain my tax home in _____ (foreign country or countries) for a 12-month period that includes the entire tax year _____ . Or, if not the entire year, for the part of the tax year beginning on _____ , 20 _____ , and ending on _____ , 20 _____ .

     Based on the facts in my case, I have good reason to believe that for this period of presence in a foreign country or countries, I will satisfy the tax home and the 330 full-day requirements within a 12-month period under section 911(d)(1)(B).

Part II   Estimated Housing Cost Amount for Foreign Housing Exclusion

1 Rent	1	
2 Utilities (other than telephone charges)	2	
3 Real and personal property insurance	3	
4 Occupancy tax not deductible under section 164	4	
5 Nonrefundable fees paid for securing a leasehold	5	
6 Household repairs	6	
7 Estimated qualified housing expenses. Add lines 1 through 6	7	
8 Estimated base housing amount for qualifying period	8	
9 Subtract line 8 from line 7. This is your estimated housing cost amount	9	

Part III   Certification

     Under penalties of perjury, I declare that I have examined the information on this form and to the best of my knowledge and belief it is true, correct, and complete. I further certify under penalties of perjury that:

● The estimated housing cost amount entered in Part II, plus the amount reported on any other statements outstanding with other employers, is not more than my total estimated housing cost amount.

● If I become disqualified for the exclusions, I will immediately notify my employer and advise what part, if any, of the period for which I am qualified.

     I understand that any exemption from income tax withholding permitted by reason of furnishing this statement is not a determination by the Internal Revenue Service that any amount paid to me for any services performed during the tax year is excludable from gross income under the provisions of Code section 911(a).

Your Signature   Date

For Paperwork Reduction Act Notice, see back of form.   Cat. No. 10183Y   Form **673** (Rev. 6-2003)

Exhibit 16.3   *IRS Form 2555*

Form **2555**	Foreign Earned Income	OMB No. 1545-0067

Department of the Treasury
Internal Revenue Service   (99)

► See separate instructions.   ► Attach to Form 1040.

2003

Attachment
Sequence No. 34

For Use by U.S. Citizens and Resident Aliens Only

Name shown on Form 1040

Your social security number

Part I   General Information

1   Your foreign address (including country)

2   Your occupation

3   Employer's name ► ....

4a   Employer's U.S. address ► ....

b   Employer's foreign address ► ....

5   Employer is (check   a ☐ A foreign entity   b ☐ A U.S. company   c ☐ Self
any that apply):   d ☐ A foreign affiliate of a U.S. company   e ☐ Other (specify) ► ....

6a   If, after 1981, you filed Form 2555 or 2555-EZ to claim either of the exclusions, enter the last year you filed the form. ► ....

b   If you did not file Form 2555 or 2555-EZ after 1981 to claim either of the exclusions, check here ► ☐ and go to line 7.

c   Have you ever revoked either of the exclusions?   .   .   .   .   ☐ Yes   ☐ No

d   If you answered "Yes," enter the type of exclusion and the tax year for which the revocation was effective. ► ....

7   Of what country are you a citizen/national? ► ....

8a   Did you maintain a separate foreign residence for your family because of adverse living conditions at your tax home? See Second foreign household   on page 3 of the instructions   .   .   .   .   ☐ Yes   ☐ No

b   If "Yes," enter city and country of the separate foreign residence. Also, enter the number of days during your tax year that you maintained a second household at that address. ► ....

9   List your tax home(s) during your tax year and date(s) established. ► ....

Next, complete either Part II or Part III. If an item does not apply, enter "NA." If you do not give the information asked for, any exclusion or deduction you claim may be disallowed.

Part II   Taxpayers Qualifying Under Bona Fide Residence Test   (See page 2 of the instructions.)

10   Date bona fide residence began ► ...., and ended ► ....

11   Kind of living quarters in foreign country ► a ☐ Purchased house   b ☐ Rented house or apartment   c ☐ Rented room
d ☐ Quarters furnished by employer

12a   Did any of your family live with you abroad during any part of the tax year?   .   .   .   .   ☐ Yes   ☐ No

b   If "Yes," who and for what period? ►...

13a   Have you submitted a statement to the authorities of the foreign country where you claim bona fide residence that you are not a resident of that country? (See instructions.)   .   .   .   .   ☐ Yes   ☐ No

b   Are you required to pay income tax to the country where you claim bona fide residence? (See instructions.)   ☐ Yes   ☐ No
If you answered "Yes" to 13a and "No" to 13b, you do not qualify as a bona fide resident. Do not complete the rest of this part.

14   If you were present in the United States or its possessions during the tax year, complete columns (a)–(d) below. Do not include the income from column (d) in Part IV, but report it on Form 1040.

(a) Date arrived in U.S.	(b) Date left U.S.	(c) Number of days in U.S. on business	(d) Income earned in U.S. on business (attach computation)	(a) Date arrived in U.S.	(b) Date left U.S.	(c) Number of days in U.S. on business	(d) Income earned in U.S. on business (attach computation)

15a   List any contractual terms or other conditions relating to the length of your employment abroad. ►.........................

b   Enter the type of visa under which you entered the foreign country. ► ....

c   Did your visa limit the length of your stay or employment in a foreign country? If "Yes," attach explanation   ☐ Yes   ☐ No

d   Did you maintain a home in the United States while living abroad?   .   .   .   .   ☐ Yes   ☐ No

e   If "Yes," enter address of your home, whether it was rented, the names of the occupants, and their relationship to you. ► ....

For Paperwork Reduction Act Notice, see page 4 of separate instructions.   Cat. No. 11900P   Form **2555** (2003)

Exhibit 16.3 *(Continued)*

Form 2555 (2003)

Part III Taxpayers Qualifying Under Physical Presence Test   (See page 2 of the instructions.)

16 The physical presence test is based on the 12-month period from ▶ .... through ▶ ....

17 Enter your principal country of employment during your tax year. ▶ ....

18 If you traveled abroad during the 12-month period entered on line 16, complete columns (a)–(f) below. Exclude travel between foreign countries that did not involve travel on or over international waters, or in or over the United States, for 24 hours or more. If you have no travel to report during the period, enter "Physically present in a foreign country or countries for the entire 12-month period." Do not include the income from column (f) below in Part IV, but report it on Form 1040.

(a) Name of country (including U.S.)	(b) Date arrived	(c) Date left	(d) Full days present in foreign country	(e) Number of days in U.S. on business	(f) Income earned in U.S. on business (attach computation)

Part IV All Taxpayers

Note: Enter on lines 19 through 23 all income, including noncash income, you earned and actually or constructively received during your 2003 tax year for services you performed in a foreign country. If any of the foreign earned income received this tax year was earned in a prior tax year, or will be earned in a later tax year (such as a bonus), see the instructions.Do not include income from line 14, column (d), or line 18, column (f). Report amounts in U.S. dollars, using the exchange rates in effect when you actually or constructively received the income.

If you are a cash basis taxpayer, report on Form 1040 all income you received in 2003, no matter when you performed the service.

2003 Foreign Earned Income	Amount (in U.S. dollars)
19 Total wages, salaries, bonuses, commissions, etc. **19**	
20 Allowable share of income for personal services performed (see instructions):	
a In a business (including farming) or profession **20a**	
b In a partnership. List partnership's name and address and type of income. ▶ **20b**	
21 Noncash income (market value of property or facilities furnished by employer —attach statement showing how it was determined):	
a Home (lodging) **21a**	
b Meals **21b**	
c Car **21c**	
d Other property or facilities. List type and amount. ▶ **21d**	
22 Allowances, reimbursements, or expenses paid on your behalf for services you performed:	
a Cost of living and overseas differential **22a**	
b Family **22b**	
c Education **22c**	
d Home leave **22d**	
e Quarters. **22e**	
f For any other purpose. List type and amount. ▶ **22f**	
g Add lines 22a through 22f **22g**	
23 Other foreign earned income. List type and amount. ▶ **23**	
24 Add lines 19 through 21d, line 22g, and line 23 . . . . **24**	
25 Total amount of meals and lodging included on line 24 that is excludable (see instructions) . . **25**	
26 Subtract line 25 from line 24. Enter the result here and on line 27 on page 3. This is your 2003 foreign earned income . . . . ▶ **26**	

Form **2555** (2003)

Exhibit 16.3 *(Continued)*

Form 2555 (2003)   Page 3

Part V   All Taxpayers

27   Enter the amount from line 26   . . . . | 27 |
     Are you claiming the housing exclusion or housing deduction?
     ☐ Yes. Complete Part VI.
     ☐ No. Go to Part VII.

Part VI   Taxpayers Claiming the Housing Exclusion and/or Deduction

28   Qualified housing expenses for the tax year (see instructions) . . . . | 28 |
29   Number of days in your qualifying period that fall within your 2003 tax
     year (see instructions) . . . . | 29 | days
30   Multiply $30.77 by the number of days on line 29. If 365 is entered on line 29, enter $11,233.00 here | 30 |
31   Subtract line 30 from line 28. If the result is zero or less, do not complete the rest of this part
     or any of Part IX . . . . | 31 |
32   Enter employer-provided amounts (see instructions) . . . . . . | 32 |
33   Divide line 32 by line 27. Enter the result as a decimal (rounded to at least three places), but do
     not enter more than "1.000" . . . . | 33 | × .
34   Housing exclusion. Multiply line 31 by line 33. Enter the result but do not enter more than the
     amount on line 32. Also, complete Part VIII . . . . ▶ | 34 |
     Note: The housing deduction is figured in Part IX. If you choose to claim the foreign earned
            income exclusion, complete Parts VII and VIII before Part IX.

Part VII   Taxpayers Claiming the Foreign Earned Income Exclusion

35   Maximum foreign earned income exclusion . . . . | 35 | $80,000 | 00
36   ● If you completed Part VI, enter the number from line 29.
     ● All others, enter the number of days in your qualifying period that | 36 | days
       fall within your 2003 tax year (see the instructions for line 29).
37   ● If line 36 and the number of days in your 2003 tax year (usually 365) are the same, enter "1.000."
     ● Otherwise, divide line 36 by the number of days in your 2003 tax year and enter the result | 37 | × .
       as a decimal (rounded to at least three places).
38   Multiply line 35 by line 37 . . . . | 38 |
39   Subtract line 34 from line 27 . . . . | 39 |
40   Foreign earned income exclusion.   Enter the smaller of line 38 or line 39. Also, complete Part VIII ▶ | 40 |

Part VIII   Taxpayers Claiming the Housing Exclusion, Foreign Earned Income Exclusion, or Both

41   Add lines 34 and 40   . . . . | 41 |
42   Deductions allowed in figuring your adjusted gross income (Form 1040, line 34) that are allocable
     to the excluded income. See instructions and attach computation   . . . . | 42 |
43   Subtract line 42 from line 41. Enter the result here and in parentheses on Form 1040, line 21.
     Next to the amount enter "Form 2555." On Form 1040, subtract this amount from your income
     to arrive at total income on Form 1040, line 22 . . . . ▶ | 43 |

Part IX   Taxpayers Claiming the Housing Deduction   —Complete this part only if (a) line 31 is more than line
             34 and (b) line 27 is more than line 41.

44   Subtract line 34 from line 31 . . . . | 44 |

45   Subtract line 41 from line 27 . . . . | 45 |

46   Enter the smaller of line 44 or line 45 . . . . | 46 |
     Note: If line 45 is more than line 46 and you could not deduct all of your 2002 housing deduction
            because of the 2002 limit, use the worksheet on page 4 of the instructions to figure the
            amount to enter on line 47. Otherwise, go to line 48.

47   Housing deduction carryover from 2002 (from worksheet on page 4 of the instructions) . . . | 47 |

48   Housing deduction. Add lines 46 and 47. Enter the total here and on Form 1040 to the left of
     line 33. Next to the amount on Form 1040, enter "Form 2555." Add it to the total adjustments
     reported on that line   . . . . ▶ | 48 |

⊕   Form **2555** (2003)

If an employee qualifies for the foreign earned income exclusion, he or she can exclude the first $80,000 of foreign earned income from his or her gross income, as noted in Part VII of Form 2555.

Foreign earned income is defined as earned compensation, bonuses, cost of living allowances, tax equalization payments, and allowances for such items as moving (above actual expenses incurred), home leave, and education. If a company pays an employee a bonus, it must be split into those portions attributable to work in the United States and abroad, thereby reducing the amount of foreign earned income eligible for the exclusion. Also, employee income is based on a modified form of accrual accounting, not cash basis accounting, so an employee's foreign income must include payments made to an employee up to one year after the tax year that are attributable to the tax year being reported.

If an employee meets all the tests noted in Form 2555, does not have a housing deduction carryover from the previous year, is not claiming the foreign housing deduction, has total foreign earned income of $80,000 or less, has no self-employment income, and has no business/moving expenses, then he or she can file the shorter Form 2555-EZ instead of the Form 2555.

The Foreign Housing Cost Exclusion

If an employee qualifies for the foreign earned income exclusion, he or she can deduct some foreign housing costs exceeding a base amount that is revised annually by the government. One can elect to take the foreign housing cost exclusion on Form 2555, using Parts V, VI, and VIII of the form. Housing expenses includable in the exclusion calculation are rent for housing, furniture, and residential parking, as well as utilities, occupancy taxes, home repairs, and home parking. For the most recent list of includable housing expenses, see the IRS's instructions to Form 2555.

An employee can also include in the housing expenses the costs associated with a second residence for other family members if the country in which the primary residence is located is considered to have adverse conditions or if the employee is housed at a remote location for the benefit of the employer.

The decision tree shown in Exhibit 16.4 is a revised version of the example used in the IRS's Publication 54, giving an overview of the circumstances under which one can take the foreign earned income or foreign housing exclusions.

Payroll Tax Withholding for Employees Working Abroad

Even if an employee qualifies for the foreign earned income exclusion described earlier in this chapter, an employer must still deduct Social Security and Medicare taxes from that person's pay and match the withheld amounts. This rule does not apply in two instances. First, when an employee works for a foreign subsidiary. Second, when employees are considered to be working permanently[2] in a select

Exhibit 16.4 *Foreign Tax Exclusion Decision Tree*

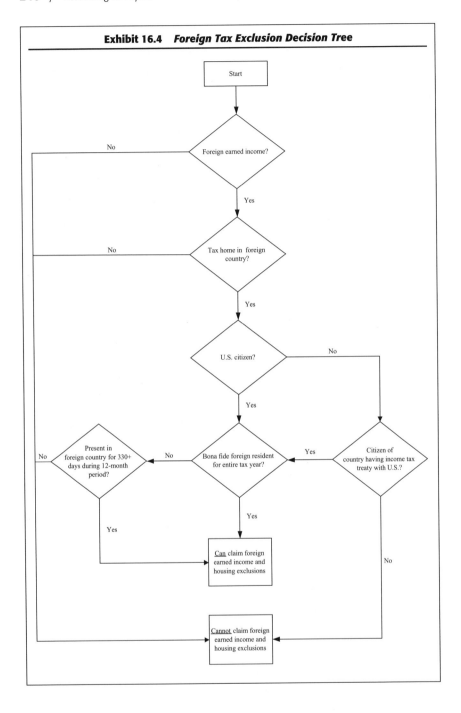

number of countries with whom the United States has a "Totalization" agreement. Under these agreements, employees are only subject to the social security taxes of those countries (thereby avoiding double taxation). The countries with which the United States currently has Totalization agreements are shown in Exhibit 16.5.

Exhibit 16.5 *Participants in Totalization Agreements*

Australia	Germany	Norway
Austria	Greece	Portugal
Belgium	Ireland	Spain
Canada	Italy	Sweden
Chile	Korea (South)	Switzerland
Finland	Luxembourg	United Kingdom
France	Netherlands	

A company should obtain written notification of an employee's coverage by a foreign social security system and retain it in the employee's files in case the company's lack of United States tax withholding is ever questioned.

If a foreign country questions an employee residing there about his or her coverage by the U.S. Social Security System, they can now go online to print a Certificate of U.S. Coverage, which can be used as proof. The access site is *www.socialsecurity.gov/coc.*

For more information about the applicability of social security in foreign assignments, consult the Social Security Administration's website at *www.ssa.gov/international.*

A domestic employer can voluntarily elect to both deduct and match payroll taxes for U.S. citizens and resident aliens working abroad for a foreign affiliate of which the company has at least 10 percent ownership. By doing so, those employees will receive coverage under the United States Social Security system. If a company chooses to take this route, it must complete Form 2032, "Contract Coverage under Title II of the Social Security Act," as shown in Exhibit 16.6. Before completing the form, be aware that one cannot rescind it unless the foreign affiliate ceases to be an affiliate.

State and federal unemployment taxes are not covered by Totalization agreements, and so must be paid in most situations. The only exception is for U.S. citizens working for foreign affiliates of a U.S. company.

State Income Taxes

A person working in a foreign country may still be subject to the income taxes of the state in which he or she officially resides. The key consideration in most cases

Exhibit 16.6 *Notification of Payroll Tax Coverage for Foreign Affiliates*

Form **2032** (Rev. September 2002) Department of the Treasury Internal Revenue Service	Contract Coverage Under Title II of the Social Security Act (For use by an American employer to extend social security coverage to U.S. citizens and resident aliens employed by its foreign affiliates.)	OMB No. 1545-0137 File three copies of this form

Name of American employer	Employer identification number
Address number and street (P.O. Box if no mail delivery to street address)	Apt. or suite no.
City, state, and ZIP code	

This Form 2032 is filed as (check applicable box(es)):

1 ☐ An original (new) agreement.
This agreement is effective for services performed on and after (for original agreements only, check one):
  a ☐ The first day of the calendar quarter in which the service center director signs this agreement.
  b ☐ The first day of the calendar quarter following the calendar quarter in which the service center director signs this agreement.
2 ☐ An amendment to an agreement previously entered into.
3 ☐ An election to apply the rules in effect after April 20, 1983, to agreements in effect on that date. By making this election, U.S. resident aliens as well as U.S. citizens will be covered by social security.

If this is an amended election or agreement, provide the following information:

_____ on _____
(Location where previous Form 2032 was filed)   (Date service center director signed original agreement on Form 2032)

4 This agreement extends the Federal insurance system under Title II of the Social Security Act to certain services performed out side the United States by U.S. citizens and resident aliens employed by any of the foreign affiliates listed below. For an amendment to an agreement without making the election to apply the post-April, 1983 rules, this amendment extends Title II social security coverage to certain services performed outside the United States by U.S. citizens employed by any of the foreign affiliates listed below.

Note: Enter foreign affiliate addresses below in the following order: city, province or state, and country. Do not abbreviate the country name, and follow the country's practice for entering the postal code. If this agreement includes more than four foreign afflia tes, attach a separate sheet of paper identified as a part of this agreement with the name and address of each additional foreign affiliate.

a Name and address of foreign affiliate	c Name and address of foreign affiliate
b Name and address of foreign affiliate	d Name and address of foreign affiliate

5 Estimated number of employees to be initially covered by this agreement, amendment, or election:
Nonagricultural employees ▶   Agricultural employees ▶

This agreement applies to all services performed outside the United States by each U.S. citizen or resident alien employed by a ny of the foreign affiliates named. However, the agreement applies only to the extent that payments to each employee for the services would be co nsidered wages if paid by the employer for services performed in the United States. This agreement does not apply to any service that is consi dered employment for purposes of the employee tax and the employer tax under the Federal Insurance Contributions Act.

For an original agreement, an amendment to an agreement that was entered into after April 20, 1983, or an election to apply the rules in effect after April 20, 1983, to agreements in effect on that date, the American employer declares that it owns at least a 10% interest (dire ctly or through one or more entities) in the voting stock or profits of each foreign entity named above. It also declares that Code section 3121(l) do es not prevent this agreement.

For an amendment to an agreement in effect on April 20, 1983, without making the election to apply the new rules in effect afte r that date, the domestic corporation declares that (a) it owns at least 20% of the voting stock of each foreign corporation named above, or (b) it owns at least 20% of the voting stock of a foreign corporation that owns more than 50% of the voting stock of a foreign corporation named above. It also declares that Code section 3121(l) does not prevent this agreement.

The American employer agrees:
1. To pay amounts equal to the taxes that would be imposed by Code sections 3101 and 3111 if the payment for the services were con sidered wages;
2. To pay, on written notification and demand, amounts equal to the interest, additions to taxes, and penalties that would apply i f the payment for the services were considered wages; and
3. To comply with the applicable regulations under Code section 3121(l).

This agreement (or amended agreement or election) is entered into under the provisions of section 3121(l) of the Internal Revenue Code and the applicable regulations.

Signature of individual authorized to enter into this agreement for the American employer	Title	Date
Director, Internal Revenue Service Center	Location	Date

For Privacy Act and Paperwork Reduction Act Notice, see back of form.   Cat. No. 49954D   Form **2032** (Rev. 9-2002) is whether the employee maintains a permanent home in a state to which he or she intends to return after a period of foreign work has been completed. Evidence of being *domiciled* in a state includes home ownership, residence by the person's family, issuance of a driver's license, or ability to cast a vote.

State taxes can also apply based on *residence*. Evidence of residency includes living or working in a state for a significant period of time, as well as where an employee's children attend school and members of their immediate family live.

The rules on income tax applicability vary by state. A state will typically require income tax payments if a person is domiciled there and resides there for a significant proportion of the year.

To further complicate matters, some states do not allow the foreign earned income exclusion or housing cost exclusion, while others do not allow a credit for foreign income taxes paid.

Given the significant variability in state tax laws, an employer should consult with their particular state tax division for the most recent tax laws pertaining to this topic.

Business Expense Reimbursement

If a company employee is on temporary assignment in a foreign country, payments made by the company to the employee for substantiated travel and living costs, as well as storage costs while they are abroad, are not considered reportable income to the employee. However, if the employee is reimbursed for lavish expenditures, capital expenditures, or the cost of domestic labor, these reimbursements are considered to be reportable income to the employee.

If a company reimburses an employee for moving expenses incurred and the amount paid exceeds the amount incurred, the difference must be reported as income to the employee.

Moving expenses paid by the employer will be considered income to the employee if the distance between the employee's new residence and old workplace, subtracted from the distance between the employee's old residence and old workplace, is less than 50 miles. This is highly unlikely when a person moves to a foreign country. A second rule is much more likely—moving expenses will be considered income to the employee if the employee resides in the new location for less than 39 weeks during the 12 months beginning at the completion date of the move.

Summary

International payroll regulations are quite detailed and change regularly, so this is an ideal area in which to retain the services of a knowledgeable tax advisor. Without such an advisor, the best source of information is the IRS's excellent Publication 54, which is available in PDF format from its website at *www.irs.gov*. This publication contains detailed information about filing requirements, deductions and credits, moving expenses, special rules for U.S. government employees, travel restrictions, and tax treaties.

Notes

1. Residency is the employee's place of employment or, if there is no regular place of employment, the employee's home.
2. With the intention of being in the foreign country for at least five years.

17

Setting Up the Payroll Department

Introduction

In most cases, a payroll manager only takes over an existing payroll department when hired, which requires a modest amount of systems reviews and upgrades to manage. However, a manager hired into a newly formed company has much more work to do to set up the payroll department from scratch. In this chapter, we cover the broad range of activities required to bring a new payroll department into compliance with all legal, procedural, and control requirements. In addition, we address the timing of basic payroll data collection, as well as other improvement issues that can be addressed once the initial payroll system has been created.

The Payroll Set-Up Checklist

The following list of steps assumes that a payroll manager is beginning from scratch—a company has just been founded and there is absolutely no payroll (or other) information on hand with which to process the first payroll or create a database of payroll-related information. Though not all of the following steps will be needed to create a payroll system and the order of events may change in specific cases, the list of presented activities is a good basis for creating a payroll system. The steps are:

1. *Obtain a federal employer identification number.* The federal government identifies payroll tax remittances by the federal employer identification number (EIN). Though one can apply for an EIN with the Form SS-4, it will take four weeks to obtain the number, which will arrive too late for the first company payroll. A better approach is to call the government's "Tele-TIN" number at 866-816-2065 to obtain an EIN on the spot.

2. *Obtain state identification numbers.* At a minimum, the payroll manager will need a state employer number for each state in which the company has employees and possibly also a state unemployment identification number (some states use the same number for both functions). A number of states allow one to apply for these identification numbers online; if not, it can take several

weeks to obtain a number. Generally, one can obtain the state identification number through the Secretary of State's office or some subsidiary business department. A Labor and Unemployment department (or some variation on that name) usually issues the unemployment identification number.

3. *Determine the new employer tax rate for the state unemployment tax.* The first payroll must include the state unemployment tax rate for a new employer. This information can be obtained from Chapter 11, "Unemployment Insurance," of this book; however, states regularly change the amount of this tax or the range of pay over which the tax percentage applies. A better approach is to look up the latest state unemployment rate on the Internet (CCH offers an excellent unemployment tax site at *www.toolkit.cch.com/text/P07_1294.asp*). It is also possible to contact the state government directly for this information, though there is no common countrywide department name to contact.

4. *Set up a payroll bank account.* Though payroll checks can certainly be issued on the main corporate bank account, the accounting is somewhat easier if a separate account is used. If the payroll manager feels this is necessary, she should obtain one immediately so the bank can order a supply of checks. Typically, enough temporary checks will be issued to address the first payroll. If payroll is outsourced, then the supplier will issue paychecks from its own account and will only deduct total payroll expenses from the company's bank account in a single entry, which does not call for a separate payroll account.

5. *Create a payroll permanent file.* As taxpayer identification numbers come in, do not lose the documentation! Instead, create a permanent file for assigned tax numbers and unemployment tax rates and absolutely do not store it with other accounting records. The reason is that nearly all accounting records will eventually be archived and marked for destruction at some later date. Instead, store the permanent file in a locking file cabinet, and prominently mark on the file "Do Not Archive—Permanent File."

6. *Set up a timecard system.* If there will be hourly employees, then they should start filling out timecards as of their first day of work, so accurate hourly payment information is available by the time the first payroll is ready to be processed. At its simplest level, this calls for a paper time sheet that can be constructed with an electronic spreadsheet or word processing program. A slightly more complex approach is to purchase a time clock and timecards from a business supply store. Do not initially invest in a computerized time clock using badges, since these typically take a few weeks to set up and will arrive too late to process information for the first payroll.

7. *Flowchart the system.* It is prudent to lay out the process flow for all aspects of the payroll system as soon as possible. Though the resulting process flow may change significantly before the payroll system has been installed, it provides a visual plan for how processing will be achieved. The flowcharts shown in Chapter 1 can be used as a starting point for all three types of payroll systems—computerized, manual, or outsourced—but there will be com-

pany-specific variations in most cases, requiring a unique flowchart. A good approach is to dedicate an entire white board to the flowchart, so the diagram is large enough to read from a distance and can easily be changed.

8. *Create a Gantt chart.* With a flowchart in place that gives a payroll system overview, the payroll manager can now create a Gantt chart itemizing each action step required to build a payroll system, as well as the likely duration of each step. A Gantt chart gives more rigor to the system development process and is useful not only for tracking upcoming tasks but also for spotting missing steps, potential missed deadlines, and bottleneck tasks.

9. *Create payroll-processing procedures.* There are a great many possible payroll policies and procedures. However, early in the development of the payroll department, the only procedure that matters is one for processing the payroll (which includes timecard processing, tax and deduction calculations, and printing and distributing paychecks). By installing a regimented approach to processing payroll right away, there is much less chance of having to deal with time-consuming processing errors. Once completed, have at least one other person walk through the procedure to see if there are any missing or incorrect steps. This is the most important procedure in the payroll department and it must be done right the first time.

10. *Create a tax remittance deadline calendar.* If a company outsources its payroll processing, then it can rely on the supplier to remit taxes on its behalf. However, if payroll is processed internally, remitting taxes becomes a very important task, given the significant government-imposed penalties if remittances are sent too late. Accordingly, create a tax remittance calendar right away that shows not only the remittance dates for all state and federal taxes but also the dates by which W-2 and 1099 forms must be sent to employers and suppliers, respectively. Further, the calendar should note the filing date for the annual Form 940 or 940-EZ for the federal unemployment tax report, as well as the quarterly Form 941 federal tax return. There will also be a variety of unemployment tax and income tax remittance forms to send to state governments, for which the filing requirements will vary by state.

11. *Create a database backup system.* Losing the payroll database is disastrous, since so much detailed information must be recreated from paper documents. Accordingly, as soon as the initial payroll processing has been completed, obtain backup equipment, create a backup procedure, and follow it rigorously. The backup system should include multiple backup copies, so an earlier backup will be available if a later one is corrupted. Also, the backup procedure should include the rotation of a recent backup copy into an off-site location. One alternative is backup suppliers that dial into the payroll system from an outside location and periodically perform the backup for the company. Of course, if payroll processing is outsourced, then the database is already off-site and no backup policy is needed.

12. *Create payroll policies and complete additional procedures.* Once the preceding steps have been completed, there is now some breathing room in

which to complete other payroll procedures besides the payroll-processing procedure. Typical procedures can include record archiving, changing deduction amounts, changing employee payroll data, and updating payroll forms. In addition, any necessary payroll policies can be implemented at this time, typically with formal approval from the controller or CFO. Payroll policies are frequently included in the employee manual, which is created by the human resources department, so the timing of payroll policies may be driven by the production schedule for the employee manual.

13. *Create employee files.* Though the human resources department is supposed to maintain employee files, smaller companies may not have this department. If so, the payroll department usually maintains them. Obtain a locking file cabinet to store these files. Files should contain a checklist itemizing all documents required to be in each employee's file, such as a W-4 form, confidentiality agreement, noncompete agreement, I-9 form, and so forth. Other likely contents are signed deduction authorizations, garnishments, reviews, and authorized pay rate changes.

14. *Create payroll deductions.* Since there are so many key steps to complete for the first company payroll, it is unwise to add another layer of complexity and start making voluntary deductions for such items as medical and dental insurance, short-term or long-term disability insurance, or 401k deductions. Instead, wait until a later payroll period, after the bugs are ironed out of the initial system, before adding this information. The controller may push for early adoption of deductions, on the grounds that this represents a deduction from company-incurred expenses and therefore impacts reported profits. A reasonable response is that the controller can still accrue estimated deductions until such time as the payroll manager is comfortable enough with the payroll system to make actual deductions. This will, of course, require somewhat higher deductions in order to make up for the earlier absence of deductions. However, if official garnishment documentation arrives, action *cannot* be delayed—the company is required to begin deductions at once or risk incurring penalties from the issuing court.

15. *Accrue sick and vacation time.* As was the case with voluntary deductions, it is not necessary to create a vacation and sick time accrual as of the first payroll. Few employees will make inquiries about their accrued balances during their first few weeks of work, so there is no rush. Once the basic payroll system is complete, create a basic accrual system on an electronic spreadsheet to calculate this information. Once there is programming time available, it may be possible to have an Intranet-based vacation and sick time accrual system (see the section on "Finetuning the Payroll Department" below) that employees can manage on their own. Alternatively, if payroll is outsourced, the payroll supplier can report this information on paycheck remittance advices.

16. *Create an employee manual.* The human resources department should create the employee manual, but smaller companies typically lack this department. Instead, the task falls on the payroll manager. From the payroll perspective,

the employee manual is important for laying out such payroll policies as when time sheets are due, how much vacation and sick time can be taken, when the payroll week ends, business hours, employment classifications, handling of severance pay, and how errors in pay are dealt with. Since the employee manual should be considered a legal document that employees can use to assert their rights against the company, it is best to consult with a labor lawyer or local employers' trade association to expand upon an initial rough draft of an employee manual. It is also possible to have a consultant write the entire manual. Once complete, employees should be required to sign a document stating that they have received and read the manual. This document should be stored in their employee files.

17. *Establish performance metrics.* Once the initial department setup is completed, the payroll manager should develop an interest in the department's level of performance. This calls for the establishment of metrics, such as the time required to complete a payroll, the number of payroll transaction errors requiring fixes, or the total department cost divided into the total number of company employees. The exact metrics used will vary by company, depending on the circumstances. A key point is to ensure that the same calculation is used to track metrics from period to period, so the metrics are comparable over time.

18. *Create management reports.* Most payroll department reports are based on the basic reports generated either by the in-house payroll software or the supplier to whom payroll processing is outsourced. However, the payroll summary and register do not always supply sufficient information. Consider generating additional reports, such as the names of those people not yet using direct deposit, or the specific types and number of payroll transaction errors created in each payroll cycle. The payroll manager can use this sort of operational information to improve the performance of the department.

19. *Create a department budget.* During the initial rush to create a payroll system and produce the first payroll, a planning feature like a budget is usually ignored. However, after a few months have passed and one has a better idea of the company growth rate and related payroll processing requirements, it is time to create one. This can easily be contained within one or two pages, itemizing major expense categories by month. Typically, there are only two expense drivers for the payroll department. The first is whether or not the payroll processing task will be outsourced and the second is the total number of company employees expected to be serviced by the payroll department. Both expense drivers have a major impact on the number of people working in the payroll department, and the payroll expense is usually the largest department expense.

20. *Schedule an internal auditor controls review.* Another task that usually waits until the initial department setup is done is a controls review by an independent group, typically either the internal audit department or a group of independent certified public accountants. The purpose of this review is to ensure

that a complete set of controls is in place to ensure that the risk of losing company assets is minimized. This task is occasionally completed at the initial formation of the department, since this allows excellent controls to be built into the initial department procedures. However, payroll managers rarely have time during the initial setup phase to meet with auditors, and so delay this step until later.

Collecting Employee Information

In addition to the preceding tasks, it is also necessary to obtain information about employees for the payroll database. Though it is possible to issue manually calculated paychecks to employees with a minimum of employee data, it is best to collect a complete set of data at the beginning of the setup process and avoid multiple iterations of the data collection process at some later date. Nonetheless, if there is only time to initially collect a minimum data set, here are the clusters of information to obtain:

1. *Minimum required data.* The minimum data set is defined by a company's legal requirement to remit taxes to the government on behalf of each employee. This means that each person's Social Security number, tax withholding information, marital status, name, and address must be obtained. The best way to obtain this data set is to issue a W-4 form to all employees. Obviously, one also needs the salary or wage rate for each employee, which should be verified and approved by an authorized manager.

2. *Organizational data.* The accounting staff will probably want to track payroll expenses by department, so a department code should be entered into the payroll database for each employee at the earliest opportunity.

3. *Voluntary withholding data.* A company can save money by arranging for the deduction of expenses from employee paychecks. However, this information does not absolutely have to be available for the first check run, since a company can simply increase the size of later deductions in order to offset the missing deductions from the first paychecks. Typical deduction data would cover medical, dental, 401k, cafeteria plan, life insurance, garnishments, long-term disability insurance, and short-term disability insurance. Of all these deduction types, the one that may require immediate action is garnishments, since a court mandates the size and timing of this deduction.

4. *Direct deposit data.* Sending money directly into an employee's bank account is more a convenience than a necessity and so can wait until a later check run to complete.

5. *EEO data.* Equal employment opportunity reports are unlikely to be required during the early stages of a company's formation, so sex and ethnic background codes can be collected after most other data.

6. *Key employee dates data.* This data is most commonly used to determine the next date on which employees are due for a pay review, which is frequently a

year from the initial company formation. Thus, the addition of employee hire dates and last pay change dates to the payroll database can be safely delayed for some months. However, if a 401k plan is to be integrated into the payroll system, then employee birth dates and hire dates must be entered into the payroll system prior to the plan start date.

Finetuning the Payroll Department

Once the accounting department has been set up, there are still a number of actions the payroll manager can take to ensure that the department's efficiency and effectiveness continue to improve over time:

- *Create activity consistency.* Absolutely the first priority once a payroll system has been set up is ensuring that the basic payroll tasks are completed on time and in a consistent manner. To do so, create an activity calendar for each payroll employee, itemizing precisely what key tasks are to be completed during each day of the month. The payroll manager should revise these calendars at the end of each month and review them with the payroll staff prior to the beginning of the next month in order to make last-minute revisions or explain changes. Next, write procedures for the payroll tasks listed in the activity calendar, so that employees not only know when to complete tasks, but also how to do them. Since procedures can take a long time to write, first complete those procedures needed by the most junior (and presumably least trained) staff, or those procedures where errors are most likely to arise.

- *Cross-train the staff.* A task closely linked to activity consistency is cross-training the staff. When employees tasked with key activities either leave the company or are unavailable for short periods, the quality of the work performed by their replacements typically drops. To avoid this, cross-train the staff on key tasks as soon as possible. To ensure that the training "sticks," regularly shift payroll tasks to different staff members, so everyone has a chance to practice on the most important items.

- *Tailor additional training to staff and job requirements.* Besides cross-training, the payroll manager should determine the need for additional training in such areas as process improvement, workflow management, computer systems, management techniques, and specific payroll legal issues. It is rarely necessary to pay for a massive training program for individual employees, such as a college degree. Instead, the payroll manager should authorize training that is tightly focused on the needs of the department, while balancing this training with a moderate amount of peripheral training for those employees whose morale may be improved by it. It is best to research available training in the region, create a formal list of approved training classes, obtain advance approval of a training budget, and make the training opportunity known to the payroll staff.

- *Report errors.* Another way to improve consistency is to generate a periodic report itemizing all errors caused by the payroll department. By regularly reviewing this report with the staff, it is possible to gradually trace the causes of errors and eliminate them. Such a report might list incorrect employee addresses that caused checks to be returned in the mail, incorrect hours worked that required manual checks to be created, or incorrect vacation time calculations requiring manual recalculations. A key element in the successful accumulation of error information is the cooperation of the payroll staff in reporting this information to the manager; the only way this will occur is by emphasizing a focus on resolving the reported problem, rather than chastising the person reporting it.

- *Link payroll changes to specific events.* Payroll changes typically occur when key employee dates arise, such as the inception of voluntary deductions for health insurance once a 90-day probationary period has passed. Since it is easy to miss these dates and have to scramble to make retroactive changes later on, the payroll staff should either manually track key employee dates or (better yet) see if the payroll software can automatically track it for them. Similarly, install a system to make payroll changes based on the modification of related data; for example, if an employee's address changes, notifications must be sent to the health insurance provider and pension plan administrator to alter the address in their systems, too.

- *Controls review following procedural changes.* Controls may be created at the initiation of a department that are perfectly adequate, but the payroll manager must review the controls situation every time a procedural change is made to ensure that the level of control is still adequate. Though the assumption is that new controls will be added, the reverse may also be true—a control may become redundant and can be removed, thereby enhancing departmental efficiency.

- *Ask the staff.* No matter how well steeped in operations the payroll manager may be, the payroll staff is truly the most knowledgeable in how operations can be improved, since they handle transactions all day long. The payroll manager can access this excellent knowledge base most effectively by maintaining constant contact with her staff. This should certainly involve repeated daily contacts to make the staff comfortable with the manager, but also a periodic operational review meeting with the staff to go over any improvement suggestions they may have. If the payroll manager elects to conduct such meetings, she should issue written documentation of the meeting to the staff immediately following the meeting, and report back to them at the next meeting (or sooner) regarding progress made on their suggestions.

- *Give the staff continual feedback.* If the staff has made valuable contributions to the department or the reverse, tell them. This can involve frequent informal job reviews, which give feedback immediately after an event, so employees will know at once how their actions have impacted the company. Though a formal annual job review does have certain uses from a documentation perspective, the positive impact on employee behavior of frequent informal reviews cannot be emphasized enough. Also, the payroll manager should create a small pool of awards, such as gift certificates to local restaurants and shops that she can give to employees for spot recognition of any unusually excellent contributions to the department.

Besides the basic management tasks noted in the preceding bullet points, anyone setting up a payroll system should also strongly consider installing a select group of best practices that can have a strong impact on departmental efficiency. They are:

- *Automate vacation accruals.* Employees are always curious about the remaining balance of their vacation time available for use, so they regularly contact the payroll staff regarding this balance. Constantly recalculating it can waste a considerable amount of staff time. One way to avoid this problem is to include the remaining vacation balance on the payroll remittance advice, if this feature is available either in the in-house payroll processing software or from a payroll supplier. Another alternative is to track the information on an electronic spreadsheet, though this requires continually updating the spreadsheet with vacation hours used for each employee. An excellent alternative if programming time is available is to create a web-based timekeeping system that incorporates vacation tracking and modeling. Under this approach, employees enter their own time into an online timekeeping database that also allows them to calculate available vacation time as of user-defined dates. Though this approach is the most expensive of the alternatives to implement, it completely removes the payroll staff from the vacation accrual issue.
- *Consolidate payroll systems.* If a company uses a different payroll system at each location or acquires companies using alternative systems, the corporate payroll staff will endure the ongoing headache of using different procedures and processing schedules for each one. Though it is time-consuming to do so, make an effort to gradually consolidate the payroll systems into the smallest possible number. By doing so, the payroll function will operate with a much higher degree of efficiency.
- *Disallow prepayments.* Whenever an employee asks for an advance on a future paycheck, the payroll staff must cut a manual check, create a journal entry for the payment, enter it in the payroll system, and create a deduction to offset the advance, which introduces a great deal of inefficiency to the payroll process. The payroll manager should work with the company president to formulate a policy forbidding the use of advances, which can be difficult for low-wage companies where employees frequently ask for advances. One can make the policy more effective by arranging with local providers of short-term loans to handle employee cash problems.
- *Minimize payroll cycles.* Processing a payroll requires a great deal of time, so reducing the number of payrolls will automatically require less staff time. Also, if there are a great many payrolls to process, it can be quite difficult for a small payroll department to arrange for staff vacations around the processing dates.

An excellent alternative is to lengthen each payroll period, at least to twice a month. The problem for companies currently providing weekly payrolls is how to ensure that employees do not run out of money during the first payroll period when the longer pay cycle is in use. The best approach is to make payroll advances available to those needing them, but to gradually reduce the size of the advances over several payroll cycles until employees are accustomed to the new, longer pay periods.

- *Outsource payroll processing.* Outsourcing is available for virtually all accounting functions, but payroll is the area in which the arguments for doing so are the most compelling. The payroll staff no longer has to concern itself with updating payroll tax tables, remitting taxes, or submitting direct deposit information to a bank. Also, payroll providers can now accept payroll information either verbally over the phone, by dial-up modem, or through web access. The only downsides to this approach are the processing fees charged and the inaccessibility of payroll data that may be needed for automatic integration into other accounting reports.

- *Post payroll forms on the company website.* Employees are always asking the payroll staff for a variety of forms—W-4 forms, vacation permission forms, cafeteria deduction forms, and so forth. These requests disrupt the staff. If a company already has an intranet site, it is a simple matter to add a page on which links are provided to a number of these forms. If the IRS issues a form (such as a W-4 form), then it can be downloaded from the IRS website at *www.irs.gov* in PDF format and posted in that format directly onto the intranet site. If a form is more specialized, it may require more elaborate reconstruction in some other software package prior to being converted into a more universally readable PDF format.

- *Use bar-coded time clocks.* If there are a large number of hourly employees, the payroll staff's primary chore is probably the ongoing compilation of hours worked from timecards. This process is tailor-made for errors, given the large number of calculations required, which in turn leads to time-consuming payroll errors. An excellent alternative is to issue employee-specific bar-coded badges that they scan through a computerized time clock. The clock automatically calculates their hours worked, while also providing a number of other controls. Though these clocks are expensive, they completely eliminate timecard calculations and associated errors.

There are other best practices besides the group of core items just noted. Chapter 4 provides more information about these and other best practices.

Once a payroll manager has completed the basic departmental improvement tactics noted in this section, it may seem as though no further enhancements can be made. Though an aggressive payroll department may think it has brought itself up to a "world class" level of efficiency, it can be quite startling for the department to benchmark its results against those of other organizations and find that its performance is subpar. Evaluations can be done by hiring a consulting firm to compile benchmarking information from a selection of other companies, though the payroll manager can also arrange for the direct exchange of performance information with other companies. A common result of such benchmarking activities is a new knowledge of additional actions the payroll department can take to improve its operations.

Summary

The payroll department is an extremely regimented place, where activities are driven by the timing of payroll cycles and tax remittance dates. Consequently, one should approach the department setup task as a highly engineered approach, involving fixed schedules, control points, and procedures that must subsequently be reviewed on an iterative basis to ensure that every last drop of efficiency has been wrung out of the department.

18

Government Payroll Publications and Forms

Introduction

The Internal Revenue Service (IRS) maintains a current list of approximately 400 publications and 150 forms. It is a daunting task to even obtain a general knowledge of this vast body of regulations, much less a detailed grasp of their nuances. In this chapter, we will specify those publications and forms pertaining specifically to the corporate payroll function, so the payroll manager can focus his or her attention on the minimum amount of government paperwork. In addition, we will note website links to other government entities having an additional impact on the payroll department.

For direct access to all IRS publications and forms, go to its main webpage, located at *www.irs.gov*. From the main page, look under the "Contents" header and click on the "Business" category. Alternatively, you can enter a form or publication number directly into a forms search field on the home page, which takes you straight to the desired document. Please note that the IRS changes its website regularly, so these instructions may vary from the actual page layout over time.

IRS Publications

It is impossible to adequately summarize the vast amount of information contained within all IRS publications. Instead, only the main topic headers are described for each of the primary payroll-related IRS publications. Surprisingly, the bulk of all payroll topics are contained within just three IRS publications, numbers 15, 15-A, and 15-B. The other six publications and notices described in this section either address only niche topics or happen to include some payroll-related information in addition to other topics. In addition, the IRS issues a number of brochures and posters describing its Electronic Funds Transfer Payment System; they are easily identified on the IRS's publications page, which is located at *www.irs.gov/formspubs*.

A short description of the key payroll publications is noted in the following bullet points, which are sorted in order by publication number. In addition, the same information is reorganized in a matrix format in Exhibit 18.1, with topics listed down the left side and publication numbers across the top.

- *Publication 15, "Employer's Tax Guide."* Discusses the employer identification number, calendar of key tax-related dates, employee definitions, compensation, tips, supplemental wages, the payroll period, wage withholding, the Advance Earned Income Credit, depositing taxes, filing Form 941, FUTA, and income tax withholding tables.

- *Publication 15-A, "Employer's Supplemental Tax Guide."* Discusses employee definitions, independent contractors, compensation, sick pay, pensions, and alternative withholding methods.

- *Publication 15-B, "Employer's Tax Guide to Fringe Benefits."* Discusses cafeteria plans, accident and health benefits, achievement awards, dependent care assistance, educational assistance, employee discounts, employee stock options, group-term life insurance, meals, moving expense reimbursement, retirement planning services, and commuting benefits.

- *Publication 393, "Federal Employment Tax Forms."* Includes a complete list of tax forms as well as an order form and directions for contacting the IRS for additional information.

- *Publication 463, "Travel, Entertainment, Gift, and Car Expenses."* Discusses travel and entertainment expenses, gifts, car expenses, and recordkeeping.

- *Publication 560, "Retirement Plans for Small Business."* Discusses Simplified Employee Pensions (SEP), SIMPLE retirement plans, and qualified retirement plans.

- *Publication 583, "Starting a Business and Keeping Records."* Discusses the employer identification number, the tax year, the accounting method to use for tax purposes, types of business taxes, penalties, business expenses, and recordkeeping requirements. It is important from a payroll perspective because of its discussion of business taxes and recordkeeping requirements.

- *Publication 1542, "Per Diem Rates."* Notes the localities eligible for different per diem rates as of the publication date.

- *Notice 931, "Deposit Requirements for Employment Taxes."* This is an IRS bulletin rather than a publication, but is important because it lists a variety of tax deposit schedules for the current payroll year.

Exhibit 18.1 presents the same information just noted for each key IRS publication, but does so in a more easily searchable matrix format, with topics listed in alphabetical order down the left side and publication numbers across the top.

Worthy of separate mention is Publication 54, "Tax Guide for U.S. Citizens and Resident Aliens Abroad." As the title implies, this excellent manual is only applicable to international payroll situations and so was excluded from the more general publications listed earlier. It can also be accessed from the IRS's website at *www.irs.gov.*

Exhibit 18.1 *Reference Table for Key Publications*								
Publication Number:	**15**	**15A**	**15B**	**393**	**463**	**560**	**583**	**1542**
401k plans						✔		
941 Form	✔							
Accident benefits			✔					
Achievement awards			✔					
Advance earned income credit	✔							
Cafeteria plans			✔					
Car expenses					✔			
Commuting benefits			✔					
Compensation	✔	✔						
Contractor definition		✔						
Dependent care assistance			✔					
Educational assistance			✔					
Employee definition	✔	✔						
Employee discounts			✔					
Employee stock options			✔					
Entertainment expenses					✔			
Federal unemployment tax	✔							
Filing dates	✔							
Forms ordering information				✔				
Gifts					✔			
Group-term life insurance			✔					
Health benefits			✔					
Meals			✔					
Moving expense reimbursement			✔					
Payroll period	✔							
Pensions		✔						
Per diem rates								✔
Qualified retirement plans						✔		
Recordkeeping requirements					✔		✔	
Retirement planning services			✔					
Sick pay		✔						
SIMPLE retirement plan						✔		
Simplified employee pension						✔		
Tax deposits	✔						✔	
Tax tables	✔							
Taxes, employment							✔	
Tips	✔							
Travel expenses					✔			
Wage withholding	✔	✔						
Wages, supplemental	✔							

IRS Forms

The IRS maintains about 150 forms, most of which can be accessed from the *www.irs.gov/formspubs* page. Fortunately, the payroll department needs to be aware of only a few of these forms. The following bullet points note the 14 most commonly used forms, sorted by form number, with a brief description of each one:

- *Form 668-W, "Notice of Levy on Wages, Salary, and Other Income."* A multipart notice issued by the IRS to an individual, warning of an impending levy. The employee must complete Part 6 of the form and return it to the employer for subsequent routing to the IRS.

- *Form 673, Statement for Claiming Exemption from Withholding on Foreign Earned Income Eligible for the Exclusions Provided by Section 911."* Despite the massive title, this form fulfills a simple function—it gives an employer justification not to withhold federal income taxes from an employee's pay if the employee expects to qualify for a foreign earned income exclusion.

- *Form 940, "Employer's Annual Federal Unemployment (FUTA) Tax Return."* A form used to report annual unemployment taxes paid to the federal government.

- *Form 941, "Employer's Quarterly Federal Tax Return."* A form used to summarize a company's quarterly withholding of Social Security and Medicare taxes from employee pay, as well as actual payments made to the government of these amounts.

- *Form 943, "Employer's Annual Federal Tax Return for Agricultural Employees."* A form used to summarize a company's periodic liability for agricultural employee income taxes withheld and actual payments made to the government of these amounts.

- *Form 945, "Annual Return of Withheld Federal Income Tax."* A form used to summarize a company's periodic liability for employee income taxes withheld and actual payments made to the government of these amounts.

- *Form 1099, "Miscellaneous Income."* A multipart form issued to qualified recipients, based on W-9 form returns, detailing payments made by the company to the recipients.

- *Form 2032, "Contract Coverage under Title II of the Social Security Act."* An employer uses this form to elect to deduct payroll taxes from the pay of U.S. citizens who work for foreign affiliates.

- *Form 4070, "Employee's Report of Tips to Employer."* A monthly report given by employees to the employer, detailing the general sources of tips and the total amount of tips received.

- *Form 8027, "Employer's Annual Information Return of Tip Income and Allocated Tips."* A form used to report the total amount of tip income reported by company employees during a calendar year.

- *Form SS-4, "Application for Employer Identification Number."* The first form a company should complete when it is initially formed; this is a request for an employer identification number, which is used on all payroll correspondence with and remittances to the federal government.

- *Form SS-8, "Determination of Worker Status for Purposes of Federal Employment Taxes and Income Tax Withholding."* This form is filed in order to request a determination from the IRS if a company should pay employment taxes and withhold income from a person's wages.

- *Form W-2, "Wage and Tax Statement."* A multipart form issued by an employer to anyone who was paid compensation during a calendar year, itemizing the amount of gross pay, deducted taxes, and net pay.

- *Form W-4, "Employee's Withholding Allowance Certificate."* Each employee fills out this form, authorizing the employer to withhold a specific amount of taxes from that person's pay.

- *Form W-5, "Earned Income Credit Advance Payment Certificate."* A form filed by employees, requesting advance payment of a portion of their earned income credit, if they are entitled to receive it.

- *Form W-9, "Request for Taxpayer Identification Number and Certification."* Companies issue this form to their suppliers, requiring them to submit their organizational status and employer identification number. Under certain circumstances, the issuing company uses this information to report to the government some payments made to the supplier.

Other Government Entities

Though the IRS has the greatest impact on the payroll department, a few other government entities have a peripheral impact. This section describes the roles of three other government entities and the websites where additional information can be found.

- *Department of Labor (DOL).* This agency requires federal contractors to annually file the VETS-100 form, detailing the proportion of military veterans employed by a company. The best source of information about the form can be found at a site operated by the University of Denver, *http://vets100.cudenver.edu/.* In addition, the DOL maintains a library of forms located at *www.dol.gov/libraryforms/FormsByTitle.asp.* Nearly all of these forms are of more interest to the human resources department than the payroll department, dealing with such topics as accident report forms, discrimination complaints, and specialty worker visa applications.

- *Social Security Administration (SSA).* A company has no direct need to access the publications and forms of the SSA, but the payroll department may receive occasional queries from employees about Social Security that can be answered most easily by accessing its website at *www.ssa.gov.* Forms and Publications are separate topics listed under the "Resources" section of its home page. The publications section is especially good, with sections devoted to disability benefits, retirement benefits, survivor benefits, the Supplemental Security Income program, the appeals process, the Social Security number, earnings, and a variety of other special topics.

■ *U.S. Immigration and Citizenship Services.* This agency requires companies to have all employees complete the Form I-9, "Employment Eligibility Verification," in which the employer must verify the employee's identity and right to work at the inception of that person's employment. Its website is located at *http://uscis.gov/graphics/index.htm.* For information about the Form I-9, access the "Employer Information" button on the home page.

Summary

Even if you have successfully located and downloaded from a government website any of the publications and forms noted in this chapter, do not continue to rely upon them for very long. The government regularly updates its publications and forms, so be sure to mark on the department activities calendar a date on which someone accesses the government sites to obtain annual updates. Otherwise, a payroll manager may find herself working with outdated information that may result in government penalties or returned documents.

Sources of Payroll Information

This appendix contains Internet linkages to an array of payroll sources. Please note that these are by no means the only Internet sources of information and services available. In particular, there are dozens of Internet-based payroll processing companies available—the five shown here are only a representative sample. Also, some linkages will change over time. If so, the best source of alternative information is the search engine Google, located at *www.google.com*.

Internet-Based Payroll Processing

- Advantage Payroll Services (*www.advantagepayroll.com*)
- Fidelity (*www.fidelitypayroll.com*)
- Payroll Online Corp. (*www.payrollonline.com*)
- Payroll.com (*www.payroll.com*)
- Wells Fargo (*www.wellsfargo.com/biz*)

Internet Informational Sites

- CCH (*business.cch.com/linkexpress*) Contains research tools for IRS regulations, investment plans, and tax rates
- Department of Labor (*www.dol.gov*) Contains lists of labor statistics, wage-related laws, and form downloads.
- Internal Revenue Service Forms Site (*www.irs.gov/formspubs*) Contains comprehensive list of downloadable tax forms
- Internal Revenue Service Small Business Site (*www.irs.gov/smallbiz/index*) Lists downloadable forms, a tax deadline calendar, a business startup checklist, how to apply for an employer identification number, and more.
- Office of Child Support Enforcement (*www.acf.dhhs.gov/programs/cse*) Contains links to state programs, as well as a variety of new hire information
- PaycheckCity (*www.paycheckcity.com*) Contains a number of paycheck calculation tools.

- Payroll Taxes (*www.payroll-taxes.com*) Contains a large database of payroll tax information and related articles, as well as links to all state government tax sites.
- Social Security Administration (*www.ssa.gov*) Contains information related to benefit, disability, and survivor rules for social security benefits.

Payroll Organizations

- American Payroll Association (*www.americanpayroll.org*) American Society for Payroll Management (*www.aspm.org*)
- Institute of Payroll and Pensions Management (*www.ippm.org*)

Payroll-Related Laws

- Consolidated Omnibus Budget Reconciliation Act (*www.dol.gov/pwba/pubs/cobrafs*)
- Contract Work Hours and Safety Standards Act (*www.arnet.gov/far/current/html/Subpart_22_3*)
- Davis-Bacon Act (*www.lectlaw.com/files/emp16*)
- Employee Retirement Income Security Act (*www.dol.gov/dol/topic/retirement/erisa*)
- Fair Labor Standards Act (*www.lectlaw.com/files/emp39.htm*)
- Family and Medical Leave Act (*www.employer-employee.com/fmla*)
- Health Insurance Portability & Accountability Act (*www.hcfa.gov/medicaid/hipaa*)
- Self-Employment Contributions Act (*www.taxguide.completetax.com/text/Q15_3110.asp*)
- Service Contract Act (*www.arnet.gov/far/current/html/Subpart_22_10*)
- Walsh-Healey Public Contracts Act (*www.rbpubs.com/ls/ls27*)

Traditional Payroll Service Providers

- Automatic Data Processing, Inc. (*www.adp.com*)
- Ceridian (*www.ceridian.com*)
- Paychex (*www.paychex.com*)

Dictionary of Payroll Terms

401k Plan. A retirement plan set up by an employer, into which employees can contribute the lesser of $13,000 or 15 percent of their pay (as of 2004), which is excluded from taxation until such time as they remove the funds from the account.

403b Plan. A retirement plan similar to a 401k plan, except that it is designed specifically for charitable, religious, and education organizations that fall under the tax-exempt status of 501(c)(3) regulations.

ABC Test. A test used to determine the status of an employee under a state unemployment insurance program, where a person is a contractor only if there is an **A**bsence of control by the company, **B**usiness conducted by the employee is substantially different from that of the company, and the person **C**ustomarily works independently from the company.

Alien. The citizen of a country besides the United States.

Automated Clearing House (ACH). A banking clearinghouse that processes direct deposit transfers.

Benefit Ratio Method. The proportion of unemployment benefits paid to a company's former employees during the measurement period, divided by the total payroll during the period. This calculation is used by states to determine the unemployment contribution rate to charge employers.

Benefit Wage Ratio Method. The proportion of total taxable wages for laid off employees during the measurement period divided by the total payroll during the period. This calculation is used by states to determine the unemployment contribution rate to charge employers.

Cafeteria Plan. A flexible benefits plan authorized under the Internal Revenue Code allowing employees to pay for a selection of benefits with pay deductions, some of which may be pretax.

Clear Card. A credit card from which payments are deducted over subsequent time periods.

Compensation. All forms of pay given to an employee in exchange for services rendered.

Consolidated Omnibus Budget Reconciliation Act (COBRA). A federal Act containing the requirements for offering insurance to departed employees.

Consumer Credit Protection Act. A federal Act specifying the proportion of total pay that may be garnished.

Contract Work Hours and Safety Standards Act. A federal Act requiring federal contractors to pay overtime for hours worked exceeding 40 per week.

Contribution Rate. The percentage tax charged by a state to an employer to cover its share of the state unemployment insurance fund.

Coverdell Education IRA. A form of individual retirement account whose earnings during the period when funds are stored in the IRA will be tax free at the time when they are used to pay for the cost of advanced education.

Current Tax Payment Act of 1943. A federal Act requiring employers to withhold income taxes from employee pay.

Davis-Bacon Act of 1931. A federal Act providing wage protection to nongovernment workers by requiring businesses engaged in federal construction projects to pay their employees prevailing wages and fringe benefits.

Defined Benefit Plan. A pension plan that pays out a predetermined dollar amount to participants, based on a set of rules that typically combine the number of years of employment and wages paid over the time period when each employee worked for the company.

Defined Contribution Plan. A qualified retirement plan under which the employer is liable for a payment into the plan of a specific size, but not for the size of the resulting payments from the plan to participants.

Direct Deposit. The direct transfer of payroll funds from the company bank account directly into that of the employee, avoiding the use of a paycheck.

Educational Assistance Plan. A plan that an employer creates on behalf of its employees covering a variety of educational expenses incurred on behalf of employees, for which they can avoid recognizing some income.

Electronic Federal Tax Payment Systems (EFTPS). An electronic funds transfer system used by businesses to remit taxes to the government.

Employee. A person who renders services to another entity in exchange for compensation.

Employer. A person or entity that directs and controls the work of individuals in exchange for compensation.

Employee Retirement Income Security Act of 1974 (ERISA). A federal Act that sets minimum operational and funding standards for employee benefit plans.

Employee Stock Ownership Plan (ESOP). A fund containing company stock and owned by employees, paid for by ongoing contributions by the employer.

Equal Pay Act of 1963. A federal Act requiring that both sexes receive equal pay in situations where work requires equivalent effort, responsibility, and skills, performed under similar working conditions.

Escalating Price Option. A nonqualified stock option that uses a sliding scale for the option price that changes in concert with a peer group index.

Fair Labor Standards Act of 1938. A federal Act creating standards of overtime pay, minimum wages, and payroll recordkeeping.

Family and Medical Leave Act. A federal Act containing the rules for offering health insurance to employees who are on leave.

Federal Employer Identification Number. A unique identification number issued by the federal government used for payroll purposes to identify the company when it deals with the Internal Revenue Service.

Federal Insurance Contributions Act of 1935 (FICA). A federal Act authorizing the government to collect Social Security and Medicare payroll taxes.

Federal Unemployment Tax Act (FUTA). A federal Act requiring employers to pay a tax on the wages paid to their employees, which is then used to create a pool of funds to be used for unemployment benefits.

FICA. The acronym for the Federal Insurance Contributions Act, also used to describe the combined amount of Social Security and Medicare deductions from an employee's pay.

Flexible Spending Account. A form of cafeteria plan allowing employees to pay for some medical or dependent care expenses with pretax pay deductions.

Form 1099. A form used by businesses to report to the government payments made to certain types of suppliers.

Form 4070. A form used by employees to report to an employer the amount of their tip income.

Form 668-W. The standard form used for notifying a company to garnish an employee's wages for unpaid taxes.

Form 8027. The form used by employers to report tip income by their employees to the government.

Form 940. A form used to report federal unemployment tax remittances and liabilities.

Form 940-EZ. A shortened version of the Form 940.

Form 941. A form used to identify to the government the amount of all quarterly wages on which taxes were withheld, the amount of taxes withheld, and any adjustments to withheld taxes from previous reporting periods.

Form I-9. The Employment Eligibility Verification form, which must be filled out for all new employees to establish their identity and eligibility to work.

Garnishment. A court-ordered authorization to shift employee wages to a creditor.

Green Card. The I-551 Permanent Resident Card, held by a resident alien.

Gross Pay. The amount of earnings due to an employee prior to tax and other deductions.

Health Insurance Portability and Accountability Act of 1996 (HIPAA). A federal Act expanding upon many of the insurance reforms created by COBRA. In particular, it ensures that small businesses will have access to health insurance, despite the special health status of any employees.

Heavenly Parachute Stock Option. A nonqualified stock option that allows a deceased option holder's estate up to three years in which to exercise his or her options.

Hourly Rate Plan. A method for calculating wages for hourly employees that involves the multiplication of the wage rate per hour times the number of hours worked during the work week.

Illegal Immigration Reform and Immigrant Responsibility Act of 1996 (IIRIRA). A federal Act shielding employers from liability if they have made a good-faith effort to verify a new employee's identity and employment eligibility.

Immigration Reform and Control Act of 1986. A federal Act requiring all employers having at least four employees to verify the identity and employment eligibility of all regular, temporary, casual, and student employees.

Incentive Stock Option. An option to purchase company stock that is not taxable to the employee at the time it is granted nor at the time when the employee eventually exercises the option to buy stock.

Individual Retirement Account. A personal savings account into which a defined maximum amount may be contributed, and for which any resulting interest is tax deferred.

Individual Retirement Annuity. An IRA comprised of an annuity that is managed through and paid out by a life insurance company.

Internal Revenue Code. Refers to all federal tax laws as a group.

Internal Revenue Service. A federal agency empowered by Congress to interpret and enforce tax-related laws.

McNamara-O'Hara Service Contract Act of 1965. A federal Act requiring federal contractors to pay those employees working on a federal contract at least as much as the wage and benefit levels prevailing locally.

Minimum Wage. An hourly wage rate set by the federal government below which actual hourly wages cannot fall. This rate can be increased by state governments.

Net Pay. The amount of an employee's wages payable after all tax and other deductions have been removed.

Nonqualified Retirement Plan. A pension plan that does not follow ERISA and IRS guidelines, typically allowing a company to pay key personnel more than other participants.

Nonqualified Stock Option. A stock option not given any favorable tax treatment under the Internal Revenue Code. The option is taxed when it is exercised, based on the difference between the option price and the fair market value of the stock on that day.

Outsourcing. The process of shifting a function previously performed internally to a supplier who is responsible to the company for its ongoing operations and results.

Overtime. A pay premium of 50 percent of the regular rate of pay that is earned by employees on all hours worked beyond 40 hours in a standard work week

Paycard. A credit card into which a company directly deposits an employee's net pay.

Payroll Cycle. The period of service for which a company compensates its employees.

Payroll Register. A report on which is summarized the wage and deduction information for employees for a specific payroll.

Payroll Stabilization. This calculation is used by states to determine the unemployment contribution rate to charge employers and links the contribution rate to fluctuations in a company's total payroll over time.

Per Diem. A fixed rate paid to employees traveling on behalf of a business, which substitutes for reimbursement of exact expenses incurred.

Personal Responsibility and Work Opportunity Reconciliation Act. A federal Act requiring the reporting of new hires into a national database.

Piece Rate Plan. A wage calculation method based on the number of units of production completed by an employee.

Premium Grant. A nonqualified stock option whose option price is set substantially higher than the current fair market value at the grant date.

Profit Sharing Plan. A retirement plan generally funded by a percentage of company profits, but into which contributions can be made in the absence of profits.

Qualified Retirement Plan. A retirement plan designed to observe all of the requirements of the Retirement Income Security Act (ERISA), which allows an employer to immediately deduct allowable contributions to the plan on behalf of plan participants.

Reserve Ratio. This calculation is used by states to determine the unemployment contribution rate to charge employers. The ongoing balance of a firm's unclaimed contributions from previous years is reduced by unemployment claims for the past year and then divided by the average annual payroll, resulting in a "reserve ratio."

Rollover IRA. An IRA that an individual sets up for the express purpose of receiving funds from a qualified retirement plan.

Roth IRA. An IRA account whose earnings are not taxable at all under certain circumstances.

Savings Incentive Match Plan for Employees (SIMPLE). An IRA set up by an employer with no other retirement plan and employing fewer than 100 employees, into which they can contribute up to $9,000 per year (as of 2004).

Section 83(b) Election. The decision by an employee to recognize taxable income on the purchase price of an incentive stock option within 30 days following the date when an option is exercised and withhold taxes at the ordinary income tax rate at that time.

Self-Employment Contributions Act (SECA). A federal Act requiring self-employed business owners to pay the same total tax rates for Social Security and Medicare taxes that are split between employees and employers under the Federal Insurance Contributions Act.

Sick Pay. A fixed amount of pay benefit available to employees who cannot work due to sickness. Company policy fixes the amount of this benefit that can be carried forward into future periods.

Signature Card. A bank document containing the signatures of all approved signatories that a company has approved to sign checks.

Signature Plate. A stamp on which is inscribed an authorized check signer's signature and which is used to imprint the signature on completed checks.

Social Security Act of 1935. A federal Act establishing Old Age and Survivor's Insurance, which was funded by compulsory savings by wage earners.

State Disability Tax. A tax charged by selected states to maintain a disability insurance fund, from which payments are made to employees who are unable to work due to illness or injury.

Target Benefit Plan. A defined benefit plan under which the employer makes annual contributions into the plan based on the actuarial assumption at that time regarding the amount of funding needed to achieve a targeted benefit level.

Termination Pay. Additional pay due to an employee whose employment is being terminated, usually in accordance with a termination pay schedule contained within the employee manual.

Timecard. A document or electronic record on which an employee records his or her hours worked during a payroll period.

Time Clock. A device used to stamp an employee's incoming or outgoing time on either a paper document or an electronic record.

Totalization Agreement. An agreement between countries whereby an employee only has to pay Social Security taxes to the country in which he or she is working

Unclaimed Pay. Net pay not collected by an employee, which is typically transferred to the local state government after a mandated interval has passed from the date of payment.

Uniform Interstate Family Support Act. A federal Act specifying which jurisdiction shall issue family support-related garnishment orders.

Uniformed Services Employment and Reemployment Rights Act of 1994. A federal act that minimizes the impact on people serving in the Armed Forces when they return to civilian employment by avoiding discrimination and increasing their employment opportunities.

W-2 Form. A form used to report gross pay and tax deductions for each employee to the IRS for a calendar year.

W-4 Form. A form on which an employee declares the amount of federal tax deductions to be deducted from his or her pay.

W-9 Form. A form issued to a company's suppliers, requesting that they identify their form of legal organization and tax identification number.

Walsh-Healey Public Contracts Act of 1936. A federal Act that forces government contractors to comply with the government's minimum wage and hour rules.

Work Week. A fixed period of 168 consecutive hours that recurs on a consistent basis.

Workers' Compensation Benefits. Employer-paid insurance that provides their employees with wage compensation if they are injured on the job.

Index